Rhetorical Questions

Hituzi Language Studies

No. 1 *Relational Practice in Meeting Discourse in New Zealand
       and Japan*   Kazuyo Murata
No. 2 *Style and Creativity*   Saito Yoshifumi
No. 3 *Rhetorical Questions*   Goto Risa

Hituzi Language Studies
No. 3

Goto Risa

Rhetorical Questions

A Relevance-Theoretic
Approach to Interrogative Utterances
in English and Japanese

HITUZI
SYOBO

Copyright © Goto, Risa 2018
First published 2018

Author: Goto Risa

All rights reserved. Except for the quotation of short passages for the purposes of criticism and review, no part of this publication may be reproduced, stored in a retrieval system, or transmitted in any form or by any means, electronic, mechanical, photocopying, recording or otherwise, without the written prior permission of the publisher.

In case of photocopying and electronic copying and retrieval from network personally, permission will be given on receipts of payment and making inquiries. For details please contact us through e-mail. Our e-mail address is given below.

Hituzi Syobo Publishing

Yamato bldg. 2f, 2-1-2 Sengoku
    Bunkyo-ku Tokyo, Japan 112-0011
Telephone: +81-3-5319-4916
Facsimile: +81-3-5319-4917
e-mail: toiawase@hituzi.co.jp
http://www.hituzi.co.jp/
postal transfer: 00120-8-142852

ISBN978-4-89476-883-3
Printed in Japan

Acknowledgments

This book is based on my doctoral thesis, submitted to the Graduate School of Nara Women's University in 2012. I wish to thank all the people who gave me valuable suggestions on the research that would eventually grow into this book.

First, I am extremely grateful to my supervisor Professor Seiji Uchida and sub-supervisor Professor Akiko Yoshimura. This study would not have come into existence without their patient support and warm encouragement during my graduate years. Professor Uchida enlightened me on the cognitive-pragmatic analyses of languages and showed me, with step-by-step guidance, how linguistic arguments should be presented. My observations and analyses of Japanese sentence-final particles in questions were highly influenced by his views. I consider meeting him at the beginning of my PhD program at Nara Women's University one of the most important turning points in my life. Professor Yoshimura also shared her deep insight with me, particularly through thoughtful and detailed comments on the behavior of polarity-sensitive expressions. She made me realize the importance of the sentential biases they affect to the interpretation of questions. I would also like to give a special mention to Associate Professor Ayumi Suga, who was one of my PhD examiners and offered insightful comments from a different perspective.

I heartily thank Professor Diane Blakemore of the University of Salford, who attentively read an earlier version of Chapters 2 and 8 of this book and guided me in the right direction by pointing out some fundamental problems. I would also like to thank the Rotary Foundation, whose 2007–08 Rotary Foundation Ambassadorial Scholarship supported my studies at the University of Salford, and offer much gratitude to Mr. and Mrs. Shepherd, my mentors at my host Rotary Club.

I am deeply indebted to Emeritus Professor Seisaku Kawakami of Osaka University for his warm and patient comments on my research. It was my good fortune to study rhetoric in languages through his lectures and seminars, and one of the core analyses of this book is based on his cognitive theory of irony, for which inspiration I offer special gratitude.

I am also indebted to my seniors in the academic world: Professors Yuji Nishiyama, Michiko Takeuchi, Mayumi Nishikawa, and many others for their instructive comments on my presentations and papers over the years while I was a student at the Graduate School of Nara Women's University. Their constant support encouraged me to continue my linguistic analyses.

I have been blessed with my colleagues at Nara Women's University. During my graduate years, we spent endless hours discussing issues in cognitive pragmatics. I extend my special thanks to Tatsuya Taguchi, Mark Donnellan, Leila Kardan, and many other friends in the academic world who read earlier drafts and gave me helpful suggestions on parts of this study. I apologize that I cannot list all the people whose assistance I am thankful for.

The publication of this book was supported by the Grant-in-Aid for the Publication of Scientific Research Results of Japan Society for the Promotion of Science (JSPS), grant number 17HP5064 (2017). Special thanks go to Isao Matsumoto and Eri Ebisawa of Hituzi Syobo Publishing, as well as the copy editor, Matt Treyvaud. They taught me a great deal about how the book contents should be presented; in particular, Matt carefully copyedited every page of this book.

Last but not least, my deepest thanks go to my family. I would like to dedicate this book to them for their love and support.

Goto Risa
January 2018

Abbreviations and Notations

AUX	auxiliary verb
COMP	complementizer
CON	conditional affix
COP	copula or copular construction (*da, desu, de aru, no da, no desu, no*)
DM	discourse marker
DO	direct object marker (*o*)
FN	formal noun (*mono, koto*)
GEN	genitive marker (*no*)
HON	honorific
IO	indirect object marker (*ni*)
LOC	locative
NEG	negative form
NPM	negative polarity marker
PASS	passive voice
PAST	past form
PPM	positive polarity marker
Q	interrogative (also exclamative) marker
QUO	quotative (hearsay) marker (*to, tte*)
S	subject marker (*ga*)
TOP	topicalizer (*wa*)

An asterisk (*) indicates an utterance that is not acceptable in the context given.
Two question marks (??) indicate an utterance whose acceptability is not clear.

Some Japanese words show discrepancies between script and pronunciation. For example, there are two ways to romanize the hearsay particle と い う: script-based *to iu* and phonemic *to yuu*. I use the former in accordance with recent practice in Japanese studies (Tanaka, 2006, 2015). However, the particles を and は are romanized *o* and *wa* (i.e., phonemically). These rules have also been silently applied to examples from other authors where it does not affect the authors' arguments.

Contents

Acknowledgments — I
Abbreviations and Notations — III

CHAPTER 1
Are Interrogative Utterances Asking Anything?

CHAPTER 2
What Rhetorical Questions Are: The Pragmatic Properties of Interrogative Utterances

2.1	Classical Views	7
2.2	Defining Rhetorical Questions	8
2.3	What Are Information-Seeking Questions?	10
2.4	The Speech Act Theoretic Approach	12
2.4.1	The Classification of Speech Acts	12
2.4.2	Requests for Information and Indirect Requests	13
2.4.3	The Limitations of Speech Act Theory	14
2.5	Against Speech Act Theory: Wilson and Sperber	15
2.5.1	Types of Questions	16
2.6	Against Speech Act Theory: A New Analysis	18
2.6.1	Assertive Force and Directive Force	18
2.6.2	Can Assertive Force Be Measured?	20
2.6.3	Do Rhetorical Questions Assert Polarity-Reversed Assumptions?	23
2.7	The Answer to a Rhetorical Question	24
2.8	Conclusion	29

CHAPTER 3
The Continuum of Rhetoricity

3.1	Borderline Cases: Information-Seeking or Rhetorical?	32

3.1.1	Complex Questions and Rhetoricity	34
3.1.2	Vain Questions and Rhetoricity	35
3.1.3	Other Rhetorically Biased Question Types	37
3.2	Rhetorically Ambiguous Questions	40
3.2.1	Felicitous Conditions for Information-Seeking Questions	41
3.3	Rhetoricity as Scale and Continuum	44
3.4	Clues to Rhetorical Bias in Questions	45
3.4.1	Interrogative Mood	45
3.4.2	Expressive Function	47
3.4.3	Answers and Retorts in Question-Answer Sequences	49
3.5	Conclusion	52

CHAPTER 4
Triply Interpretive Use: Relevance Theory and Interrogative Utterances

4.1	The Principles of Relevance	55
4.2	Interpreting Utterances and Thoughts	58
4.2.1	Explicit Meaning, Implicit Meaning, and Speakers' Attitudes	58
4.2.2	Propositional Attitudes in Interrogative Utterances	60
4.2.3	Rhetorical Questions and Speakers' Attitudes	62
4.3	Interpretive Resemblance	64
4.3.1	Descriptive and Interpretive Representation	64
4.3.2	Interrogatives and Desirable Thoughts	67
4.4	Metaphor and Irony in Interrogative Utterances	69
4.4.1	Metaphorical Expressions and Narrowing/Broadening	69
4.4.2	Irony as Attributive Use	71
4.4.3	Triply Interpretive Use in Echoic Interrogative Utterances	72
4.5	Meanings and Truth Conditions	76
4.5.1	Gricean Conversational Implicature	76
4.5.2	Conventional Implicature	79
4.5.3	An Alternative Approach: Conceptual and Procedural Meanings	80
4.6	Conclusion	82

CHAPTER 5
Rhetorical Questions and Irony: The Echoic Hypothesis

5.1	The Continuum of Rhetoricity Revisited	86
5.2	Ironical Questions	89
5.2.1	Traditional Accounts of Verbal Irony	89
5.2.2	Kawakami's Cognitive Theory of Irony	90
5.2.3	Polarity-Reversed Assumptions in Rhetorical Questions	95
5.2.4	Non-Polarity-Reversed Rhetorical Questions: Recognizing Discrepancies	97
5.3	Echoic Interpretation	99
5.3.1	Wilson and Sperber's Echoic Hypothesis	99
5.3.2	Universal Desires and Echoing	101
5.3.3	Other Echoic Approaches: Allusional Pretense and Implicit Display	103
5.3.4	What Do Borderline Cases of Verbal Irony Refer To?	105
5.4	Echo in Rhetorical Questions	106
5.4.1	Echo in Polarity-Reversed Rhetorical Questions	107
5.4.2	Echo in Non-Polarity-Reversed Rhetorical Questions: Possible Worlds as Echoed Source	109
5.5	Conclusion	114

CHAPTER 6
Rhetorical Questions in Japanese

6.1	Sentence-Final Expressions (SFEs) in Japanese	121
6.2	Conclusion	123

CHAPTER 7
SFEs in Japanese Interrogatives 1: The Case of To Iu No Ka

7.1	Ka As Interpretive Use Marker	127
7.2	The Meaning of To Iu No (Desu) Ka	129
7.2.1	To Iu/Tte Iu in Declarative Utterances	130
7.2.2	The Meaning of Tte	134
7.3	Tte and Tte-Iu No (Desu) Ka in Interrogative Utterances	135
7.4	Does Tte Alone Function as an Echoic Reformulation Marker?	142

7.5	Strong and Weak Implicatures	146
7.6	To Iu/Tte Iu in Wh-Interrogatives	150
7.7	Conclusion	151

CHAPTER 8

SFEs in Japanese Interrogatives 2: The Case of Mono Ka

8.1	The Mono Da Construction	157
8.1.1	Background Studies	157
8.1.2	Deontic and Epistemic Interpretations of Mono Da	159
8.1.3	Explicit and Implicit Meanings of Mono Da	161
8.2	The Mono Ka Construction in Interrogatives	168
8.2.1	Mono in the Mono Ka Construction	168
8.2.2	Mono Ka in Wh-Interrogatives	173
8.2.3	Mono Ka in Exclamatives	179
8.3	Degrees of Dissociation and Speaker Emotion	182
8.4	Conclusion	183
	Afterword	185
	References	187

CHAPTER 1
Are Interrogative Utterances Asking Anything?

Consider the utterances in the following extracts from *The Second Bakery Attack*, a short story by Murakami Haruki (2001) translated into English by Jay Rubin.

(1) [The narrator and his wife are hungry]
We took turns opening the refrigerator door and hoping, but no matter how many times we looked inside, the contents were never changed…
"Would madame care for some French dressing sautéed in deodorizer?"
I expected her to ignore my attempt at humor, and she did.
(Murakami, 2001, p. 37)

(2) [The narrator and his wife are robbing at McDonald's]
My wife counted the finished hamburgers and put them into two small shopping bags, fifteen burgers to a bag.
"Why do you have to do this?" the girl asked me. "Why don't you just take the money and buy something you like? What's the good of eating thirty Big Macs?" (Murakami, 2001, pp. 47–48)

All four utterances are all interrogative in form, but they don't seem to be purely asking something. Many readers might be happy to call them rhetorical questions that are not really asking anything. But is there any decisive evidence for this interpretation? There are some clues: the speaker's humorous intentions in (1), the use of three continuous questions without a break in (2). It seems that these clues lead the reader to *rhetorically biased* readings.

However, are those clues sufficient to arrive at the speaker's (or author's) intended meaning? For instance, what is the evidence that the speaker of (2), a female worker at the McDonald's, did *not* seek answers to any of her three questions? It seems to me that in fact she might have wanted at least some answers, i.e., she might have been partly seeking information.

The intentions of the speaker of a rhetorical question are not always clear. Rhetorical questions can fall into grey areas regarding the hearer's interpretation of these intentions, and the mechanism of the hearer's interpretation remains mysterious. This book aims to clarify our understanding of such grey areas and identify the factors that lead hearers to the correct interpretation of such interrogative utterances.

Some say that the point of uttering a rhetorical question lies in the speaker's not expecting an answer to it. Zarefsky (2011) argues that "a rhetorical question is one for which no answer is really expected. Instead, simply asking the question can cause an audience to think about the answer" (p. 241). In line with this view, I argue that a rhetorical question is a question that performs or pretends to perform the speech act of asking but which does not expect the hearer to provide an answer.

Miscommunication can occur where there is ambiguity as to whether a question is genuinely seeking information or not. In fact, many interrogative utterances in daily interactions are ambiguous in this way: not decisively rhetorical but still susceptible to rhetorically biased readings. For instance, the rhetorical readings of the two utterances below are totally dependent on context (for further analysis, see Chapter 3):

(3) Who knows?
(4) Did you read that trashy novel?

This book seeks a theoretical approach that can explain the pragmatic ambiguity of interrogative utterances like these with respect to rhetoricity. Traditional accounts of rhetorical questions (Quirk, Greenbaum, Leech, & Svartvik, 1985) have focused on polarity reversal: rhetorical questions conveying assertions opposite in polarity to the propositional content. The utterance in (3) would fit this description if it were uttered to convey the assertion *Nobody knows*. There are, however, non-polarity-reversed and rhetorically ambiguous interrogatives which do not seem to be covered by Quirk et al. For example, the utterance in (4) might be rhetorical whether or not it conveys the polarity-reversed assertion *You didn't read that trashy novel*.

An alternative approach is offered by the cognitive-pragmatic theory called *relevance theory*, originally proposed by Sperber and Wilson (1986). The relevance-theoretic account accommodates any type of interrogative utterance (Sperber & Wilson, 1995; Wilson & Sperber, 1988/2012; Blakemore, 2002). According to their *principle of relevance*, a hearer's cognitive processing seeks an optimal balance between processing effort and cognitive effects. The relevance-theoretic view implies that questions might be rhetorical to various degrees, rather than simply rhetorical or not. The hearer of an utterance accesses clues to rhetoricity, if any exist, in the search for optimally relevant assumptions. The validity of these clues is then examined. Even if the clues within an utterance are weak or indecisive, the hearer's cognition eventually arrives at a relevant assumption.

A reinterpretation of rhetoricity through the lens of relevance theory holds the promise of combining various possible degrees of understood rhetoricity into a single continuum. This hitherto uncharted territory will be explored throughout this book. By the end of the book, the details of our cognitive processing of rhetorical questions will be made clear. The itinerary for this adventure is as follows.

Chapter 2 reviews previous studies of rhetorical questions and discusses their strengths and weaknesses. The study of rhetorical questions can be traced back to ancient Greek and Roman times, when skilful use of questions enabled orators to control their audience. By contrast, modern studies of rhetoric take as their subject only figurative expressions with non-literal meanings. Study of rhetorical questions in discourse has only recently begun to appear in semantic and pragmatic analyses by authors such as Searle (1969, 1975) and Grice (1975). According to these studies, rhetorical questions can be treated as non-ordinary cases: Rhetoricity is recognized in such utterances' violation of the maxims of conversation. Such an analysis requires the intrepreter to distinguish ordinary cases from non-ordinary (i.e., non-literal) cases. In other words, the hearer of an interrogative utterance must examine its literalness to distinguish whether it is an ordinary (information-seeking) or non-ordinary (rhetorical) question.

These accounts, however, seem to ignore the fact that many interrogative utterances in daily interactions are ambiguous: neither fully information-seeking nor fully rhetorical. A speaker of an interrogative utterance may exhibit a slight (non-salient) sarcastic attitude but still seek information. The hearer of the utterance, however, might process the speaker's sarcasm as a strong clue to a rhetorically biased reading. Moreover, if the speaker is not interested in whether the hearer interprets the question as information-seeking or rhetorical, the speaker may not have any particular expectation regarding the hearer's answer. This sort of apathetic interpretation might arise between participants with rather intimate relations such as close friends or spousal partners. In light of this, Chapter 3 proposes a *continuum of rhetoricity* for interrogative utterances.

The fourth and fifth chapters of this book propose a solution for understanding rhetorical interrogatives based on relevance theory. Chapter 4 gives an overview of relevance theory, introducing the main concepts proposed by Sperber and Wilson (1986, 1995; see also Wilson & Sperber, 1988/2012, 1992, 2002), and subsequent relevance theorists (Carston, 1999, 2002;

Blakemore, 1992, 1998, 2002). The most important concept is *interpretive resemblance*. Sperber and Wilson (1995) state that any utterance is understood in terms of two *interpretive* relationships: one "between its propositional form and a thought of the speaker's, and one . . . between that thought and what it represents" (p. 231). As for interrogative utterances, they are said to involve "an interpretive relation between the speaker's thought and *desirable* [emphasis added] thoughts" (p. 231). *Desirability* is an important concept in this analysis; it enables us to explain the distinction between a variety of interrogative utterances.

Chapter 5 argues that rhetoricity has an *ironical* aspect. In relevance theory, irony can be explained by the concept of *interpretation of attributive (echoic) thought*. This means that the processing of rhetorical interrogative utterances can be understood based on the idea of blending desirability and attribution. The idea of such blending has already been introduced as *triply interpretive use* of utterances in Wilson and Sperber's (1988/2012) example of free indirect speech. In this book I argue that the concept of triple interpretation is also useful for analyzing the cognitive processing of rhetorical questions.

The final three chapters, Chapter 6 through Chapter 8, apply the framework of relevance theory to two case studies of rhetorical markers in Japanese interrogative utterances. These studies focus on the cognitive effect brought about by the semantic and/or pragmatic functions of two distinct sentence-final expressions (SFEs) in Japanese interrogative utterances: *to iu no ka* (Chapter 7) and *mono ka* (Chapter 8).

SFEs are common in Japanese utterances. Some allow the hearer to recognize the sentential mood of the utterance: *Ka* in (5b) and *no* in (5c) below both indicate the interrogative mood.

(5) a. Watashi wa   pātii ni   ikimasu.
       I   TOP   party to   go
       'I (will) go to the party.'
    b. Anata wa   pātii ni   ikimasu *ka*?
       you   TOP   party to   go   Q
       'Will you go to the party?'
    c. Anata wa   pātii ni   iku *no*?
       you   TOP   party to   go   Q
       'Will you go to the party?'
    d. Anata wa   pātii ni   iku *no desu ka*?
       you   TOP   party to   go   COP Q
       'Will you go to the party?'

Although the utterances in (5b) through (5d) could be used as purely information-seeking questions, there is still a distinction of nuance between them. Intuitively, (5c) and (5d) are felt to indicate a greater confirmatory intention on the part of the speaker than (5b). Also note that, as in (5d), although *ka* often appears as part of an SFE in interrogative utterances, it remains a sentence-final particle in its own right.

I argue that combinations of interrogative sentence-final particles with other elements, such as *to iu* and *mono*, often occur in rhetorical questions and tend to lead the hearer to a correct interpretation in terms of rhetoricity. Chapters 7 and 8 investigate the mechanism by which the hearer of an interrogative utterance with a particular sentence-final expression recognizes the speaker's rhetorical intentions. Chapter 7 focuses on *to iu no ka* interrogatives, which incorporate the hearsay construction *to iu*, and Chapter 8 explores *mono ka* interrogatives, which incorporate the formal noun *mono*. Both chapters confirm that interrogative utterances containing SFPs are successfully explained by relevance-theoretic analyses.

The presence of these SFEs suggests that Japanese interrogatives have more salient linguistic clues to rhetoricity than those in English. However, it does not necessarily follow that understanding rhetoricity in Japanese interrogative utterances requires less processing effort than understanding rhetoricity in English. In both languages, when an utterance lacks a decisive linguistic clue, hearers search for weaker clues, including contextual information. Relevance theory claims that, with or without strong clues, the hearer seeks an optimal balance between maximizing cognitive effects and minimizing processing effort (see Chapter 4). The hearer's process of understanding concludes when a relevant interpretation achieves a certain cognitive effect with the least effort. Therefore, one the most important factors in the processing of rhetorical interrogative utterances is cognitive effect. I will draw on examples of both English and Japanese interrogative utterances to unravel the relationships between linguistic and non-linguistic factors and cognitive effects.

CHAPTER 2

What Rhetorical Questions Are: The Pragmatic Properties of Interrogative Utterances

What makes rhetorical questions *rhetorical*? Many linguists have tried to answer this question. This chapter traces the study of rhetorical questions from classical civilization to current linguistic thinking, particularly from the viewpoints of semantics and pragmatics.

2.1 Classical Views

The literature on rhetorical questions reaches back to ancient Greek and Roman oratory. Ancient orators used questions to control their audience and defeat opposing arguments. In his works *Topics* (350 BCE/1960) and *Rhetoric* (350 BCE/1924), Aristotle distinguishes *dialectic*, a technique of argumentation, from *rhetoric*, the art of persuasion. Dialectic was used to pose and answer questions in logical argumentation, whereas rhetoric was used to persuade an audience, whether judge, jury, legislators, voters, or spectators. What we call rhetorical questions were therefore used as both dialectical and rhetorical devices.

In *Rhetoric*, Aristotle proposes a rhetorical triad of *ethos*, *pathos* and *logos*. *Ethos* is defined as "to say the truth," *pathos* "to bring the audience to the right state of emotion," and *logos* "to gain the consent of the audience." The Roman philosopher Cicero (84 BCE/1949) and the Roman rhetorician Quintilian (95 BCE/1856, 1920) developed the Aristotelian triad into *five canons of rhetoric*. The five canons of rhetoric outline the processes of persuasion in a practical way, and are summarized in (1) below.

(1) The five canons of rhetoric:
    a. invention: preparing your arguments
    b. arrangement: organizing the discourse structure of arguments
    c. style: using persuasive expressions, e.g., figures of speech, diction

d. memory: memorizing the speech
  e. delivery: using non-verbal communication, e.g., voice, gestures

(Prus, 2010)

Style, the third of the canons, involves the selection of figures of speech, including rhetorical questions. On the other hand, from a dialectic point of view, Quintilian introduced several types of rhetorical question, giving examples such as:

(2) a. How long…will you abuse our patience? Do you not see that your machinations are discovered?
    b. Has Caius Fidiculanius Falcula…been brought to judgment?
    c. How is it possible?   (Quintilian, 95 BCE/1856, 9.2.7)

Quintilian states that both utterances in (1a) are useful for attacking the audience. The utterance in (1b) is a question that cannot be denied, whereas the utterance in (1c) is a question that is difficult to answer.

As I will argue, "answerability" is a key factor when assessing the rhetoricity of a question. Recent studies recognize multiple unanswerable question types, including *vain questions* (Driver, 1998) and *loaded questions* (Walton, 1988), both of which are explored later in this chapter. Such questions do not purely seek information: They can be used as rhetorical questions too.

2.2 Defining Rhetorical Questions

Many authors have offered definitions of rhetorical questions, often contrasting them with information-seeking questions. This can be seen in Quintilian's distinction between two types of questions, *interrogare* and *percontari* (Quintilian, 95 BCE/1856, 9.2). Both mean 'to ask,' but *interrogare* implies merely seeking information whereas *percontari* implies a concern with establishing proof. *Interrogare* therefore corresponds more closely to what we call information-seeking questions, and *percontari* to rhetorical questions.

More recently, Struyker Boudier (1988, p. 25) cited Ernst Mach's distinction in his 1905 *Erkenntnis und Irrtum* between answerable and meaningless (i.e., unanswerable) questions. Struyker Boudier characterizes this as an opposition between strictly scientific, meaningful questions, which are answerable, and non-scientific, meaningless questions, which are not.

How can a scientific, meaningful question be recognized? One solution can be found in Jeffreys (1948). Jeffreys proposes three conditions for judging the question *Is Mr. Johnson at home?*: (a) "I do not know whether Mr. Johnson is at home"; (b) "I want to know whether he is at home"; and (c) "I believe that you know whether he is at home" (p. 378). These conditions can be reduced to two felicity conditions for information-seeking questions equivalent to those proposed by Searle (1969, 1975), in which the speaker of a request for information (i.e., information-seeking question) (a) does not know the answer (i.e., the expressed proposition), and (b) wants to elicit this information from the hearer. Similar felicity conditions for information-seeking questions are provided by Kawakami (1984): (a) the speaker does not know the answer, and (b) the speaker wants to know the answer.

Are, then, the felicity conditions for rhetorical questions the inverse of those for information-seeking questions? That is, is a rhetorical question an utterance for which the speaker (a) knows the answer, and (b) does not want the hearer to provide the answer?

It is clear that the examples in (2a)–(2c) above do not satisfy the felicity conditions for information-seeking questions in Seale (1975) and Kawakami (1984): A speaker of such utterances does not know or want to know the answers to them. Do they satisfy the inverse conditions as described above? That is, does a speaker of (2a)–(2c) not want an answer because they already know it?

Before we consider this, we must clarify our definition of the answer to a question. The answer to an interrogative utterance can be explained in terms of logical form (for yes-no questions) or the completion of logical form (for *wh*-questions). What, then, is the answer to a rhetorical question? As one solution, the answers that the speaker of the utterances in (2a)–(2c) have in mind might be restated as declarative equivalents as follows:

(3) a. You have abused our patience *for a long time*; your machinations *are* discovered.
b. Caius Fidiculanius Falcula has *not* been brought to judgment.
c. There is *no* way it is possible.

According to Quintilian, saying something using rhetorical questions is more animated than saying it using declarative equivalents. In other words, Quintilian believed that a speaker of (2a)–(2c) intended to communicate the assumptions in (3a)–(3c) respectively. Some modern authors also argue that rhetorical questions assert the thoughts or propositions they express (Quirk et al., 1985; Huddleston & Pullum, 2002; Han, 2002). According to these views, Quintilian's examples in (1) might be explained as asserting the declarative equivalents in (3). If this is correct, however, what is the difference between asking a rhetorical question and stating its declarative equivalent? The authors mentioned above do not answer this question, which is one of the major issues addressed in this book.

I outline some previous studies of the uses of rhetorical interrogative utterances below. One of the most important questions for this chapter is whether rhetorical questions are clearly distinguished from information-seeking questions. To answer this question, we must consider a wide variety of information-seeking and non-information-seeking questions.

2.3 What Are Information-Seeking Questions?

According to Huddleston and Pullum (2002), a question is an utterance in one of the following four interrogative forms:

(4) a. Did they see her? (open interrogative)
    b. Who broke the window? (closed interrogative)
    c. He's rather aggressive, isn't he? (interrogative tag)
    d. He's rather aggressive, don't you think? (interrogative parenthetical)
    (Huddleston & Pullum, 2002, pp. 853, 891)

In Huddleston and Pullum's classification, an *open interrogative* as in (4a) or a *closed interrogative* as in (4b) can be used as a so-called ordinary question in which the speaker requests information (i.e., the answer to the question). Note that this view is grounded in the speech act theoretic approach to interrogatives (Searle, 1975, 1979).

According to Huddleston and Pullum, the utterances in (4a) and (4b) seek not just an answer but a truthful answer. The speaker of (4a) seeks the truthfulness of the proposition expressed by the utterance (i.e., *They saw her*), whereas the speaker of (4b) seeks to know who broke the window. In this view, these examples meet the felicity conditions for information-seeking questions given in the previous section: (a) the speaker does not know the answer, and (b) the speaker expects the hearer to provide it.

On the other hand, tag questions such as (4c) and (4d) can be used for confirmation, or "verification" in Huddleston and Pullum's terminology (2002, p. 894). The speaker of (4c) intends to confirm that "he" (i.e., the subject of the utterance) is aggressive, and similarly the speaker of (4d) intends to confirm that the hearer thinks "he" is aggressive.

However, is the distinction between tag questions such as (4c) and (4d) and open/closed questions such as (4a) and (4b) justified? If so, on what basis should this distinction be drawn? Is the distinction based on syntactic form, or on semantic properties or pragmatic functions?

In fact, tag questions are not the only form that can be used for confirmation questions. The confirmatory interpretation of interrogative utterances seems to depend on pragmatics. In his analysis of rhetorical questions, Gutiérrez-Rexach (1998, p. 143) claims that both open interrogatives (particularly negative ones) and tag questions can be used for confirmation. Consider the following example:

(5) Isn't Fred coming to dinner? (Gutiérrez-Rexach, 1998, p. 144)

According to Gutiérrez-Rexach, the utterance in (5) can be used for confirmation in a context such as when the speaker of (5) assumes that Fred is coming to dinner but Fred does not appear. The speaker might utter (5) to attempt to confirm the *initial* assumption *Fred is coming to dinner*. In other words, the speaker does have an assumption in mind, but does not have full confidence in it and wants the hearer to confirm it.

In Gutiérrez-Rexach's view, then, the speaker utters a confirmation question to find out if there is any information she is unaware of that might mean that her existing belief is untrue. If, as Gutiérrez-Rexach observes, both positive and negative tag questions such as (4c) and (4d) can be used for confirmation, then not only negative yes-no questions such as (5) but also positive yes-no questions such as (4a) should be usable in this way. For example, if a speaker believes that *they didn't see her* but then encounters possible evidence that *they saw her*, that speaker might utter (4a) *Did they see her?* to confirm this initial assumption.

The distinction between ordinary information-seeking questions and confirmation questions might therefore lie in the speaker's awareness of her intention to confirm her existing belief. If the speaker of (4a) has neither a belief that *they didn't see her* nor a new assumption *they saw her*, then (4a) might be uttered as a purely information-seeking question and not convey any surprise or doubt. The speaker in this case does not communicate any biased assumption: Both positive and negative answers are considered equally likely. Hence, confirmation questions can be classified as a subtype of information-seeking questions, in the sense that the speaker seeks a true answer and expects the answer to be provided by the hearer.

Gutiérrez-Rexach further claims that a negative interrogative is similar to a rhetorical question in that in both cases the speaker assumes a polarity-reversed answer. What, then, distinguishes confirmation questions from rhetorical questions? Gutiérrez-Rexach argues that the distinction lies in the speaker's confidence in their belief regarding the assumption or true answer. This in turn implies that there should be borderline cases whose rhetoricity cannot be clearly classified. This gray area between information-seeking and rhetorical questions is the main interest of this book.

Note that a view that accepts borderline cases is in conflict with the speech act theoretic approach. The reasons for this are explored in the next section.

2.4 The Speech Act Theoretic Approach

Many authors have applied speech act theory to their study of interrogative utterances. The main interests of speech act theorists were traditionally taxonomy and classification: Understanding an interrogative utterance involves identifying the speech act performed by the utterance, which in turn requires a taxonomy of speech acts. I review the outlines of this analysis below.

2.4.1 The Classification of Speech Acts

According to speech act theory, language is a vehicle of action. By uttering something, we can ask a question, issue a request, make a promise, and so on. In his analysis of speech acts, Austin (1962) explains that we generally perform three distinct types of actions when we make an utterance: *saying* something, *performing a certain action* by saying it, and/or *affecting the hearer* by saying it. Austin dubs these the "locutionary," "illocutionary," and "perlocutionary" act, respectively (pp. 98–102).

The *illocutionary act* plays a central role in speech act theory. The identification of the illocutionary force of an utterance is a prerequisite for understanding the utterance. Searle (1979, pp. 12–17) built on Austin's speech act theory to suggest five types of illocutionary force:

(6) a. *Assertives* commit the speaker to a certain belief in the truth of the expressed proposition (e.g., *suggesting that P*, *insisting that P*)
b. *Directive* attempt to get the hearer to do something (e.g., *asking, ordering, requesting*)
c. *Commissives* commit the speaker to a future action (e.g., *promising*)
d. *Expressives* express an emotional attitude towards the state of affairs described (e.g., *thanking, congratulating, apologizing*)
e. *Declarations* guarantee that the propositional content corresponds to the world (e.g., *appointing someone chairman, declaring war, marrying someone*)

Searle assumes that illocutionary verbs and sentential mood can indicate certain illocutionary forces. Typically, declarative sentences have assertive force, whereas imperative and interrogative sentences have directive force. Consider the following examples:

(7) a. The capital of Japan is Tokyo.
    b. Pass me the salt.
    c. Are you coming to the party?

The declarative utterance in (7a) is interpreted as communicating the speaker's assertion that the capital of Japan is Tokyo, whereas the imperative utterance in (7b) and the interrogative utterance in (7c) both have the directive force of a request, with the difference lying in the type of request. (7b) is interpreted as a request for action (i.e., to pass the salt to the speaker), whereas (7c) is interpreted as a request for information (i.e., whether or not the hearer is coming to the party).

2.4.2 Requests for Information and Indirect Requests

Requests for action like (7b) above can also be made using interrogative utterances in at least two distinct ways. Consider these examples:

(8) a. Can you pass me the salt?
    b. Can you reach the salt?   (Seale, 1975, p. 60)

According to Searle, the utterances in (8a) and (8b) are *not* requests for information: The speaker does not want to know whether the hearer is able to pass or reach the salt. The speaker of (8a) simply wants the hearer to *pass the salt*; similarly, the speaker of (8b) wants the hearer to *reach the salt* (and, implicitly, to *pass it* to the speaker).

Interrogative utterances like (8a) and (8b) are called *indirect requests*, contrasting with direct requests like the utterance in (7b) above. The traditional definition of indirect speech acts is Searle's: "cases in which one illocutionary act is performed indirectly by way of performing another" (1975, p. 60; see also Bach & Harnish, 1979). The interrogative utterance in (8a) functions like an imperative utterance in that it tends to be interpreted as a request for action rather than a request for information. (Sadock, 1971, calls such utterances *whimperative*, highlighting their ambiguous relationship to the typical uses of both interrogatives and imperatives.) In other words, the utterance in (8a) can be understood as indirectly performing a directive speech act.

A direct speech act is performed by an utterance whose speech act type is conventionally associated with the type of speech act performed. The question, then, is how hearers arrive at the intended interpretation of indirect speech acts. Here Searle (1975, 1979) mainly invokes Grice's (1975) conventional implicatures and conversational maxims (see Chapter 4 for discussion). Searle's claim is that indirect requests such as (8a) and (8b) would, if interpreted more literally, flout conversational maxims. For example, (8a) would first be interpreted as a *direct* speech act (asking whether the hearer has the ability to pass the salt), but as this interpretation would flout the maxim of quality, the hearer is led to an interpretation of the utterance as an *indirect* speech act, i.e., an indirect request.

2.4.3 The Limitations of Speech Act Theory

Searle (1975, pp. 65, 67) classifies indirect requests into five basic categories according to the properties of the desired activity. The classification includes:

(9) a. H[earer]'s ability to perform A[ction]
  e.g., [= (8b)] Can you reach the salt?
 b. S[peaker]'s desire that H do A
  e.g., I would like you to go now.
 c. H's doing A
  e.g., Would you kindly get off my foot?
 d. H's desire or willingness to do A
  e.g., Would you mind not making so much noise?
 e. Reasons for A
  e.g., How many times have I told you not to eat with your fingers?

(Searle, 1975)

In Searle's view, each utterance in (9) is an indirect request with directive force intended to get the hearer to do an action. Speech act theory, however, does not explain why or how a certain interrogative utterance can be a request for action rather than information—why, for instance, an utterance like *Can you X?* should be understood as performing the speech act of requesting action rather than the speech act of questioning (i.e., requesting information). (Searle does claim that the auxiliary verb *can* itself has a force of a request, but does not discuss the matter further.)

In fact, there are some contexts in which *Can you X?* cannot be interpreted as a request for action. Consider (9a) [= (8b)], included again below:

(9) a. Can you reach the salt?

Suppose that the speaker and the hearer are brothers who are competing to jump high enough to reach the salt on the top shelf. The taller elder brother suggests that the younger try to jump and reach (touch) the salt, uttering (9a). In this case, the utterance would not be interpreted as a request that the hearer pass the speaker the salt. Rather, it would be interpreted as a genuine request for information: The speaker really does want to know whether the hearer can reach the salt.

There are also cases in which the utterance in (9a) cannot be interpreted as a request for information and must be interpreted as a rhetorical question. Consider the two brothers again. If it were easy for the elder brother to touch the salt but impossible for the younger to do so, and the elder brother uttered (9a), the utterance might be interpreted as communicating the speaker's doubt regarding the expressed proposition, i.e., *The hearer (i.e., younger brother) can reach the salt*.

2.5 Against Speech Act Theory: Wilson and Sperber

Wilson and Sperber (1988/2012) point out that illocutionary force of a speech act is a purely pragmatic matter. This implies, in contradiction to speech act theory, that the identification of an utterance's illocutionary force is not a prerequisite for its interpretation. For instance, imperative sentences are not always used to perform directive speech acts. Consider the following counterexamples to the speech act theoretic account (all emphasis added):

(10) a. Threats and dares:
 [Seeing Peter about to throw a snowball to her, Mary says:]
 Go on. *Throw it*. Just you dare.
 b. Good wishes:
 [Visiting Peter in the hospital, Mary says:]
 Get well soon.
 c. Permission:
 Peter: Can I open the window?
 Mary: Oh, *open it*, then.
  (Wilson & Sperber, 1988/2012, pp. 212–213)
(11) Figurative: Reach for the stars.   (Blakemore, 1992, p. 111)

As Wilson and Sperber observe, the imperative utterances in (10a)–(10c) do not have the directive force of a request. The utterance *Throw it* in (10a) does not encourage the hearer to throw the snowball; indeed, it discourages him from doing so. The speaker of (10b) knows that the action described is not under the hearer's control, so the utterance cannot be viewed as an attempt to get the hearer to perform an action. The same is true of (10c), because there is no reason to think that Mary cares whether Peter performs the action described, and (11), which obviously is not interpreted as a literal instruction to attempt to reach the stars.

Similar problems arise for declaratives and interrogatives. Wilson and Sperber note that declarative utterances may not perform assertive speech acts in cases involving metaphor, irony, and jokes, for example. Similarly, metaphorical or ironical interrogative utterances may not always perform directive speech acts either. Consider the following interrogative utterances that do not seek information, i.e., do not seek to ascertain the truthfulness of the proposition expressed by the utterance.

(12) [Ichirō, a baseball player for the Mariners in the U.S., met Kitajima, a breaststroke gold medalist who set a new world record at the 2008 Beijing Olympics, and uttered:]
Are you a fish? (*Kimi wa sakana ka?*)
("Ichirō, Kitajima," 2008)

(13) [Susan and Mary are co-workers at a company. Susan often wears sunglasses. On a rainy day, when Susan comes into the office, Mary sarcastically utters:]
Did you bring your sunglasses?
(D. Blakemore, personal communication, 2008)

The expressed proposition of (12) is *You are a fish*. As the hearer is obviously human, the speaker clearly does not seek the truthfulness of the proposition expressed. In other words, the utterance in (12) is not a request for information about whether the hearer *is a fish*. In (13), the answer (i.e., the proposition expressed by the utterance) is *You brought your sunglasses*, but because the utterance is ironical, the speaker cannot be said to seek the truthfulness of the proposition expressed.

The utterances in (12) and (13) obviously do not satisfy the felicity conditions for information-seeking questions: It is not the case that the speakers do not know the answer but want to. Are these, then, rhetorical questions? If so, is it the use of metaphor or irony that makes them so? Metaphorical and ironical interrogative utterances are discussed further in Chapter 5, but let us first consider other types of interrogative utterance that do not satisfy the felicitous conditions for information-seeking questions.

2.5.1 Types of Questions

Wilson and Sperber (2012/1988) argue against speech act theory by showing a variety of interrogative utterances that are neither requests for information nor requests for action. Consider these examples encouraging the hearer to provide an answer the speaker already knows:

(14) a. [An examiner utters to a student:]
       What are the binding principles?
   b. [A mother, hiding a chocolate in her hand, utters to her child:]
       Which hand is it in?   (Wilson & Sperber, p. 222)

The answers to (14a) and (14b) can be provided by substituting a value for the variable X in the following incomplete logical forms:

(15) a. The binding principles are X.
   b. The chocolate bar is in the X hand. [X = either *left* or *right*]

Both utterances in (14) can be distinguished from ordinary information-seeking questions by the fact that the speaker already knows the answer to the question. The utterance in (14a) is an *exam question*: The speaker (i.e., the examiner) knows the answer to the utterance, whereas the hearer might know it or might not. The utterance in (14b) is a *guess question*: The speaker knows both the answer to the utterance and the fact that the hearer doesn't know it, but still encourages the hearer to attempt to provide it.

As Wilson and Sperber observe, speech act theory suggests that an exam or guess question "would have the force of a request for an answer, but not a request for information" (p. 23). In other words, speech act theory would claim that the speaker of an exam or guess question requires an answer from the hearer but does not seek information. Thus, exam or guess questions do not satisfy the felicity conditions for requests for information (i.e., information-seeking questions).

It might be argued that the point of uttering an exam or guess question is to encourage the hearer to participate in a particular activity, i.e., demonstrating knowledge of the answer or the ability to guess accurately (Clark, 1991, p. 150). The speaker expects the hearer to provide the answer to the utterance, and the provided answer demonstrates the hearer's ability to do so. This view is not incompatible with Wilson and Sperber's claim that exam/guess questions are not requests for information. Wilson and Sperber argue that questions seeking information the speakers already have do not fit the speech act theoretic account of interrogative utterances.

Let us consider some other non-information-seeking questions:

(16) a. Expository questions:
       What are the main objections to this approach? First...
   b. Speculative questions (self-addressed):
       Why do the leaves of different trees go different colours in autumn?
                           (Sperber & Wilson, 1995, pp. 251–252)

(17) Speculative questions/musings:
    Now, who is going to win the by-election tomorrow?
                                               (Blakemore, 1992, p. 115)

Just as in the case of an exam question, the speaker of an expository question like (16a) knows the answer whereas the hearer might or might not. These questions are nevertheless different from exam or guess questions in that the speaker has no interest in ascertaining the hearer's answer, intending rather to provide the answer themselves immediately after uttering the question. Similarly, a self-addressed question like (16b) can be produced in the absence of any audience. The speaker of (16b) neither knows the answer nor, given the absence of a hearer, expects any to be provided. Finally, the speaker of the utterance in (17) does not know the answer, but also knows that the hearer does not know it either and so does not expect the hearer to provide it.

Sperber and Wilson state that rhetorical questions such as (18) below are also cases of non-information-seeking interrogative utterances:

(18) [Hearer has claimed that he would give up smoking, but later the speaker sees the hearer smoking, and utters:]
    When did you say you were going to give up smoking?
                                           (Sperber & Wilson, 1995, p. 251)

According to Sperber and Wilson, the utterance in (18) is not an information-seeking question but a rhetorical question: The speaker communicates the thought (i.e., the answer) *The hearer has said they would give up smoking at a certain time in the past*. They claim that the thought is relevant as it functions as a "reminder" (Sperber & Wilson, 1995, p. 252). This approach to interrogative utterances, grounded in relevance theory, will be explored in detail in Chapter 4.

2.6 Against Speech Act Theory: A New Analysis

2.6.1 Assertive Force and Directive Force

Many authors claim that the most salient property of a rhetorical question is assertion: A rhetorical question, they argue, performs an *assertive speech act*. The following definition given in Quirk et al. (1985) is also invoked in other studies of rhetorical questions, including Rohde's (2006) and Han's (2002):

(19) The rhetorical question is interrogative in structure, but has the force of a

strong assertion   (Quirk et al., 1985, p. 825)

According to Quirk et al., a yes-no rhetorical question like those in (20a) and (20b) below communicates an assertion with the opposite polarity of the proposition expressed by the utterance, whereas a *wh*-rhetorical question communicates an assertion developed from the incomplete logical form by replacing the variable with either an empty value such as *nobody*, as in (21a), or a universal quantifier such as *everybody*, as in (21b).

(20) a. Is that a reason for despair?
     Speaker's assertion: Surely that isn't a reason for despair.
   b. Isn't the answer obvious?
     Speaker's assertion: Surely the answer is obvious.
(21) a. Who knows?
     Speaker's assertion: Nobody knows.
   b. Who doesn't know?
     Speaker's assertion: Everybody knows.

                                               (Quirk et al., 1985, p. 826)

Although Quirk et al. is not based on speech act theory, the definition given in (19) is recognized as one based on a speech act theoretic approach by writers such as Han (2002) and Rohde (2006). Rohde claims that the asserted content is equivalent to a *possible* answer to the question. For example, this suggests that the answer to the utterance in (21a) is *Nobody knows*.

Here we can see two distinct views based on speech act theory: A rhetorical interrogative utterance either has assertive force, functioning as a reminder that something is the case, or directive force, functioning as a reminder that the speaker wants the hearer to do something. Recall (9e):

(9) e. How many times have I told you not to eat with your fingers?

The utterance in (9e) is not an information-seeking question but a rhetorical question: It is obvious that the speaker does not expect the hearer to provide the answer . In Searle's (1975) view, the utterance in (9e) is an indirect request for action: It has a directive force encouraging the hearer not to perform the action of eating with fingers. By contrast, Quirk et al. and those who agree with their view would say that (9e) has an assertive force, asserting something like *The speaker has told the hearer countless times not to eat with his fingers*. A similar case is given by Huddleston and Pullum (2002):

(22) [At eight o'clock, her child's bedtime, Mother says to her child:]

Do you know what time it is?   (Huddleston & Pullum, 2002, p. 861)

Huddleston and Pullum provide example (22) as a typical indirect request for action. The utterance has the directive force of causing the child to go to bed. By contrast, if the utterance in (22) were interpreted as a rhetorical question, Quirk et al. might say that it *asserts* that *you (the hearer; i.e., the child) should know that it is eight o'clock* or that *it is time for the child to go to bed*.

However, it seems strange that an utterance should have two distinct illocutionary forces. Indeed, these speech act theoretic accounts do not fit in the case of some rhetorical questions. In other words, there are contexts in which the same utterance might be neither a request for action nor an assertion. Consider example (22) with a new context:

(23) [At an evening conference, when the guest of honor does not appear on time, the speaker says to her friend:]
Do you know what time it is?

Suppose that the speaker is attending an evening conference and the guest of honor is late. If the speaker utters (23) to a friend also attending the conference, the utterance implies the assumption *It is time for the guest speaker to appear*. Clearly this assumption does not have directive force as a request. The speaker does not indicate any request for action on the guest of honor's part; indeed, such a request would be impossible because the guest of honor is not participating in the interaction. The difference between (22) and (23), therefore, lies in whether some individual is expected to perform an action or not.

Consider another example. In this case, an individual is expected to perform an action, but the utterance still does not have directive force:

(24) [Someone arrives late for a meeting. As the chair of the meeting enters, they utter:]
Do you know what time it is?

As the utterance in (24) is made after the time at which the meeting was scheduled to start is already past, it is clearly impossible to request that the hearer come on time. The thought communicated by the utterance might be interpreted as an admonishment rather than a request.

2.6.2 Can Assertive Force Be Measured?

Another problem with the speech act theoretic analysis of rhetorical questions is that although many authors who view rhetorical questions as assertive speech acts adopt Sadock's (1971) syntactic tests for declarativity (Gutiérrez-Rexach, 1998; Han, 2002; Rohde, 2006), which Han states are "to show that rhetorical yes-no questions are formally assertions" (p. 203), these tests do not seem capable of determining whether an utterance has assertive force.

Sadock's tests involve the use of *after all*, *by any chance*, and a *yet*-clause. According to Sadock, utterances introduced by *after all* or followed by *yet*-clauses must be interpreted as rhetorical rather than ordinary information-seeking questions. On the other hand, utterances co-occurring with *by any chance* cannot be interpreted as rhetorical questions and must be information-seeking questions.

However, although the first two tests (i.e., use of *after all* and a *yet*-clause) seem to be valid ways of confirming the declarativity of questions, it does not follow that they are also valid for conforming assertive force. Assertive force is not, after all, equivalent to declarativity. Most authors do not mention this distinction; they appear to simply use Sadock's tests to confirm assertive force. Consider the following examples:

(25) a. *After all*, do phonemes have anything to do with language?
    b. Do phonemes have anything to do with language?
       Yet people continue to believe in them.
    c. Are the gazanias blooming, *by any chance*?

                                            (Sadock, 1971, pp. 225, 227)

According to Sadock, (25a) and (25b) are rhetorical questions, whereas (25c) is an information-seeking question. *After all*, as in (25a), can occur with a rhetorical question, but not with an information-seeking question. Similarly, a rhetorical question can be followed by *yet*-clause felicitously as in (25b), but an information-seeking question cannot. Finally, Sadock argues, *by any chance* can co-occur with an information-seeking question, as in (25c), but not with a rhetorical question.

Gutiérrez-Rexach (1998) applies these tests to his examples of yes-no questions as follows:

(26) a. *After all*, are you coming to the party?
    b. Did I receive help from anybody?
       Yet, I managed to complete my tasks on time.
    c. Is John coming, *by any chance*?   (Gutiérrez-Rexach, 1998, p. 142)

However, Gutiérrez-Rexach reaches a different conclusion, arguing that *by any chance* can occur with a rhetorical question as well. He claims that (26a) and (26b) are always interpreted as rhetorical questions, whereas the utterance in

(26c) is preferably interpreted as a rhetorical question (1998, p. 142).

Han (2002) applies the tests to *wh*-interrogatives, using the following examples:

(27) a. *After all*, who helped Mary?
   b. Who helped Mary?
      Yet she managed everything by herself.
   c. ?Who helped Mary, *by any chance*? (Han, 2002, p. 204)

Han's examples support Sadock's claim that *after all* and *yet*-clauses can co-occur only with rhetorical questions whereas *by any chance* can co-occur only with information-seeking questions. Han does observe, however, that the utterance in (27c) is "a bit degraded for reasons which I do not understand yet" (p. 204), which is why she marks it "?".

Note that, in addition to the *yet*-clause test, contrastive discourse markers such as *although* and *but* also imply declarativity in questions. They can also appear in responses to rhetorical questions, as in the following examples:

(28) A (Mother): *Do you know what time it is?*
   B (Child): *But* I don't want to go to bed yet, Mom.
(29) A: *Do you know what time it is?* I'm fed up with your friends.
      They're late and my meal is getting spoilt.
   B: *Although* I guess they could have got lost.
                        (D. Blakemore, personal communication, 2008)

The claim by Quirk et al. (1985) and their followers that such rhetorical questions have assertive force is too strong. Furthermore, they do not attempt to explain why speakers should not simply use declarative equivalents to assert the same content. If rhetorical questions are to be interpreted as having assertive force, a clear distinction must be drawn between saying something with a rhetorical interrogative utterance and saying the same thing with a declarative utterance.

In my view, the thought communicated by the rhetorical question *Who knows?* is not the same as the thought communicated by the declarative equivalent *Nobody knows*. Quintilian is right to argue that asking a rhetorical question is *more animated* than saying its declarative equivalent (95 B.C.E/1856, 9.2). Rhetorical questions communicate more emotional and expressive thoughts than their declarative equivalents. In other words, the speaker of the utterance *Who knows?* communicates not only the thought *Nobody knows* but also a set of related thoughts such as *It could be anyone but I don't care*, rich in feelings such as incuriosity and sarcasm regarding the previous question.

2.6.3 Do Rhetorical Questions Assert Polarity-Reversed Assumptions?

Another problem with the idea that rhetorical questions are assertive can be found in the idea, as argued by Han (2002), that rhetorical questions like those in (20) and (21) negate the proposition expressed by the utterance: they are *polarity-reversed*. This, as I will show below, is not always true.

Polarity-reversed rhetorical questions have been discussed by a number of authors, including Sadock (1971), Progovac (1993), Gutiérrez-Rexach (1998), and Han (2002). According to Han, rhetorical questions are semantically distinguished from ordinary information-seeking questions by this polarity reversal. Han argues that at the post-logical form (i.e., semantic) level, *wh*-words in positive *wh*-rhetorical questions act as negative quantifiers, whereas covert *wh*-words (i.e., *whether*) in yes-no rhetorical questions act as ¬ (*no* or *not*), as in the following examples:

(30) a. What has John done for you?   (Adapted from Han, 2002, p. 220)
    b.

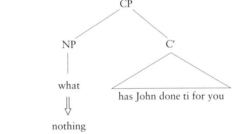

    c. ¬ ∃ x [John has done x for you]

(31) a. Did I tell you that writing a dissertation was easy?
                                           (Adapted from Han, 2002, p. 219)
    b.

    c. ¬ [I told you that writing a dissertation was easy]

Han states that the *wh*-word of (30a) is mapped onto a negative quantifier at the post-logical form level as in (30b) (p. 220). The interpretation of (30a) is then (30c). Similarly, the covert *wh*-word (i.e., *whether*) of (31a) is mapped onto a negation, as in (31b), giving the interpretation (31c).

However, there are some rhetorical questions whose assertions are not thoughts with reversed polarity. Consider the following example:

(32) A: What company's computer will you buy?
    B: Well, *what company do I work for?*   (Lee-Goldman, 2006, Slide 10)
       Speaker's assertion: The speaker works for a (particular) computer company

Lee-Goldman (2006) gives (32B) as an example of a rhetorical question, but it obviously does not communicate a polarity-reversed assertion such as *I don't work for any company*.

Rohde (2006) takes another approach, claiming that the assertion of a rhetorical question is equivalent to the answer to the question. On this analysis, the speaker's assertion in (32B) should be its answer: *I work for a (particular) computer company*. This view seems plausible, except the use of term *assertion*, as it fits not only polarity-reversed but also other types of rhetorical question. However, the felicity conditions for rhetorical questions Rohde offers, which involve the obviousness of the answer and the shared knowledge, remain problematic. The final section in this chapter outlines Rohde's approach based on common ground theory as a platform for reconsidering felicitous conditions for rhetorical and information-seeking questions.

2.7 The Answer to a Rhetorical Question

Rohde (2006) argues that, regardless of whether an utterance is an ordinary information-seeking question or a rhetorical question, the discourse participants assume a set of *possible* answers to it. This is based on the speech act theoretic account that rhetorical questions communicate *assertions*: As noted in the preceding section, Rohde holds that the assertion of a rhetorical question is equivalent to its answer.

Rohde argues that rhetoricity can be analyzed in terms of the obviousness of the answer. The answer to a rhetorical question should be obvious and constitute *common ground* between the speaker and hearer before the utterance is made.

Rohde's views on common ground are based on Gunlogson's (2001) common ground discourse model, itself based on Stalnaker's (1974/1999) conception of common ground developed as part of his pragmatic account of presuppositions. Gunlogson's formalization of common ground is framed in terms of participants' beliefs or *commitments* (Rohde, 2006) regarding the proposition expressed by an utterance. For example, according to Gunlogson, a falling declarative utterance (e.g., *It's raining*) can be used in contexts in which the *speaker* is already committed to the proposition expressed by the utterance, a rising declarative utterance (e.g., *It's raining?*) can be used as a question in contexts where the *hearer* is committed to the proposition expressed, and an interrogative utterance (e.g., *Is it raining?*) can be used in contexts where *no one* is committed to the proposition expressed by the utterance (e.g., *It is raining*).

Rohde (2006) develops Gunlogson's theory and applies it to her analysis of rhetorical questions, saying:

> Rhetorical questions...require that both participants already be committed to a joint mutual belief. Joint commitments require all participants to not only believe a proposition *P* but also be aware that other participants believe *P* as well. Shared knowledge about others' beliefs and about the real world is precisely what licenses rhetorical questions.
>
> (p. 145)

Consider the following example:

(33) A: So, who's your favorite team?
    B: *Who do you think?* The Dallas Cowboys!   (Rohde, 2006, p. 140)

Rohde claims that the rhetoricity of (33B) is successfully understood because both participants in (33) "already know or can derive the answer to (33B) from their knowledge about B's public commitments (e.g. B's silver and blue jacket)" (2006, p. 140).

There are two problems with this argument. First, the *answer values* (i.e., true answers) of rhetorical questions are not always obvious to discourse participants. Second, rhetorical questions can be uttered in contexts in which the answers to the utterances are not necessarily shared by the discourse participants as common ground before the utterance is made.

Regarding the first problem, the following example shows that the answer values of rhetorical questions are not always obvious:

(34) [Watching a news story about a child who had been murdered, the speaker utters to her husband]
    What monster would dare to harm a sleeping child?

(Sperber & Wilson, 1995, p. 247)

Neither the speaker of (34) nor its hearer knows which individual killed the child, but the speaker is not really interested in who the monster is anyway. The point of uttering (34) lies in implicit speaker assumptions such as *The murderer is monstrous* and *(Therefore) the news is terrible*. The speaker does not intend to convey an answer such as *The monster is the individual* X.

Consider a similar example in Japanese:

(35) [After watching a movie, the speaker says to her boyfriend:]
 Doko no baka ga wazawaza konna hidoi eiga tsukuru no kashira?
 where GEN idiot S dare to do such terrible film make Q
 'What idiot would dare to make such a terrible film?'
                                    (Murakami, 1988/1991, p. 263)

Just like we saw in (34), neither the speaker of (35) nor its hearer knows who exactly made the film they have just watched. The speaker knows that the hearer doesn't know the answer to the utterance (i.e., the individual who made the film) but is not interested in the answer anyway. The point of uttering (35) lies in implicit speaker assumptions like *Only an idiot would make such a film* or *The film is terrible*.

To summarize, the answer values of rhetorical questions like (34) and (35) are obvious to neither hearer nor speaker. Thus, the point of uttering rhetorical questions cannot lie in the answer (or *assertion* in a speech act theoretic account) as argued by Rohde (2006)

As for the second problem with Rohde's argument that rhetorical questions can be uttered even if the answers to the utterances are not necessarily shared by both discourse participants in advance, consider the following example of a declarative utterance, given by Blakemore (1992) to provide evidence that mutual (i.e., common-ground) knowledge is unnecessary. Suppose that, when asked by Mary if he has read a certain book, Peter utters:

(36) I never read books that win prizes.   (Blakemore, 1992, p. 21)

Even if Mary did not know in advance that the book in question won a prize, she can recover the intended interpretation that Peter didn't read it.

Similarly, the answer to (i.e., speaker's assumption in) the following rhetorical interrogative utterance could become obvious between the speaker and hearer as a result of the utterance. Consider:

(37) [Sue and John are friends. John feels depressed when his girlfriend is leav-

ing him, and utters:]
John: Well, she's finally leaving.
Sue: *Whose fault is that?*
Speaker's assumption (i.e., answer): It is John's fault.

To understand Sue's intention, John need not have accessed the assumption *It is John's fault* before the utterance is made: The assumption need not have been common ground. Even if John had believed that his girlfriend leaving him was not his fault, and thought that this assumption was shared by Sue, he can access Sue's actual assumption *It is John's fault* after her utterance is made. In other words, Rohde's felicity condition that the answer to a rhetorical question must be shared by the discourse participants before the utterance is made is not necessary for the utterance to be understood.

Many authors have discussed definitions of common ground, including Clark and Marshall (1981), Clark (1996), and Sperber and Wilson (1986, 1995). Clark and Marshall note that the definition of common ground provided by Schiffer (1972) (albeit using the term *mutual knowledge*) involves *iterated propositions* or what Clark calls the "common-ground-iterated" (p. 100) or *CG-iterated* as follows:

(38) CG-iterated:
    A and B mutually know that p =def
    (1) A knows that p.
    (1') B knows that p.
    (2) A knows that B knows that p.
    (2') B knows that A knows that p.
    (3) A knows that B knows that A knows that p.
    (3') B knows that A knows that B knows that p.
    et cetera ad infinitum.
                                      (Clark & Marshall, 1981, p. 17)

Some authors, however, claim that the concept of the CG-iterated is flawed (Clark, 1996; Sperber & Wilson, 1995; Clark & Marshall, 1981). As Clark puts it, "it cannot represent people's mental state because it requires an infinitely large mental capacity" (p. 95). Sperber and Wilson claim that mutual knowledge that requires access to infinitely iterated assumptions is neither necessary nor sufficient for communication.

Lewis (2002) offers an alternative model, arguing that presupposed assumptions are constructed as part of the interpretation of the utterance rather than set up in advance (p. 340). Lewis's *rule of accommodation for presupposition* attempts to answer the question of what exactly constrains the hearer's choice of context in a particular case.

(39) *The rule of accommodation for presupposition*
If at time *t* something is said that requires presupposition P to be acceptable, and if P is not presupposed just before *t*, then—*ceteris paribus* and within certain limits—presupposition P comes into existence at *t*.

(Lewis, 2002, p. 163)

According to this rule of accommodation, the hearer of an utterance accommodates the context necessary for achieving an acceptable interpretation. This principle explains why it is not necessary for Sue's assumption in (37), *It is John's fault*, to be common ground in advance.

Sperber and Wilson (1995) raise the question of how participants know that certain assumptions are genuine common ground or mutual knowledge (i.e., the CG-iterated) rather than simply shared assumptions. They argue that the notion of common ground is useless for understanding our inferential process in communication, and suggest as a replacement the notion of *mutual manifestness*. This concept requires some explanation.

In the framework of Sperber and Wilson's (1995) relevance theory, an assumption accessed by a discourse participant becomes *manifest* in that participant's cognitive environment (p. 45). Sperber and Wilson argue that mutually manifest assumptions exist in "the total shared environment of two people [which] is the intersection of their two total cognitive environments, i.e. the set of all facts that are manifest to them both" (1995, p. 41). Manifestness is defined as follows:

(40) a. A fact is *manifest* to an individual at a given time if and only if he is capable at that time of representing it mentally and accepting its representation as true or probably true.
b. A *cognitive environment* of an individual is a set of facts that are manifest to him. (Sperber & Wilson, 1995, p. 39)

Any assumption can be manifest, and some assumptions are more manifest than others. As Sperber and Wilson observe, when you hear the doorbell ringing, you might develop the assumption that there is somebody behind the door (1995, p. 40). This might be the most manifest assumption at that time, winning out over other accessible assumptions that are less manifest such as *A man behind the door is tall enough to touch the bell*.

In summary, we have seen substantial evidence that a rhetorical question does not assert anything. Speakers use rhetorical questions to communicate explicit and/or implicit assumptions that the utterance itself might or might not lead the hearer to access. Furthermore, we have also seen that rhetorical questions do not necessarily have answers that are obvious or shared by discourse participants as common ground. In fact, some rhetorical questions do not have answers accessible to participants at all.

2.8 Conclusion

This chapter has examined the properties of rhetorical questions, considering a variety of uses of interrogative utterances in English.

First, we saw claims from speech act theorists such as Searle (1975) that the interrogative mood correlates with directive speech acts: ordinary interrogatives are requests for information, whereas indirect interrogatives are indirect requests of action. However, some types of interrogative utterances seem to be beyond the limits of this account.

For example, Sperber and Wilson (1995) and Wilson and Sperber (1988/2012) provide rhetorical and other non-information-seeking questions that are counterexamples to speech act theoretic accounts of interrogative utterances. Sperber and Wilson also observe that not only these interrogatives but also some declaratives and imperatives cannot be explained by speech act theoretic accounts.

I concur with Sperber and Wilson's criticisms of speech act theoretic accounts and argue that rhetorical questions have neither assertive nor directive force. For instance, the point of uttering *Do you know what time it is?* is not to perform a directive speech act (e.g., request that the hearer go to bed) or an assertive speech act (e.g., assert that *It is 8 o'clock and it is time you went to bed*). Speech act theoretic accounts do not explain why the speaker should use an interrogative form in such cases rather than simply uttering a request like *Go to bed* or an assertion like *It is time you went to bed*.

If speech act theory cannot accommodate all interrogatives, including non-ordinary questions, it cannot provide a general account of interrogative utterances: We must seek another theoretical framework.

Rohde (2006) provided an alternative account based on common ground theory, arguing that the point of uttering a rhetorical question like *Do you know what time it is?* lies in the fact that the speaker knows the answer, e.g., *It is 8 o'clock*. Although her felicitous conditions seemed able to accommodate various types of rhetorical questions, they were not without problems of their own. In the following chapters, this book will offer a more robust account.

CHAPTER 3

The Continuum of Rhetoricity

The previous chapter showed that the rhetoricity of an interrogative utterance might be inferred from a variety of semantic or pragmatic clues, such as linguistic expressions (e.g., discourse markers), knowledge shared between the participants, knowledge shared at the time of utterance, and the speaker's emotional attitude to the proposition expressed by the utterance as understood from the speaker's tone of voice (e.g., sarcasm, irritation, or surprise; see later in this chapter).

Logically, therefore, we would expect to see cases that fall between clearly information-seeking questions and clearly rhetorical questions — cases that prevent the deduction process from being completed. For instance, a sarcastic tone of voice might cause a rhetorically *biased* interpretation. Sarcasm, which can be defined as an ironical attitude, affects the interpretation of interrogative utterances: It guides the hearer towards a rhetorically biased evaluation. However, there does not seem to be any standard by which hearers rate sarcasm as a clue to rhetorical bias. More than one clue might be involved, including facial expression, tone of voice, and contextual information such as shared knowledge or knowledge being shared at the time of the utterance. There must be cases in which the hearer cannot arrive at a single clear interpretation from the available clues; the hearer might wonder if the utterance was intended as a rhetorical question due to the ironical tone, but hesitate to identify the utterance as unambiguously rhetorical.

This chapter searches for a standard by which to evaluate the rhetoricity of interrogative utterances. The following section introduces several distinct cases of interrogative utterances from previous studies where the rhetorical bias is ambiguous, such as *confirmation questions* (Gutiérrez-Rexach, 1998), *complex questions* (Walton, 1988), *vain questions* (Driver, 1988), and others. A literal–rhetorical continuum is then proposed in the section after that.

3.1 Borderline Cases: Information-Seeking or Rhetorical?

Most rhetorical questions can be distinguished from information-seeking questions. Some confirmation questions, however, communicate similar (negatively biased) assumptions to those of rhetorical questions (Gutiérrez-Rexach, 1998). Consider:

(1) [The speaker knows that the hearer has reservations for a one-week vacation in the Bahamas in two weeks. When the hearer tells the speaker that he is too busy to finish the assigned task during the next month, the speaker says:]
Aren't you going to the Bahamas?   (Gutiérrez-Rexach, 1998, p. 143)

According to Gutiérrez-Rexach, the interrogative utterance in (1) can be interpreted as both a confirmation question and a rhetorical question. The utterance, Gutiérrez-Rexach says, represents the propositional content *You are going to the Bahamas* (p. 143), which already exists in the speaker's cognitive environment. Gutiérrez-Rexach claims that the distinction between a confirmatory and rhetorical use of the utterance (1) is not truth-conditional and depends on the speaker's confidence regarding the truthfulness of the proposition: It is a confirmation question if and only if the speaker is not sure whether the hearer is going to the Bahamas (p. 144).

Consider another example that could be either a confirmation or rhetorical question:

(2) [In a restaurant, a guest asks a waiter to total the bill, and the waiter replies:]
You can add the bill up. After all, don't you do maths?
(D. Blakemore, personal communication, 2008)

In (2), *Don't you do maths?* would be interpreted as a rhetorical question if the speaker believed that the hearer surely *does maths* (at least well enough to add up the bill). On the other hand, the utterance would also be interpreted as a confirmation question if the speaker were not sure whether the hearer did maths — for example, if the hearer (a guest) were a foreigner and did not seem to understand the figures written in the bill.

If the interpretation of these examples depends on the speaker's confidence rating of the thought or proposition expressed, then the extreme information-seeking rating and extreme rhetorical rating lie at the opposite ends of a single scale. In other words, clearly information-seeking questions have the highest information-seeking rating, equivalent to the lowest rhetorical rating, and clearly rhetorical questions have the lowest information-seeking rating, equivalent to the highest rhetorical rating. However, confirmation questions do not necessarily have the highest information-seeking rating; they may merely be biased towards the information-seeking end of the scale. Similarly, some rhetorical questions may merely be biased towards rhetoricity without reaching the extreme end of the scale. This leads us to conclude that there must be borderline cases between confirmation questions and rhetorical questions. For example, it is difficult to evaluate the rhetoricity of ironical confirmation questions such as:

(3)   [sarcastically] Have you ever read that trashy novel?

The irony might be one clue the hearer uses to evaluate the utterance's rhetoricity, but not necessarily a decisive one. That is, the hearer might interpret the irony or sarcasm in (3) is part of its rhetoricity, in which case the rhetorical reading of the utterance will be preferred. On the other hand, the hearer might interpret the utterance as a confirmation question with an ironical flavor. Where do we draw a line between the two distinct interpretations? My answer is that the matter is purely pragmatic, and therefore there should even be cases in which neither the hearer nor the speaker of (3) is sure whether the interrogative utterance seeks information or not. The one thing that is sure in this case is that the speaker intends to communicate a sarcastic attitude.

What if the speaker of (3) means it rhetorically? Can the hearer of (3) grasp its rhetoricity then? Interrogative utterances such as (3) might be classified as what Walton (1988) calls *loaded questions* (see below), which he claims are distinct from rhetorical questions. Although Walton does not provided any further comment on how the two types of questions are distinguished from each other, his description seems to be correct in that a loaded question can be a rhetorical question only if the sarcasm/irony of the communicated thought is strong enough to restrict the hearer's answer. In other words, if the hearer recognizes the presupposed thought *The novel is trashy* and also the speaker's sarcastic attitude, then a yes/no answer will not be assumed to be the main focus of the speaker's interest. The utterance will therefore be interpreted as communicating thoughts such as *One who has read such trashy novel is stupid* or *If the hearer has read it, the hearer is stupid*.

By contrast, there is a context where the utterance in (3) can be interpreted as an information-seeking (confirmation) question. Suppose that the hearer has already read the novel and agrees with the speaker's thought *The novel is trashy*. In this context, even though the hearer of the utterance in (3) recognizes the speaker's sarcastic attitude towards it, the utterance could still be interpreted as seeking information.

3.1.1 Complex Questions and Rhetoricity

According to Walton (1988), loaded questions are a subset of *complex questions*. Let us consider an example given by Manor (1979). Suppose that you are asked the question *Did you drive your car to the office today?* If you drove your car, you might answer with *Yes, I did*; if you walked to the office, you might answer with *No, I didn't*. Yes-no questions can usually be recognized by their requiring an answer that directly involves the truthfulness of the proposition expressed by the question. As another option, you might answer with *No, I drove Mark's car*. Because this answer implies that you didn't drive your car, it involves the truthfulness of the proposition, but only indirectly: The main focus is on how you got to the office.

Manor (1979) states that there are two different types of response to interrogative utterances: *answers* and *retorts*. The response *No, I drove Mark's car* is a retort as a *corrective answer*: It functions to correct the question's presupposition that the hearer has a car. In other words, the retort negates the presupposition of the previous question. The question *Did you drive your car?* implies two questions: one asking whether the hearer drove their own car or somebody else's, and one asking whether the hearer drove a car at all.

An interrogative utterance that implies more than one question in this way is called a *complex question*. In traditional logic, a complex question or *plurium interrogationum* (Latin for "[of] many questions") is a question that has multiple presuppositions (Walton, 1988). Complex questions can be fallacious, but are not necessarily so. Consider:

(4) a. Who is the king of Spain?
    b. Who is the king of France?

The question in (4a) presupposes two propositions: *There is a place called Spain* and *That place has a king*. Both propositions are true. The question in (4b), however, presupposes one true proposition, *There is a place called France*, and one false one, *That place has a king*. The question in (4b) commits the fallacy of the complex question.

A *loaded question* is a type of complex question with presuppositions involving controversial assumptions such as presumption of guilt. For example:

(5)   Have you stopped beating your wife?   (Walton, 1988)

Loaded questions such as the utterance in (5) are used to entrap the hearer in certain circumstances such as court trials (Walton, 1988). The utterance in (5) presupposes the proposition *You have beaten your wife*. If the hearer answers *Yes*, the assumption is that that proposition is true, but even if the hearer answers *No*, the presupposition still fallaciously appears to be true.

Suppose that the utterance in (5) is made in a context where the hearer has never beaten his wife. It can be interpreted as a rhetorical question whose rhetoricity is caused by the trap that the speaker has laid in committing the fallacy of the complex question. In other words, the rhetoricity is explicitly communicated when the hearer is aware of the speaker's intention: to trick the hearer into a false admission that he has beaten his wife at some point.

How does the utterance in (5), when interpreted as a rhetorical question, compare to the utterance in (3)? I repeat them below for convenience's sake:

(3) Have you ever read that trashy novel?
(5) Have you stopped beating your wife?

These can both be considered loaded questions, and a degree of sarcasm can be recognized in both. As with (3), in which the sarcasm lies in the speaker's attitude towards the thought *The novel is trashy*, the sarcasm in (5) lies in the speaker's attitude towards the thought *The hearer beat his wife*. We can predict that a rhetorical reading will be preferred if the speaker's intention to communicate this sarcastic attitude to these thoughts is stronger than their intention to seek the truthfulness of the proposition expressed by the utterance.

Hence, it seems that the hearer's recognition of the strength of the speaker's sarcastic attitude towards the thought expressed by an utterance is a strong clue to a rhetorical reading. Researchers often do not distinguish sarcasm from irony in the study of ironical interrogative utterances (Kawakami, 1984; Utsumi, 2000). The nature of irony and sarcasm in interrogative utterances will be discussed in Chapter 5.

3.1.2 Vain Questions and Rhetoricity

Another problem that should be raised here is whether types of questions that do not purely seek information but are not generally called rhetorical questions, such as vain questions (Driver, 1988) and guess/exam questions (Sperber and Wilson, 1995), are somehow rhetorical.

Vain questions are what Driver calls questions which are asked without any reason to expect an answer. According to Driver, an answer to a vain question is not expected because they are not possible to answer. Driver divides vain questions into three groups:

(6) a. questions which are (contingently) not possible to answer:
    e.g., How many drops of water?
   b. questions which are rather speculative, so that no answer (that fits the context) can be obtained:
    e.g., Are the edges of this piece of paper incommensurable?
   c. (i) questions which are even more speculative in nature than (6b) above, which may be asked as a philosophical inquiry our out of curiosity; and
    (ii) questions which have two or more logically possible answers:
    e.g., Does body exist?

Driver admits that both vain questions and rhetorical questions are uttered without any expectation of being answered, but he insists that it is important to distinguish the two, the distinction lying in *why* the answer is not expected. According to Driver, the speaker of a vain question does not expect an answer because it is obvious that the hearer has no way of knowing it, whereas the speaker of a rhetorical question does not expect an answer because they know that the answer is already obvious to both speaker and hearer.

Driver gives one example of a vain question in category (6a):

(7) A1: I can answer any question you care to ask.
    A2: What about this one: How many drops of water are there in the Atlantic Ocean? (Driver, 1988, p. 248)

However, Driver's argument that the point of rhetorical questions lies in the obviousness of the answer seems to fit Rohde's (2006) felicity conditions for interpreting rhetorical questions. In fact, Rohde has provided a similar example:

(8) How many stars are there in the sky?
    Speaker's thought: There are a number of stars in the sky.
    (Rohde, 2006, p. 156)

According to Rohde, the utterance in (8) is a rhetorical question because the answer *or the speaker's thought* is obvious between the speaker and the hearer. If one accepts that the speaker's thought may be the obvious shared information instead of the answer itself, there does not appear to be any distinction between (7) and (8) in this respect. Driver provides no argument against this view.

Furthermore, in my view, the utterance in (7A2) may be a *guess* or *exam question*. Guess and exam questions can be distinguished from rhetorical questions in that they are uttered in particular situations outside daily interactions, but a given interrogative utterance might nevertheless be interpretable as either a guess/exam question or a rhetorical question. In other words, guess and exam questions are to an extent rhetorical in the sense that they do not purely seek information and therefore do not receive the greatest information-seeking rating.

Driver's vain questions include even the famous riddle that the Sphinx asked of Oedipus:

(9) What walks on 4 legs in the morning, two legs in the afternoon, and three legs in the evening? (Driver, 1988, p. 249)

Driver argues that the utterance in (9) is a vain question because it is extremely difficult to answer, if not technically impossible. In my view, not only are riddles like this quite similar to guess/exam questions, the fact that they are not generally uttered in daily conversation makes it meaningless to argue the distinction between vain questions and rhetorical questions using this sort of example.

The utterance in (6b) resembles a speculative question, and in my analysis speculative questions are rhetorical to the extent that they are obviously non-information-seeking questions. Thus, although Driver argues that only the utterance in (6c) is similar to a rhetorical question, in my analysis all of Driver's vain questions are rhetorical to an extent.

3.1.3 Other Rhetorically Biased Question Types

Sperber and Wilson argue that guess and exam questions as non-information-seeking questions can be distinguished from rhetorical questions (Sperber & Wilson, 1995; Wilson & Sperber, 1988). The difference, they argue, is that guess and exam questions require answers that the speaker already knows, ascertaining the hearer's ability to provide or guess the answer, but rhetorical questions do not require answers at all. Consider the question *Who knows?* in the following three distinct situations:

(10) Someone must have seen who hit Billy. Come on. *Who knows?*
(11) A1: Three people in the room know my middle name. *Who knows?*
   B1: Ah, uh, Billy, John, and Ryan?
   A2: No, John, Peter, and Brian.
(12) [A school teacher finds that Billy, a student in the class, is crying, and utters to the other students:]
   a. Teacher: Who hit Billy?
   b. Student: *Who knows?*

According to Sperber and Wilson's analysis, the utterance *Who knows?* in (10) is an information-seeking question: It is obvious that the speaker wants to know who hit Billy. In (11A1), *Who knows?* is a guess question: The speaker intends to encourage the hearer to provide an answer. By contrast, in (12b), *Who knows?* functions as a response to (12a) and would be interpreted as a rhetorical question. The speaker of (12b) does not expect the answer to be provided by the hearer (i.e., the teacher); in fact, the speaker knows that the hearer does not know who knows who hit Billy. It is clear that the speaker of (12b) is not interested in ascertaining the answer to the question, and that this itself is the main thought the speaker intends to communicate. Thus, the speaker apparently communicates not only the thought *Nobody knows* (or *I don't know*) but also other thoughts such as *It could be anyone but nobody cares*, or simply *I don't care.*

Among these three examples, the difference between the rhetorical question in (12) and the non-rhetorical questions in (10) and (11A1) appears to be whether the speaker expects the hearer to answer. However, there are rhetorical questions to which speakers *do* expect an answer. Recall the following interaction, (32) from Chapter 2, included here again for convenience:

(13) A: What company's computer will you buy?
    B: Well, *what company do I work for?*

The speaker of (13B) does not want to know the answer: It is already known to them. Rather, the speaker intends to communicate the assumption (answer) *I work for a particular computer company*. However, the point of uttering (13B) does not lie solely in communicating that assumption. As the speaker utters (13B) as a response to the previous information-seeking question (13A), the speaker also communicates that the answer to (13B) is directly linked to the answer to (13A). The speaker therefore implies *I will buy a computer made by my company*. In other words, by using an interrogative utterance, the speaker intends to lead the hearer to the interpretation that the speaker will buy a computer made by the company the speaker works for.

It seems that the speaker intends to elicit an answer from the hearer, but not in the same way as might be expected if the speaker used an information-seeking question. In this sense, the question in (13B) resembles a guess question. However, there is a difference between the utterance in (13B) and guess questions such as *Which hand is it in?* The speaker of (13B) does not expect a verbal response from the hearer, whereas the speaker of a true guess question does. It seems plausible that the utterance in (13B) merely sounds as if an answer from the hearer were expected. I argue, therefore, that interrogative utterances like the utterance in (13B) should be considered rhetorically biased questions if not fully rhetorical. By contrast, guess and exam questions are biased towards the information-seeking end of the scale because they require a verbal answer from the hearer. Note that this view still supports Sperber and Wilson's categorization of guess and exam questions as non-information-seeking questions insofar as I agree that they are not *typical* information-seeking questions.

Rhetorical questions are frequently used as responses to information-seeking questions. Consider the following:

(14) [= (12), this chapter]
   [A school teacher finds that Billy, a student in the class, is crying, and utters to the other students:]
   a. Teacher: Who hit Billy?
   b. Student: *Who knows?*
(15) [The speaker and the hearer are hurrying to a party when A remembers wanting to buy something and utters:]
   A: Can I stop at Sainsbury's?
   B: *Do you know what time it is?*

The answer conveyed by the utterance in (14b) in response to (14a) is *Nobody knows who hit Billy*, whereas one possible meaning conveyed by the utterance in (15B) is *Surely you know it is 8 o'clock*, providing a response to (15A), i.e., *No, you can't stop at Sainsbury's because it is 8 o'clock*.

There are highly idiomatic cases of rhetorical questions used to respond to information-seeking questions:

(16) A: Is Clinton a liberal?
   B: *Is the Pope Catholic?* (Han, 2002, p. 216)
(17) A: Do you know me?
   B: *Does an art student know Picasso?* (Schaffer, 2005, p. 440)
(18) A: How many feet long is this ferry?
   B: *How many hamburgers are sold per month in Tartu?* (Schaffer, 2005, p. 444)

The utterances (16B), (17B) and (18B) communicate assumptions that provide answers to the previous questions: *Yes, he is* in (16B); *Yes, I do* in (17B); and *I don't know* (or *nobody knows*) in (18B). The point of these questions lies in the obviousness of the assumptions. Some authors (Schaffer, 2005; Han, 2002) claim that the speakers of these utterances imply that the answers to the previous questions are as obvious as the answers to their utterances. That is, the speaker of (16B) intends to communicate the assumption *The extent to which the assumption in (16A), i.e., Clinton is a liberal, is obvious is the same as the extent to which the assumption in (16B), i.e., the Pope is Catholic, is obvious.* Similarly, the speaker of (17B) intends to communicate the assumption *The extent to which the assumption in (17A), i.e., the speaker knows the hearer, is obvious is the same as the extent to which the assumption in (17B), i.e., an art student knows Picasso, is obvious,* and the speaker of (18B) intends to communicate the assumption *The extent to which the assumption in (18A), i.e., the speaker doesn't know well how many feet long the ferry is, is obvious is the same as the extent to which the assumption in (18B), i.e., the speaker doesn't know how many hamburgers are sold per month in Tartu is obvious.*

Note that not all interrogative utterances uttered in response to a question are rhetorical questions. Consider the following examples:

(19) A1: What's this?
    B1: You mean this?
    A2: Yeah.
    B2: It's a computer.   (Adapted from Yokoyama, 1990, p. 4)
(20) A: What's this?
    B: Where did you eat last night?   (Adapted from Yokoyama, 1990, p. 4)

Yokoyama (1990) argues that the interrogative utterances (19B1) and (20B) are information-seeking questions. The answer to the question in (19A1) is provided by (19B2), with the utterance (19B1) and its answer (19A2) inserted in between. The speaker of (19B1) does not ignore the previous question (19A1): The repetition of the word *this* from (19A1) in (19B1) conveys that the speaker retains the *subject* of the utterance. On the other hand, as Yokoyama points out, it is obvious that the speaker of (20B) is communicating that the subject is being ignored because the propositional content of (20B) is not relevant to the question (20A). Sperber and Wilson (1986) observe that this sort of utterance might be interpreted as communicating that the speaker wants to "change the subject" (p. 121).

3.2 Rhetorically Ambiguous Questions

Here are some examples of rhetorically ambiguous questions in an extract from a Japanese novel. Consider the utterance in (21c), provided below in my translation.

(21) [Hiwako and her husband Shōzō have been married for more than 10 years]
    "Let's eat," said Hiwako as usual. Shōzō doesn't say the words, but he still

doesn't start eating until Hiwako says them. It's a habit between them.
"I like a habit," said Hiwako, and Shōzō nodded. Hiwako laughed,
(a) *wondering why he nodded.*
"(b) *Why are you laughing?*"
"(c) *Why did you nod?*" Hiwako threw a question back at him, though (d) *she expected no reply to it.* (Ekuni, 2005)

In context, the utterance (21c) is ambiguous between information-seeking and rhetorical. The contextual information in (21a) suggests that the speaker Hiwako doesn't know the answer to the question (21c). A natural interpretation of a speaker asking a question to which she does not know the answer would be that she wants to know the answer to that question. However, further contextual information in (21d) makes explicit that the speaker of (21c) expects no answer to it, which means that the utterance has more or less self-oriented nuance. I argue, however, that because it has an audience (the hearer Shōzō), it is not a self-oriented question, but rather similar to a speculative question. Note also that the utterance (21c) seems to be generated as a reply to Shōzō's question (21b), *Why are you laughing?*

In summary, there is a conflict between two contextual clues — (21a) suggesting an information-seeking-biased reading and (21d) suggesting a rhetorically biased reading — but, when one also considers its status as a response to (21b), ultimately (21c) can be interpreted more naturally as a rhetorically biased question than an information-seeking question.

Let us consider rhetorical ambiguity in more detail.

3.2.1 Felicitous Conditions for Information-Seeking Questions

Can we explain the ambiguity seen in (21c) from a cognitive-pragmatic viewpoint? To answer this, let us return to the discussion in Chapter 2 about felicitous conditions for information-seeking questions. We saw in Chapter 2 that felicitous conditions for information-seeking questions have been proposed by several authors, including Jeffreys (1948), Searle (1969, 1975) and Kawakami (1984). Their suggestions are summarized below.

(22) Jeffreys (1948):
  Target Question: Is Mr. Johnson at home?
  a. Speaker does not know whether Mr. Johnson is at home.
  b. Speaker wants to know whether he is at home.
  c. Speaker believes that hearer knows whether he is at home.
(23) Kawakami (1984):
  a. Speaker does not know the answer to the question.

b. Speaker wants to know the answer to it.
(24) Searle (1969, 1975):
　　a. Speaker does not know the answer (i.e., the proposition of the utterance), and therefore:
　　b. Speaker wants to know the answer or to elicit the answer from the hearer.

I maintain that we need another condition that can properly distinguish information-seeking questions and speculative questions. Consider my amended list of felicitous conditions for information-seeking questions in (25) below, which goes beyond the proposals in (22) through (24):

(25) Amended felicitous conditions for information-seeking utterances:
　　a. Speaker does not know the answer to the question.
　　b. Speaker wants to know the answer to the question.
　　c. Speaker expects the answer to the question to be provided by the hearer.

These conditions capture the differences between typical cases. An interrogative utterance is a genuine information-seeking question if and only if all the conditions in (25) are met. Conversely, if one or more conditions are not met, the question can be interpreted as a non-information-seeking question. Recall the three different types of questions seen in Chapter 2.

(26) a. Exam question:
　　　[An examiner utters to a student:] What are the binding principles? [= (14a) in Chapter 2]
　　b. Speculative question:
　　　Now, who is going to win the by-election tomorrow? [= (17) in Chapter 2]
　　c. Rhetorical question:
　　　[Hearer has claimed that he would give up smoking, but later the speaker sees the hearer smoking, and utters:]
　　　When did you say you were going to give up smoking? [= (18) in Chapter 2]

The point of an exam question like (26a) is to encourage the hearer to demonstrate knowledge of the answer. The speaker of an exam question already knows the answer but expects the hearer to provide it anyway. Hence, for an exam question, the second and third of my felicitous conditions, (25b) and (25c), are met, but the first condition, (25a), is not.

　　By contrast, the speaker of the speculative question in (26b) does not know the answer and knows that the hearer does not know the answer either. Therefore, the speaker does not expect the hearer to provide information, which means that my felicitous conditions (25a) and (25b) are met but (25c) is not.

Finally, the utterance in (26c) is not an information-seeking but a rhetorical question. The speaker intends to communicate the thought that the hearer said he was going to give up smoking at a certain time in the past — that is, the answer. None of the felicitous conditions from (25a) to (25c) are met in this case.

The relation between these question types and the meeting of felicitous conditions is summarized in Table 1 below.

Felicitous condition	(25a) S doesn't know answer	(25b) S wants to know answer	(25c) S expects H to provide answer
Information-seeking Q	✓	✓	✓
Speculative Q	✓	✓	×
Exam Q	×	✓	✓
Rhetorical Q	×	×	×

Table 1. Question Types vs. Felicitous Conditions

Note, though, that exam questions are given in a particular setting (examinations), differentiating them from the other three question types, which can be uttered in daily interaction. Also note that rhetorically biased questions and rhetorically ambiguous questions are quite different in terms of the meeting of felicitous conditions. The rhetorically ambiguous question given in (21c) meets the felicitous condition (25a), doesn't meet (25c), and is unclear with respect to (25b), as shown in Table 2 below. This demonstrates that ambiguous questions are different not only from (typically) information-seeking questions but also (typically) rhetorical questions.

Felicitous condition	(25a) S doesn't know answer	(25b) S wants to know answer	(25c) S expects H to provide answer
Rhetorically ambiguous Q	✓	?	×

Table 2. Rhetorically Ambiguous Questions vs. Felicitous Conditions

I argue nevertheless that the cognitive process of understanding an interrogative utterance does not require identifying the question type in advance. Instead of identifying whether a question meets each of the three felicitous conditions, the interpreter (hearer) searches for one (or more than one) thought that the speaker intends to make mutually manifest between them. In example (21c), those thoughts would be along the following lines:

(27) a. Hiwako's laugh is somehow related to Shōzō's previous action of nodding.
b. Hiwako wonders why Shōzō nodded.

3.3 Rhetoricity as Scale and Continuum

The examples provided in the preceding section lead us to the possible conclusion that a scale of rhetoricity exists in interpreting interrogative utterances. No clear-cut borderline between information-seeking questions and rhetorical questions seems to exist, and I predict that information-seeking ratings and rhetorical ratings for interrogative utterances will be found to lie on opposite sides of a single continuum. In other words, information-seeking and rhetorical ratings are parallel but reversed, as shown in Figure 1, and can be combined into a single continuum scale, as shown in Figure 2.

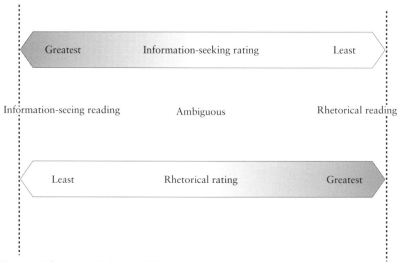

Figure 1. Information-Seeking and Rhetorical Rating Scales

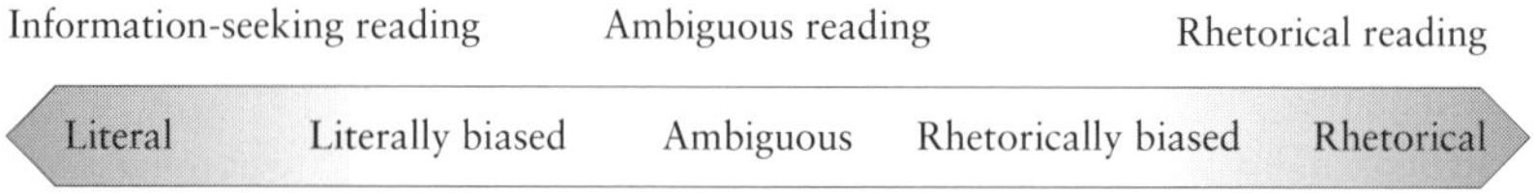

Figure 2. Literal–Rhetorical Continuum

As shown in Figure 2, information-seeking and rhetorical ratings can be described as a single continuum. This contrasts with the speech act theoretic approach, which denies that such a continuum exists. The information-seeking rating (the solid line in Figure 1) can be evaluated in terms of the extent to which the speaker seeks to know the answer because they do not know it, whereas the rhetoricity rating (the dashed line) can be evaluated in terms of whether the speaker does *not* seek to know the answer because they *do* know it. In summary, at least two distinct aspects based on my felicitous conditions (25a) and (25b) must be considered: the speaker's knowledge and expectations regarding the answer. That is, there are four possible situations:

(28) a. The speaker wants to be told the answer because they do not know it.
     (Greatest information-seeking reading is preferred)
  b. The speaker wants to be told the answer even though they do know it.
     (Somewhat information-seeking reading is preferred)
  c. The speaker does not want to know the answer because they know it already.
     (Greatest rhetorical reading is preferred)
  d. The speaker does not want to know the answer even though they do not know it.
     (Somewhat rhetorical reading is preferred)

How can the information-seeking/rhetorical rating of a guess or exam question be evaluated on this scale? Recall that the speaker of a guess or exam question wants the hearer to give an answer even though the speaker knows it already. This suggests two possible interpretations. If the interpreter (hearer) focuses on the speaker's intention to ascertain the answer, the question is rated towards the information-seeking end of the continuum and therefore can be considered a type of information-seeking question. On the other hand, if the interpreter focuses on the speaker's (background) knowledge regarding the answer, a rhetorically biased reading might be preferred, making the question a type of rhetorical question.

3.4 Clues to Rhetorical Bias in Questions

3.4.1 Interrogative Mood

As we have observed, many types of rhetorically biased questions constitute apparent counterexamples to the speech act theoretic classification of interrogative utterances. I agree with Wilson and Sperber's (1988) argument that the classification of speech acts does not say anything about the inferential process needed to identify the speaker intention behind the utterance. Wilson and Sperber(1988) claim that it is the principle of relevance that leads the hearer to recover the speaker's assumptions from the linguistic information (including sentential mood) and the context of the utterance (see Chapter 4 for the principle of relevance):

> The characteristic linguistic features of declarative, imperative, or interrogative form merely encode a rather abstract property of the intended interpretation: the direction in which the relevance of the utterance is to be sought. (p. 101)

Wilson and Sperber (1988) make it clear that sentential mood is *never* correlated with a particular illocutionary force, but rather gives a clue to the utterance's interpretation.

As seen in Chapter 2, two distinct speech act theoretic approaches to rhetorical interrogative utterances involve questions as indirect requests and as assertions. Recall:

(29) [= (22) in Chapter 2]
    [At 8 o'clock, her child's bedtime, Mother says to her child:]
    Do you know what time it is?

The utterance in (22) is a rhetorical question because the speaker does not want to know the answer (i.e., the exact time) regardless of whether it is already known to the speaker or not. According to the approach that considers the utterance in (29) as an indirect request, the utterance communicates the implicature in (30) below, which has the directive force of an indirect request that the hearer go to bed (Searle, 1975; Huddleston & Pullum, 2002).

(30) It is time you went to bed.

On the other hand, according to another approach given by Quirk et al. (1985), who consider a rhetorical question an assertion, the speaker's assertion is equivalent to the proposition expressed by the utterance. The speaker's assertion in (29) is given by substituting a value (e.g., *eight*) for the variable X in the incomplete logical form, as shown in (31a) and (31b) below.

(31) a. logical form: The hearer knows that it is X o'clock.
    b. speaker's assertion: The hearer knows that it is *eight* o'clock.

However, this raises the question of why a mother would utter (29) instead of simply saying *It is eight o'clock* to assert (30) as an indirect request. Moreover, an imperative utterance like (32) below also the same directive force encouraging the child to go to bed:

(32) Go to bed.

We could say that there are three distinct ways to encourage your child to go to bed: to utter *It is eight o'clock*, to utter (30) or to utter (32). In this case, why does the speaker utter the rhetorical question in (29) instead? Speech act theory seems to have nothing to say about this question. The same is true of the common ground approach by Rohde (2006). The problems with Rohde's arguments, as seen in Chapter 2, show that the common ground approach does not work: The point of uttering rhetorical questions does not lie in the answer because the answer values of some rhetorical questions are not obvious to the hearer *or* the speaker.

3.4.2 Expressive Function

How, then, *do* hearers distinguish rhetorical questions from other interrogative utterances such as confirmation questions? As the examples in the first part of this chapter show, the distinction between rhetorical and other questions does not seem to lie on the syntactic level. One solution involves in terms of the number and quality of clues to the utterance's interpretation. I argue that one of the most significant clues must be the speaker's attitude towards the thought or proposition expressed by the utterance, including sarcastic (ironical) attitudes as well as other emotional attitudes such as *irritation*.

Recall the utterance *Do you know what time it is?* In this case, it might be more obvious between the speaker and the hearer that the speaker utters it as a rhetorical question if the hearer observes that the speaker is explicitly or implicitly expressing a certain emotional attitude (irritation) towards the assumption that the hearer has not performed the expected action (going to bed).

By contrast, emotional attitudes such as irritation might not be expressed by the speaker in the cases of an information-seeking question as in (33B) or a confirmation question as in (34) below. Considering the hearers' responses, we can be confident that they are not focusing on the speakers' emotional attitudes. As a result, the utterances (33A) and (34A) can be interpreted as information-seeking-biased questions.

(33) A: [to a stranger in a cafe] *Do you know what time it is?*
    B: Yes, it's 3 o'clock.

(34) A: *Do you know what time it is?*
    B1: Yes, don't worry. I don't have to go yet. Bob just ran to say he won't be picking me up for another half an hour.
    B2: No, why? Is there any problem?

The utterance in (33A) is made as an information-seeking question. The speaker wants to know the time, and so an answer or information about the propositional content of the utterance (i.e., *Yes, I do* or *No, I don't*) is not required. What is relevant to the speaker is the answer to another question: *What time is it?* The speaker assumes that if the hearer knows the time the hearer can and will share that information with the speaker.

The utterance in (34A) is either an information-seeking-biased question or a confirmation question. The speaker might or might not know the exact time, but both potential hearers, B1 and B2, share the understanding that the point of the question does not lie in knowing the time. The speaker makes this utterance in order to confirm that the hearer knows the time. In other words, the speaker might intend to communicate the assumption *It is time for the hearer to go.*

Thus, the difference between a rhetorical question and a confirmation question appears to lie in the speaker's confidence in the assumption involved. In this view, the assumptions behind an interrogative utterance such as *Do you know what time it is?* might be deduced from the clues that the hearer observes. The speaker of a confirmation question is not confident in the proposition it expresses and wants to confirm its truthfulness, whereas the speaker of a rhetorical question is confident in the proposition it expresses. The hearer uses the speaker's observed or understood attitude to the thought as a clue to the speaker's intended meaning.

However, this does not mean that the level (i.e., strength) of emotion depends on the level of confidence in the thought. Even if the hearer recognizes that the speaker's emotional attitude (e.g., *irritation*) is strong, the utterance might still be understood as a confirmation question rather than a rhetorical question. In other words, an utterance might be a rhetorical question regardless of the strength of its speaker's emotional attitude: When interpreting interrogative utterances, hearers use more than one clue to reach the speaker's intended meaning.[1]

The speaker's emotional attitudes play a rather more central role in rhetorical questions uttered as responses to a previous question. Recall examples (16)–(18) in this chapter:

(16) A: Is Clinton a liberal?
    B: *Is the Pope Catholic?*

(17) A: Do you know me?
    B: *Does an art student know Picasso?*
(18) A: How many feet long is this ferry?
    B: *How many hamburgers are sold per month in Tartu?*

The point of these utterances lies in the speaker's *sarcastic* attitude to the assumptions or answers involved as well as the obviousness of the assumptions. The speaker of each utterance in (16B), (17B) and (18B) communicates that the answer is ridiculously obvious and therefore that the answer to the preceding question should also be ridiculously obvious. In other words, the speaker intends to communicate the assumption *It is silly to ask such a question*. If the hearer recognizes that the speaker's sarcastic attitude is strong enough to implicate the assumption *It is silly to ask such a question*, then the hearer will understand the question as rhetorical. Therefore, in these cases, the strength of the speaker's sarcastic attitude might lead directly to the rhetorical reading.

3.4.3 Answers and Retorts in Question-Answer Sequences

Related to the third felicitous condition given in (25c), the position of an interrogative utterance in the interactional sequence plays an important role in the hearer's cognitive process. Here I will show how this works from a socio-pragmatic viewpoint based on the question-answer sequence or adjacency pair in the conversational turn-taking rule.

Typical rhetorical questions restrict or limit the hearer's ability to answer. Interrogative utterances as the first part of an adjacency pair or at the beginning of a conversation prompt a response. Naturally, these cases tend to be information-seeking questions. Exceptional cases, however, might rate lower on the information-seeking scale. Consider the speculative question (26b) [= (17) in Chapter 2] below:

(26) b. Now, who is going to win the by-election tomorrow?

The utterance (26b) might be a speculative question if the speaker just wants to show interest in the matter. Obviously the speaker does not expect the hearer to give an answer. However, the utterance might be distinguishable from a rhetorical question in not *restricting* answers. In other words, the utterance neither requires nor blocks an answer. This type of question is a figure of speech known as *anacoenosis*: a question posed to indicate a common interest with the audience. In my view, this makes (26b) a (not typically but preferably) information-seeking question.

On the contrary, if an interrogative utterance is made as the second part of an adjacency pair (as a response to an information-seeking question), its rhetoricity can easily be recognized. Recall:

(12) a. Teacher: Who hit Billy?
   b. Student: [sarcastically] *Who knows?*

The rhetoricity of (12b) can be easily recognized because, in a context where the preceding interrogative utterance (12a) can be interpreted as an information-seeking question, (12b) should function as a response to it. The rhetoricity of (12b) is apparent because it is obvious from (12a) that the hearer of (12b) (the teacher) does not know who knows who hit Billy, and therefore (12b) blocks the hearer's answer.

Some rhetorical questions can be followed by answers immediately as in (35B) below. The first utterance in (35B) provides the answer, i.e., the second utterance in (35B).

(35) [= (33) in Chapter 2]
   A: So, who's your favorite team?
   B: Who do you think? The Dallas Cowboys!

The first utterance in (35B) highly resembles what is called an *expository question* in that the speaker immediately provides the answer; see (16a) in Chapter 2. However, it might be distinguished from an expository question in that most authors suggest that these are more natural in public speeches or academic lectures than conversational interactions (Sperber & Wilson, 1995; Wilson & Sperber, 1988/2012; Blakemore, 1992).

Nevertheless, an utterance can be a rhetorical question even if it is the first utterance of an adjacency pair or the beginning of a conversation. In the following example, the hearer's answer is not blocked: It is possible for the hearer to give a response.

(36) [On a rainy day, the speaker sees her co-worker, who usually wears sunglasses, in the office and utters:]
   A: Did you bring your sunglasses?
   B: (i) [smiling] Yeah, why not?!
     (ii) [pretending to be sad] No, I totally forgot.

Are these responses answers? Both (36B-i) and (36B-ii) seem to satisfy the felicitous condition of answerhood: They involve the truthfulness of the proposition expressed by (36A). However, if the speaker's sarcasm is mutually understood by both speaker and hearer, these responses might not be genuine answers. In other words, answers to rhetorical questions are not genuine answers insofar as the point of uttering a rhetorical question does not lie in confirming the truthfulness of the proposition it expresses. I would rather call the answer to a rhetorical question a *retort*, following Manor's (1979) terminology. Consider:

(37) a. *question*: Did you drive your car today?
   b. *answer* 1: I did drive my car today
   or
   c. *answer* 2: I did not drive my car today.
   d. *retort 1*: I don't have a car.
   e. *retort 2*: I drove Sam's VW.   (Manor, 1979, p. 16)

Suppose that the utterance in (37a) is an information-seeking question. The distinction between answers and retorts in (37) seems to lie in whether they directly involve the truthfulness of the proposition or not. As Manor points out, the retorts in (37d) and (37e) are "corrective replies" (1979, p. 10). A speaker of (37d) or (37e) negates the presupposition of the preceding utterance in (37a), implying that it was a *different* car, not the speaker's, that was driven. Consider another example:

(38) [The sound of music is bothering neighbors in the middle of night, and a neighbor says:]
   A: [irritated] Do you know what time it is!?
   B1: It's 12:45.
   B2: Sorry, I will stop it.

The utterance in (38A) is obviously a rhetorical question. A response such as (38B1) seems to be an *answer* in the sense that it meets the felicitous condition of answerhood, but it is not genuinely an answer because the hearer knows that no answer is required. In other words, (38B1) is not an *answer* but a *retort*: the hearer is aware that the speaker of (38A) is really asking the time and that an answer such as (38B1) is not helpful. The response in (38B2) can also be regarded as a retort, but in any case it might still be what the speaker expects as a response.

Rhetorical questions themselves can be uttered as retorts. Recall Schaffer's (2005) rhetorical questions used as retorts:[2]

(17) A: Do you know me?
   B: *Does an art student know Picasso?*
(18) A: How many feet is this ferry?

B: *How many hamburgers are sold per month in Tartu?*

The utterances (17B) and (18B) are retorts in the sense that they *indirectly* provide answers to the preceding questions (17A) and (18A). The speaker of (17B) intends to communicate *Yes, I know you* and the speaker of (18B) intends to communicate *No, I don't know how many*. Moreover, the utterance (10b) *Who knows?* might be called a retort in that it *indirectly* provides an answer to the preceding question in (10a), i.e., *I don't know*.

The rhetoricity of rhetorical questions as retorts like (10b), (17B), and (18B) can be recognized by the hearer without much effort due to the sequence of organization. By contrast, an utterance such as (2), which can be made as the first part of an adjacency pair or at the beginning of a conversation, imposes a greater burden on the hearer's understanding process. In order to assess its rhetoricity, the hearer of such a rhetorical question must search for more clues to the speaker's intended meaning. What is obvious in example (36) is that the information-seeking rating is rather low and a rhetorical reading is preferred. I argue that this is because of another clue: the irony of the utterance. This is explored further in Chapter 5.

3.5 Conclusion

We have observed several distinct types of interrogative utterances so far. In my view, all of these can be placed on a literal–rhetorical continuum. This raises at least two questions. First, is the distinction between information-seeking and non-information-seeking questions semantically justified, or is it rather grounded in pragmatics? Second, is there a theoretically justified semantic distinction between rhetorical and other questions?

To answer these, we must find an alternative approach that can accommodate not only rhetorical but all types of questions. As one possible solution, I argue that the concept of *interpretive use* introduced by relevance theory (Sperber & Wilson, 1995; Wilson & Sperber, 1988) is one such approach. The next chapter explores relevance-theoretic accounts of interrogative utterances.

Notes

1 Although this book does not cover the phonological aspects of rhetorical questions, irritation is often indicated by intonational properties. For example, compare the following:
> (i) Do you know what time it is? [no stress]
> (ii) a. Do you *know* what time it is? [heavy stress on *know*],
>   b. Do you know what *time* it is? [heavy stress on *time*]

When the utterance is produced with no stress, as in (i), it can be interpreted as an information-seeking question asking the time or as a confirmation question making sure that the hearer knows the time. On the other hand, when the utterance is made with a particular intonational contour such as (ii-a) or (ii-b), it conveys an attitude of irritation and can be interpreted as a rhetorical question.

2 Schaffer's (2005) use of *retort* is compatible with Manor's, both pragmatically (a retort functions as a response to the preceding question) and semantically (a retort's proposition involves a true-or-false assumption in the preceding question).

CHAPTER 4
Triply Interpretive Use: Relevance Theory and Interrogative Utterances

This chapter demonstrates the suitability of relevance theory, as established by Sperber and Wilson (1986, 1995), as a framework for analyzing rhetoricity. The basics of the theory are introduced first, followed by its account of how interrogative utterances are understood.

As discussed in Chapter 2, relevance theory rejects the speech act theoretic and Gricean accounts holding that literal and non-literal meanings are processed in separate ways. Instead, relevance theory holds that any utterance can be interpreted in terms of the notion of *interpretive resemblance*. Interpretive resemblance is a continuum: The case of no shared implication between the propositional content of the utterance and its meaning lies at one end, and full identity (i.e., the literal case) lies at the other.

Two other relevance-theoretic concepts indispensible to the analysis of interrogative utterances are also introduced in this chapter: *desirability* and *attribution of the speaker's thought*. Desirability is central to understanding the speaker's thoughts in interrogative or exclamative utterances whereas attribution is key to the analysis of rhetoricity in interrogative utterances.

4.1 The Principles of Relevance

According to Sperber and Wilson's (1995) relevance theory, human cognition and information processing is driven by the search for relevance. For example, suppose that you are working overtime and worried about being late for a party. You might pay more attention to the ticking of your desktop clock than usual, or more attention to the clock's ticking than to the other sounds in the office. The clock's ticking is more *relevant* than the other sounds in the office because it interacts with your existing assumption that you might be late for the party.

Consider another situation. If your friend has rung you to offer a lift to the party, you may shift your attention to the sound the door makes when people enter the office. The sound of the door has become more relevant than the sound of the clock. These examples illustrate the way that human cognition is driven by the search for relevant information.

Relevance theory is a cognitive pragmatic inferential theory assuming that every case of communication is an ostensive stimulus understood by the addressee through inference. Suppose that it is time for you and your partner to go to a party and you wish to leave soon. Tapping your watch to indicate this would be an ostensive stimulus. Your gesture would signal a communicative intention, and your partner might infer that it is time to go. An utterance is also an ostensive stimulus: In the same situation, you might utter *It is 8 o'clock* or *Do you know what time it is now?* rather than tapping your watch.

Sperber and Wilson claim that ostensive communication, whether linguistic or non-linguistic, is governed by two major principles:

(1) *Principles of Relevance*
   a. Cognitive Principle of Relevance: Human cognition tends to be geared to the maximization of relevance.
   b. Communicative Principle of Relevance: Every act of ostensive communication communicates a presumption of its own optimal relevance.
   (Sperber & Wilson, 1995, p. 260)

Like all other ostensive communication, utterances are interpreted based on the principles above. The first principle implies that the hearer of an utterance understands it as communicating a presumption of *optimal relevance*, defined in the following way:

(2) *The Presumption of Optimal Relevance*
   a. The ostensive stimulus is relevant enough for it to be worth the addressee's effort to process it.
   b. The ostensive stimulus is the most relevant one compatible with the communicator's abilities and preferences.
   (Sperber & Wilson, 1995, p. 270)

Optimal relevance involves a balance between maximizing cognitive effects and minimizing processing effort. An utterance is optimally relevant to the hearer if its interpretation achieves a certain cognitive effect with the least processing effort. This leads to the following comprehension procedure:

(3) *The relevance-theoretic comprehension procedure*
   Follow a path of least effort in computing cognitive effects:

a. Consider interpretations in order of accessibility.
   b. Stop when your expectations of relevance are satisfied.
                                        (Wilson, 2000, pp. 420–421)

According to Sperber and Wilson (1995, p. 108), a deduction from old and new information gives rise to cognitive effects of three main types: yielding contextual implications, strengthening existing assumptions, and eliminating existing assumptions. The strength of the interpreter's assumptions (i.e., degree of confidence in those assumptions) plays a central role in producing these effects. Sperber and Wilson define contextual implication as "a sub-type of synthetic implication" (1995, p. 112). In other words, it is a synthesis of old and new information inferred from the union of an existing assumption and a new assumption P.

For example, suppose that a mother with assumption (4a) below sees a clock and learns that it is in fact eight o'clock. The old and new assumptions (4a) and (4b) as premises yield the contextual implication (4c).

(4)   a. If it is eight o'clock, it is time my child went to bed.
      b. It is eight o'clock.
      c. It is time my child went to bed.

The strength of the hearer's assumptions influences the other two cognitive effects of strengthening and eliminating existing assumptions. The degree to which new information strengthens an existing assumption depends on the strength of that new information. For example, if you heard a pattering on the roof, you might assume *It might be raining*. If you opened the window and looked out to find that it was indeed raining, the existing assumption would be strengthened by this new information.

Existing assumptions can be eliminated through a similar process. Suppose that you heard more pattering on the roof and again thought *It might be raining*. If you then opened the window and discovered that the noise was only the wind, you would develop a new assumption such as *It's not raining, but it is windy* that would delete the existing assumption *It might be raining*.

The view that utterances are always understood through the procedure given in (3) is a clear argument against the speech act theoretic account holding that the mood of an utterance (e.g., declarative, imperative, interrogative) correlates with its speech act type (e.g., assertion, request, question). It also conflicts with the views of classical rhetoricians, who held that figurative expressions are non-literal utterances, as discussed in Chapter 1. Sperber and Wilson (1990) say:

> Note that both classical rhetoricians and their Romantic critics take as self-evident that, if there is such a thing as literal meaning, then utterances come with a presumption of literalness. We disagree. You can keep a notion of literal meaning and its analytical usefulness, and drop the presumption of literalness and its implausibility, provided you introduce a presumption of relevance. This, we will argue, makes it possible to reconcile theory and intuition. (p. 143)

Sperber and Wilson further claim that what sentence mood encodes is "not an illocutionary force but a more abstract and by itself inconclusive piece of evidence on the speaker's intentions" (p. 150). For example, a single utterance might communicate a variety of speaker attitudes. In relevance theory, one way to find evidence for the speaker's intentions is to recover such attitudes. I explore how attitudes or attitudinal assumptions are recovered in the process of understanding utterances below.

4.2 Interpreting Utterances and Thoughts

4.2.1 Explicit Meaning, Implicit Meaning, and Speakers' Attitudes

Relevance theory assumes that linguistic expressions underdetermine their semantic content: They are not semantically complete until they are developed into a fully propositional conceptual representation. For example, the following utterance is semantically incomplete:

(5) She didn't get enough units.

In relevance theory, it is assumed that an utterance communicates two different meanings: an explicit meaning called its *explicature* and an implicit meaning called its *implicature*. Explicature is defined in the following way:

> An assumption communicated by an utterance U is explicit if and only if it is a development of a logical form encoded by U. (Sperber & Wilson, 1995, p. 182)

If an assumption communicated by an utterance U is not explicit as defined above, it is implicit.

Suppose that the utterance in (5) were produced as part of the response to (6A) below.

(6) A: How is Mary feeling after her first year at university?
    B: She didn't get enough units and can't continue. (Carston, 1988, p. 155)

In the process of understanding the utterance in (6B), the incomplete conceptual representation (i.e., logical form) in (7a) below would be developed into a complete (i.e., truth-conditional) representation as shown in (7b) and (7c).

(7) a. X (she) didn't get enough units and can't continue.
    b. Mary Jones didn't get enough units and can't continue.
    c. Mary Jones didn't get enough university course units to qualify for second year study and, as a result, Mary can't continue with university study.

Recovery of the complete representation (7c) from the logical form (7a) involves three main subtasks: reference assignment, disambiguation, and enrichment. First, the proposition expressed by (7b) is recovered by assigning the reference X to Mary Jones. Next, *unit* is disambiguated to *university course unit*, whereas *enough* and *continue* are enriched to *enough to qualify for second year* and *continue with university study* respectively. At this point, (7c) has been recovered.

In addition, because any response to the utterance in (6A) should be relevant to *how Mary is feeling*, the hearer can easily recover an additional implicature like (8) below:

(8) Mary Jones is not feeling at all happy about this.

As Wilson and Sperber (1993) argue, an utterance typically has more than one explicature. Consider the exchange in (9) below. If the context is that Peter expects Mary to help him find a job, several explicatures might be recovered from (9b), such as the examples in (10):

(9) a. Peter: Can you help?
    b. Mary: (sadly) I can't.   (Wilson & Sperber, 1993, p. 5)
(10) a. Mary can't help Peter to find a job.
     b. Mary says she can't help Peter to find a job.
     c. Mary believes she can't help Peter to find a job.
     d. Mary regrets she can't help Peter to find a job.
                                                  (Wilson & Sperber, 1993, p. 5)

The propositional form in (10a) developed simply from the utterance of (9b) might be embedded in a higher-level description, like a speech act description as in (10b) or a propositional attitude description as in (10c) or (10d). For this reason, (10a) is called a *base-level* (or *basic*) explicature whereas (10b-d) are called *higher-level explicatures*.

4.2.2 Propositional Attitudes in Interrogative Utterances

The concept of higher-level explicatures explains the semantic difference between declarative and non-declarative utterances. Specifically, interrogative utterances convey a higher-level explicature about the act of asking in addition to their basic explicature about the content of the question. Consider the interrogative utterances in (11) below:

(11) a. Are you going to the party?
b. Where are you going?

The basic and higher-level explicatures of the yes-no interrogative utterance in (11a) and *wh*-interrogative utterance in (11b) are equivalent to (12) and (13) respectively:

(12) a. *Basic explicature:* The hearer is going to the party.
b. *Higher-level explicature:* The speaker is asking the hearer whether the hearer is going to the party.
(13) a. *Basic explicature:* The hearer is going somewhere.
b. *Higher-level explicature:* The speaker is asking the hearer where the hearer is going.

However, questions come in many varieties (see Chapter 1) and not all interrogative utterances can be explained in terms of a higher-level representation of the speech act *asking*. Nishikawa (2010) introduces the higher-level explicatures of a *surprise question* using the following example:

(14) [Tom loves Mary and invited her to the Christmas party held in Tom's house on the 24th of December. But Mary did not appear at his house. The next day Tom meets Mary and says.]
a. Tom: Why didn't you come to the party yesterday?
b. Mary: I went to the zoo.
c. Tom: Did you go to the zoo yesterday?!   (Nishikawa, 2010, p. 136)

The explicatures recovered from Tom's second utterance, (14c), are as follows:

(15) a. You went to the zoo the previous day.

b. Mary went to London Zoo on the 24th of December, 2005.
c. Tom is asking Mary if she went to London Zoo on the 24th of December, 2005.
d. Tom is surprised that Mary went to London Zoo on the 24th of December, 2005.   (Nishikawa, 2010, p. 136)

In the process of understanding (14c), the proposition expressed by the utterance is first recovered from the logical form (15a), giving (15b). Then, Nishikawa explains, the propositional form (15b) can be embedded under a higher-level description such as a speech act description as in (15c) or an attitudinal description as in (15d). Tom's feeling of *surprise*, which can be indicated by an exclamation mark, implies the gap between the speaker's existing assumption and some new assumption. In this example, the speaker's existing assumption may be something like *Mary did not go to the zoo the previous day*, which creates a gap with the assumption recovered from (14b), i.e., *Mary did go to the zoo that day*.

Some surprise questions are more information-seeking, whereas others are more rhetorical: this is to be expected, because a feeling of surprise can accompany either type of question. Indeed, in my view the utterance in (14c) is not a purely information-seeking (confirmatory) surprise question but in fact somewhat rhetorical. The speaker's surprise in (14c) may not be at the assumption in (15b); it may rather come from the gap between new information given in (14b) and some old information or the speaker's existing beliefs. The new information, i.e., the assumption in (15b), does not require confirmation because Mary has already confirmed it in (14b).

By contrast, in some confirmatory surprise questions the speaker's surprise and confirmatory intention can both be recovered from higher-level explicatures. Reconsider the example from Gutiérrez-Rexach (1998) that we saw in Chapter 3.

(16) [= (1) in Chapter 3] [The speaker knows that the hearer has reservations for a one-week vacation in the Bahamas in two weeks. When the hearer tells the speaker that he is too busy to finish the assigned task during the next month, the speaker says:]
Aren't you going to the Bahamas?   (Gutiérrez-Rexach, 1998, p. 143)

Possible higher-level explicatures of this utterance include:

(17) a. The hearer is not going to the Bahamas.
    b. The speaker is asking whether the hearer is not going to the Bahamas.
    c. The speaker is wondering whether the hearer is not going to the

Bahamas.
d. The speaker is surprised that the hearer is not going to the Bahamas.
e. The speaker is doubtful that the hearer is not going to the Bahamas.

If the hearer had no reason to interpret (16) as anything but a confirmation question, the attitudinal higher-level explicature (17c) might be recovered in addition to the higher-level explicature of the interrogative mood (17b). In other words, if the hearer had no concrete evidence that the speaker's belief was strong enough to explicate an attitudinal higher-level description involving doubt like (17e), such an explicature would not be recovered. In this case, the hearer would interpret (16) as a confirmation question: The speaker would be understood as seeking to confirm the truthfulness of the proposition expressed by the utterance.

In a rhetorical reading of the question, on the other hand, the hearer *can* recover the higher-level explicature (17e) because the rhetorical reading presupposes that the truthfulness of the expressed proposition has already been confirmed with the hearer: The hearer perceives a gap between old (existing) and new information. (See Chapter 1 for the details of this example.) In this situation, the speaker's attitude communicated by (16) is identical or at least similar to (14c) above. If the speaker learns that the hearer is too busy to go to the Bahamas, the speaker's existing assumption that the hearer is going to the Bahamas might be replaced by a new assumption that the hearer is *not* going there. The gap between old and new information would trigger the speaker's *surprise* and the polarity reversal caused by the gap would guide the hearer to a rhetorical reading.

4.2.3 Rhetorical Questions and Speakers' Attitudes

The difficulty in drawing a line between rhetorical and surprise (or other) questions does not lie in the need to explain speakers' attitudes and rhetoricity on different levels. Nor need rhetorical questions communicate the feeling of surprise. Rhetorical questions can convey a variety of emotional attitudes on the part of the speaker. Consider the following example:

(18) [= (23) in Chapter 2] [At an evening conference, when the guest of honor does not appear on time, the speaker says to her friend:]
Do you know what time it is?

From (18), the hearer may recover a higher-level explicature such as (19) below:

(19) The speaker is *asking* whether the hearer knows it is eight o'clock.

The hearer may also recover one or more speaker attitudes in embedding schemas:

(20) a. The speaker is *surprised* that...
    b. The speaker is *irritated* that...
    c. The speaker is *sarcastic towards the thought* that...

However, even based on the propositional content in (21), propositional attitudes corresponding to those in (20), i.e., (22a)–(22c), cannot be *directly* recovered:

(21) *propositional content*: The hearer knows it is eight o'clock.
(22) a. ?? The speaker is *surprised* that the hearer knows it is eight o'clock.
    b. ?? The speaker is *irritated* that the hearer knows it is eight o'clock.
    c. ?? The speaker is *sarcastic towards the thought* that the hearer knows it is eight o'clock.

Instead of being recovered directly, such propositional attitudes are interpreted as part of a series of implicatures:

(23) a. It is eight o'clock, and it is time the guest speaker appeared.
    b. The guest speaker does not appear.
    c. The speaker is *surprised/irritated/sarcastic towards the thought* that the guest speaker does not appear.
    d. If the hearer knows that it is eight o'clock, then the hearer should know that it is time the guest speaker appeared.

If the series of implicatures in (23) is how the hearer is led to the correct (i.e., the speaker's intended) interpretation, the speaker's attitude in (18) is recovered not on the explicature level but rather on the implicature level.

Where, then, is the rhetoricity in this use of interrogative mood? Here we can observe a discrepancy between the *asking* of (19) and the emotional attitudes like *surprise* in (20). In example (14c), *Did you go to the zoo yesterday!?*, *asking* and *surprise* were both in the propositional content, but in (18), the *surprise* is attached to the implicature, as seen in (23c).

Discrepancies of this sort are addressed by Kawakami's (1984) cognitive approach to verbal irony (see Chapter 3). Kawakami defines irony as a discrepancy recognized between two cognitions, such as between the speaker's *prior expectation or cognition* and *posterior recognition* (pp. 217–218). The rhetoricity communicated in example (18) works similarly.

In relevance theory, the notion of *interpretive resemblance* explains discrepancies between what is encoded and what is communicated. Sperber and Wilson argue that the discrepancies of figurative utterances such as *metaphor* and *irony* can be reanalyzed in terms of the notions of *loose use* and *echoic use* as subcategories of interpretive resemblance (Sperber & Wilson, 1995; see also Wilson, 2000; Pilkington, 2000; Noh, 2000). I outline this notion of *interpretive resemblance* and show how it can be applied to the interpretation of rhetoricity in interrogative utterances below.

4.3 Interpretive Resemblance

4.3.1 Descriptive and Interpretive Representation

The concept of *interpretive resemblance* plays a major role in relevance theory. It is defined as follows:

> *Interpretive resemblance*
> We will say that two propositional forms P and Q...*interpretively resemble* one another in the context C to the extent that they share analytic and contextual implications in the context C.
> (Wilson & Sperber, 1988, p. 138)

Sperber and Wilson (1995) claim that both verbal and non-verbal communication exploits this resemblance. They say:

> In appropriate conditions, any natural or artificial phenomenon in the world can be used as a representation of some other phenomenon which it resembles in some respects. (p. 227)

For example, if your friend asks you where you go at night your answer may be to mimic the act of driving or dancing to indicate this. To indicate that you are bored of a lecture, you might (intentionally) sigh or yawn.

An utterance is more or less interpretive depending on how closely the proposition that utterance expresses resembles the thought the speaker wants to convey. Relevance theory recognizes two distinct kinds of representation: *descriptive* and *interpretive*. Descriptive representation involves a relation between the representation (thought or utterance) and a state of affairs. Interpretive representation, on the other hand, involves a relation between a representation and other representations (thoughts or utterances) that resemble it in content. Any representation, including "public representations, e.g. utterances; mental representations, e.g. thoughts; and abstract representations, e.g. sentences, propositions" (Wilson, 2000, p. 414), is held to fall into one of these two categories.

The distinction between descriptive and interpretive representation is summarized in Figure 1 below.

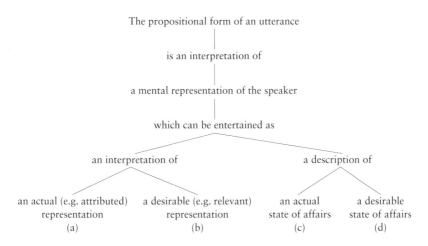

Figure 1. Descriptive and Interpretive Representation

(Sperber & Wilson, 1995, p. 232)

Sperber and Wilson (1995) offer the following comments on Figure 1:

> Metaphor involves an interpretive relation between the propositional form of an utterance and the thought it represents; irony involves an interpretive relation between the speaker's thought and attributed thoughts or utterances; assertion involves a descriptive relation between the speaker's thought and a state of affairs in the world; requesting or advising involves a descriptive relation between the speaker's thought and a desirable state of affairs; interrogatives and exclamatives involve an interpretive relation between the speaker's thought and desirable thoughts. (p. 231)

Let us examine this model more closely. The speaker can view a state of affairs in at least four distinct ways: *actual*, *possible*, *potential*, or *desirable* (Sperber & Wilson, 1986, 1995; Wilson & Sperber, 1988/2012; see also Clark, 1991 for extended analysis). Declarative utterances are descriptive representations of actual (i.e., existing in the real world) or possible (i.e., existing in some possible world) states of affairs. Consider the following example:

(24) Russell sang a few songs at the charity concert. His voice fascinated the audience.

A state of affairs is actual or not. If it is not actual, it may be interpreted as possible. The speaker of the utterances in (24) believes that the propositional content of each utterance describes an actual state of affairs. However, the speaker may have mistaken someone else for Russell, if for example there were many performers at the concert. In this case, the propositional content of the utterances (24) might be false, but it could still describe a possible state of affairs.

Imperative utterances, on the other hand, represent *potential* states of affairs. For example, the utterance in (25) represents a potential state of affairs in the real world (the hearer opening the window).

(25) Open the window, please.

Logically, if the utterance is imperative the *potential* state of affairs will also be *desirable* from the viewpoint of either hearer or speaker. If the speaker of (25) believes that the hearer is unable to stand the heat in the room, the state of affairs is desirable from the hearer's viewpoint. If it is the speaker who feels too hot in the room, the thought is desirable from the speaker's own viewpoint.

Unlike declarative or imperative utterances, interrogative and exclamative utterances do not describe any (definite) state of affairs because they represent incomplete logical forms. Consider the following examples:

(26) [In a store, the speaker takes one item, and utters:]
    a. How expensive is it?
    b. How expensive it is!

The logical form represented by both (26a) and (26b) is:

(27) It is _____ expensive.

An incomplete logical form does not *descriptively* represent a state of affairs, but the propositional form obtained by completing the logical form *interpretively* represents a belief or thought that is desirable from the viewpoint of the speaker or hearer (Wilson & Sperber, 1988/2012). The speaker of a *wh*-interrogative such as (26a) communicates that the thought (i.e., answer) is desirable from the speaker's viewpoint. The thought is desirable if it is relevant, i.e., brings about cognitive effects such as making the speaker decide to buy or not to buy something after knowing the price. On the other hand, the speaker of an exclamative such as (26b) communicates that she already has the incomplete logical form (27) in her mind and that its completion is relevant to her for its cognitive effects like making her decide not to buy the item (Clark, 1991; Itani, 1995).

Yes-no interrogatives can also be explained in terms of interpretive representation. The utterance in (28) represents either of the two desirable thoughts (i.e., possible answers) in (29):

(28) Is it expensive?
(29) a. It is expensive.
    b. It is not expensive.

The speaker of (28) communicates that the desirable thought may be either (29a) or (29b) depending on which corresponds to the state of the world at the time of the utterance. If (28) is an ordinary question, as Clark (1991, p. 184) claims, the speaker might assume that the positive answer (29a) is more relevant than the negative (29b), or that (29a) and (29b) are equally relevant. (Clark argues that, by contrast, the speaker of a negative yes-no question might assume that a negative answer is more relevant.) The thought is relevant to the speaker when it achieves cognitive effects such as making the speaker decide to buy or not to buy after knowing the answer.

4.3.2 Interrogatives and Desirable Thoughts

Wilson and Sperber (1988/2012) observe that we might be able to successfully explain the differences between a variety of interrogative utterances in terms of *interpretation of desirable thoughts*. They claim that interrogative utterances, like imperative utterances, are semantically indeterminate, expressing incomplete logical forms rather than complete propositions, and that this indeterminacy must be pragmatically resolved in terms of desirable thoughts.

What distinguishes one kind of utterance from another is to whom the speaker thinks the thought or proposition it expresses is desirable. According to Wilson and Sperber (1988/2012, pp. 226–227), interrogative utterances fall into two broad pragmatic categories: information-seeking, surprise, guess, exam, self-addressed, and speculative questions, in which the desirable thought is relevant from the *speaker's* viewpoint; and rhetorical and expository questions, in which the desirable thought is relevant from the *hearer's* viewpoint.

Wilson and Sperber claim that the hearer of an interrogative utterance needs to access further contextual assumptions in order to distinguish between these two categories. Consider the following two interactions:

(30) a. Mary: Where did I leave my keys?
   b. Peter: In the kitchen drawer.   (Wilson & Sperber, 1988/2012, p. 226)
(31) a. Peter: Will they keep their promises?
   b. Mary: Have politicians ever kept their promises?
(Wilson & Sperber, 1988/2012, p. 227)

Regarding the utterance in (30a), Wilson and Sperber state that, if Mary regards an answer to her question as desirable to herself and expects that the hearer knows and will provide the answer, then the utterance will be interpreted as an information-seeking question. However, if Mary regards an answer to her question as desirable to herself but doesn't realize that Peter is in the room, (30a) will be interpreted not as a request for information addressed to him but rather as a self-addressed question.

By contrast, consider the utterance in (31b). Depending on contextual clues, the hearer may be led to the interpretation that the answer or thought in question is desirable to the hearer rather than the speaker. For example, if Mary regards the answer as desirable to Peter in a context where she knows and is willing to provide it to him, the utterance can be interpreted as an expository question. However, the same utterance might be interpreted as a rhetorical question if Mary believed the answer to be mutually manifest between Peter and her.

This framework for interpreting interrogatives also accommodates *wh*-interrogatives. Recall the three distinct uses of *Who knows?*:

(32) [= (10) in Chapter 3]
   Someone must have seen who hit Billy. Come on. *Who knows?*
(33) [= (11) in Chapter 3]
   A1: Three people in the room know my middle name. *Who knows?*
   B1: Ah, uh, Billy, John and Ryan?
   A2: No, John, Peter and Brian.
(34) [= (12) in Chapter 3]
   [A school teacher finds that Billy, a student in the class, is crying, and utters to the other students:]
   a. Teacher: Who hit Billy?
   b. Student: *Who knows?*

In (32), the speaker wants to identify an individual who knows who hit Billy and expects the hearer(s) to provide the information: The answer to the question is desirable to the speaker. Furthermore, the answer to the question *Who knows?* is directly related to another question, *Who hit Billy?*, the answer to which is also desirable from the speaker's viewpoint. The desirability to the speaker of both answers is manifest — they are relevant enough to achieve cognitive effects leading the speaker to a decision such as who to scold for hitting Billy.

The speaker of a guess question like (33A1) also expects the hearer to provide information, but because the speaker already knows the answer, we can conclude that the speaker simply wants to know whether the hearer can provide the information. B's response in (33B1) is relevant and desirable from A's viewpoint, as it achieves cognitive effects like proving B's ability to guess the answer (see Chapter 2 for details).

By contrast, the speaker of the rhetorical question in (34B) does not expect the hearer to provide information. Instead, the speaker expects a thought the speaker has, like *Nobody knows* or *I don't know*, to become manifest between speaker and the hearer. The thought, therefore, is desirable from the hearer's viewpoint.

4.4 Metaphor and Irony in Interrogative Utterances

The notion of interpretive resemblance can also be fruitfully applied to the interpretation of metaphor or irony. Metaphorical or ironical expressions appearing in interrogative utterances often seem to affect how the rhetorical bias of those utterances is interpreted. Before considering the cognitive process of understanding such utterances, however, let us review relevance-theoretic accounts of metaphor and irony.

4.4.1 Metaphorical Expressions and Narrowing/Broadening

Consider the following examples involving metaphorical interpretations:

(35) a. The room is a pigsty. (Sperber & Wilson, 1995, p.236)
    b. The leaves danced in the breeze. (Wilson & Sperber, 2002, p. 219)

Pigsty typically implies a state of *being filthy and untidy*, whereas *dance* typically implies *move in a lively way*. Therefore, the thoughts expressed by these utterances may share contextual implications with the thoughts expressed in the utterances in (36) below:

(36) a. The room is filthy and untidy.
    b. The leaves moved in the breeze as if they were dancing.

In other words, the thoughts (35a) and (36a) interpretively resemble each other, as do the thoughts (35b) and (36b). Because the specific metaphors used in (35) are common in speech, they are typical cases in which the hearer can easily access contextual implications like (36).

Sperber and Wilson regard metaphorical utterances as examples of *loose use* of language. Interpretive resemblance can be considered a continuum with two extremes: no resemblance at one end and full propositional identity at the other (see also Ifantidou, 2002, p. 92). The more logical and contextual implications two propositions share, the closer they are to the latter end of the continuum; utterances sharing fewer implications resemble each other more *loosely* (Wilson & Sperber, 1992, p. 65; Sperber & Wilson, 1995, pp. 233–234). This view clashes with classical rhetorical and Gricean analyses, which divide meanings into two categories, literal and figurative.

If an utterance and the thought it expresses share the same propositional content, the utterance is regarded as literal (or *fully faithful*). In this case, the contextual implication can be processed as a strong implicature. However, even if metaphors used in the utterance mean that it does not share a decisive or typical contextual implication with the thought that can be processed this way, the utterance and the thought might still share a wide range of contextual implications that can be processed as weaker implicatures. For example, consider the utterance in (37) below:

(37) Robert is a bulldozer. (Sperber & Wilson, 1995, p. 236)

The utterance in (37) places more responsibility for its interpretation on the hearer than do utterances such as (35a) because no single strong implicature is accessible to the hearer. What might come to the hearer's mind instead are somewhat weaker implicatures "having to do with Robert's persistence, obstinacy, insensitivity and refusal to be deflected" (Sperber & Wilson, 1995, p. 236).

As Carston (2002, p. 350) points out, however, it is not clear from (37) where these ideas of persistence or obstinacy come from. To resolve this problem, Carston (2002, pp. 350–358) and the updated analysis of Wilson (2009) invoke an immediately created ad hoc concept that is broader than the encoded concept. According to these analyses, what "bulldozer" in the utterance in (37) communicates is not the meanings in the encyclopedic entry for *bulldozer* (e.g., *heavy machinery*) but rather an ad hoc concept that can be applied to people who share some of the characteristics found in that encyclopedic entry.

For example, the representations recovered in the process of understanding *bulldozer* in (37) may be as follows:

(38) a. Lexical (encoded) meaning of bulldozer: bulldozer (e.g., heavy

machinery)
b. ad hoc concept of bulldozer: BULLDOZER*
c. explicature: [Robert is] a BULLDOZER*
d. implicatures: [Robert is] persistent, obstinate, insensitive, [Robert] refuses to be deflected, etc.

Wilson and Carston (2006) state that the explicit content, in addition to disambiguation and reference assignment, undergoes the modification (or modulation) of one or more of its encoded concepts to the new ad hoc concept. They further argue that this process is not unique to the interpretation of metaphor: Hyperbole, approximation, and even literal utterances are "the by-products of the same relevance-guided mutual adjustment process" (p. 409). Literal utterances, they note, involve lexical narrowing of the encoded concepts whereas non-literal cases such as metaphor, hyperbole, and approximation involve lexical broadening, albeit to different degrees.[1] Consider:

(39) This policy will *bankrupt* the farmers.   (Wilson & Carston, 2006, p. 410)

In the utterance in (39), *bankrupt* can be understood as typically literal, as an approximation (communicating the ad hoc concept BANKRUPT*), or as hyperbole (communicating a different ad hoc concept BANKRUPT**). The hyperbolic interpretation likely involves "more substantial broadening of the encoded concept and hence a greater departure from the encoded meaning" (Wilson & Carston, 2006, p. 410) than the approximate one.

4.4.2 Irony as Attributive Use

Relevance theory holds that verbal irony involves attributive (or *echoic*) interpretive use (Wilson & Sperber, 1992; Wilson, 2000). Wilson and Sperber's view is based on the distinction between *use* and *mention* proposed in Sperber and Wilson (1981). Consider the following example:

(40) a. Natasha is a beautiful child.
     b. "Natasha" is a beautiful name.   (Wilson & Sperber, 1992, p. 57)

The word *Natasha* in (40a) is used to refer to a child, whereas in (40b) it is used to refer to itself. Sperber and Wilson (1981, p. 554; see also Wilson & Sperber, 1992, p. 57) call such self-referential use of words *mention* to distinguish it from the ordinary *use* of words as in (40a). In spoken language, however, the distinction may not be clear, as in the following example:

(41) a. Peter: What did Susan say?
   b. Mary: I can't speak to you now.
   c. Mary: She couldn't speak to me then.   (Wilson & Sperber, 1992, p. 58)

In the interaction in (41), Mary's response in (41b) has two possible interpretations in terms of *use* and *mention*, i.e., whether the referent of *I* is *Mary* or *Susan*. In the latter case, Mary would be quoting Susan's words directly. Note, however, that Wilson and Sperber argue that not only direct quotation but also indirect quotation such as (41c) can be analyzed as a case of *mention*.

Wilson and Sperber claim that indirect quotations can be used for two different purposes: *reporting* and *echoing*. Reporting involves merely giving information about the content of the original utterance or thought, whereas echoing involves the speaker's attitude to what is said or thought.

Echoic utterances are used to express different attitudes. Verbal irony is one example: It expresses the speaker's *dissociative* attitude towards what is echoed. Compare (42b) through (42d) below:

(42) a. Peter: That was a fantastic film.
   b. Mary: [happily] Fantastic.
   c. Mary: [puzzled] Fantastic?
   d. Mary: [scornfully] Fantastic!   (Wilson, 2000, p. 432)

Wilson (2000) argues that the attitudes expressed by echoic utterances fall into three main categories: *endorsing*, *questioning*, and *dissociative*. These are (respectively) exemplified by Mary's echoic responses (42b) through (42d) above. These attitudes may become part of higher-level schemas of metarepresentations as in:

(43) a. She believes that I was right to say/think P.
   b. She is wondering whether I was right to say/think P.
   c. She believes I was wrong to say/think P.   (Wilson, 2000, p. 432)

The next section explores the application of this notion of echo to interrogative utterances.

4.4.3 Triply Interpretive Use in Echoic Interrogative Utterances

Wilson (2000) points out that an interrogative utterance can be treated as the metarepresentational counterpart of an imperative utterance, because it represents a desirable thought whereas an imperative utterance represents a desirable state of affairs. This view is based on the information-seeking use of interrogative utterances, which is a *doubly interpretive* use: It involves the interpretive relationships between the propositional form of the utterance and the thought it expresses and the thought it expresses and a desirable thought, as depicted in Figure 1 above.

However, some interrogative utterances are also echoic, making them *triply interpretive* (Wilson & Sperber, 1988/2012). Consider the example of free indirect speech:

(44) John sighed. Would she never speak?
(Wilson & Sperber, 1988/2012, p. 229)

Wilson and Sperber argue that the second sentence in (44) is triply interpretive because it is "a more or less literal interpretation of a thought of the speaker's or writer's, which is itself an echoic interpretation of a thought attributed to John, which is in turn an interpretation of a desirable thought, namely, the answer to the question" (p. 229). In other words, triply interpretive use involves an interpretation not only of (a) but also (b) in Figure 1 above.

The relevance-theoretic view based on multi-interpretive use may be adapted to the interpretation of metaphorical or ironical interrogative utterances as introduced in Chapter 2:

(45) a. [= (12) in Chapter 2]
[Ichirō, a baseball player for the Mariners in the U.S., met Kitajima, a breaststroke gold medalist who set a new world record at the 2008 Beijing Olympics, and uttered:]
Are you a fish? (*Kimi wa sakana ka?*)
b. [= (13) in Chapter 2]
[Susan and Mary are co-workers at a company. Susan often wears sunglasses. On a rainy day, when Susan comes into the office, Mary sarcastically utters:]
Did you bring your sunglasses?

The utterance in (45a), which uses metaphor, is doubly interpretive: It involves the interpretation between the encyclopedic entry of *fish* and what the word expresses in the utterance, i.e., *a good swimmer*, as well as the interpretation of a desirable thought, i.e., the answer *You are a fish*.

The utterance in (45b), on the other hand, is both echoic and interrogative, and therefore triply interpretive. As discussed above, echoic interrogative utterances involve three distinct interpretations: an interpretation of the thought the speaker expresses; an interpretation of the thought attributed to someone else; and an interpretation of a desirable thought or the answer to the question.

Wilson and Sperber (1988) claim that the indeterminacy of echoic interrogatives must be solved in terms of two questions: *who regards the answer as desirable*, and *to whom the answer is desirable*. In the case of the utterance in (45b), however, it is difficult to see which thought is desirable at all, i.e., what could be the answer to the question. The speaker, after all, does not indicate any interest in knowing the answer — she simply wants to make fun of the hearer. In such a case, does it fall to the interpreter to find clues as to whether the answer to the question is positive, i.e., *The hearer brought her sunglasses*, or negative, i.e., *The hearer did not bring her sunglasses*?

Note that I do not argue that a sarcastic speaker's attitude allows recovery of attitudinal higher-level representations such as those in (46) below:

(46) a. The speaker is *sarcastic* towards P (i.e., that the hearer brought her sunglasses).
b. The speaker is *sarcastic* towards ¬ P (i.e., that the hearer did not bring her sunglasses).

If the speaker's interest in (45b) lies solely in the act of making fun of the hearer, the answer to the question that the speaker intends to communicate is irrelevant, making the utterance in (45b) a highly rhetorical question. In other words, the thought that the speaker intends to make manifest to the hearer must be a thought that can be elicited in an ironical context by the relationship between *rainy days* and *sunglasses*. This raises two questions. First, what thought is represented by ironical (rhetorical) interrogative utterances? Second, is there any relationship between irony and rhetoricity in interrogative utterances?

Taking the second question first, I argue that, in a broader sense, rhetorical questions are always ironical to an extent. In other words, rhetoricity is associated with echo because a rhetoric question conveys the speaker's dissociative attitude. Consider the example of rhetorical questions used as retorts:

(47) [≑ (17) in Chapter 3]
    a. Tom: Do you know me?
    b. Mary: *Does an art student know Picasso?*
(48) [≑ (32) in Chapter 2, (13) in Chapter 3]
    a. Matt: What company's computer will you buy?
    b. Catherine: Well, *what company do I work for?*

Each rhetorical question implicitly gives the answer to the preceding information-seeking question. The interaction in (47), however, cannot be extended with answers:

(49) A1: Do you know me?
 B1: *Does an art student know Picasso?*
 A2: ?? Yes.
 B2: ?? Yes.

Compare this with a structurally similar interaction that we have already observed:

(50) [= (19) in Chapter 3]
 A1: What's this?
 B1: You mean this?
 A2: Yeah.
 B2: It's a computer.

The utterance in (50B1) is information-seeking rather than rhetorical. The speaker of (50B1) expects the hearer to provide the answer, and, because the speaker does not yet know the answer, the answer is relevant and desirable to the speaker. By contrast, the speaker of (47b) does not expect the answer to be provided — it is already obvious. Rather, the speaker wants to make manifest to the hearer that to ask whether he knows her is silly. The rhetoricity in (47b) therefore appears to lie in the speaker's sarcastic attitude towards the previous utterance, which is to say towards the propositional attitude involving the speech act of asking. This may be described as in (51d) below:

(51) The interpretation of (47b):
 a. *propositional content*: An art student knows Picasso.
 b. *higher-level explicature 1*: The speaker is asking whether an art student knows Picasso.
 c. *higher-level explicature 2*: The speaker is sarcastic towards the thought that she is asking whether an art student knows Picasso.
 d. *implicature 1*: The speaker is sarcastic towards the thought that Tom is asking whether she knows him.
 e. *implicature 2*: Tom's utterance is a silly question.

The point of the utterance in (47b) is therefore the discrepancy between the thoughts in (51b) and (51c). Recognition of this discrepancy allows recovery of the implicature in (51d).

The interpretation of the *wh*-rhetorical interrogative utterance in (48b) can be analyzed in a similar way:

(52) a. *propositional content*: the speaker works for *Company X*.

b. *higher-level explicature 1*: The speaker is asking what company she works for.
   c. *higher-level explicature 2*: The speaker is sarcastic towards the thought that she is asking what company she works for.
   d. *implicature 1*: The speaker is sarcastic towards the thought that Matt is asking what company's computer she will buy.
   e. *implicature 2*: Matt's utterance is a silly question.

The speaker's sarcastic attitude in both (47b) and (48b) can be successfully explained in terms of echoic use. Both utterances echo the thought expressed by the preceding utterance while showing a dissociative attitude towards it. I argue that this dissociation is part of rhetoricity in interrogative utterances. The role of irony in rhetorical questions and the process of understanding them, which seems to be significant, will be taken up again in Chapter 5.

4.5 Meanings and Truth Conditions

We have seen that utterances have two distinct levels of meaning: explicature and implicature. Explicature is recovered through both semantic decoding and pragmatic inference; basic explicature contributes to the truth-conditional meaning of the utterance, whereas higher-level explicature contributes to both truth-conditional and non-truth-conditional meanings. Implicature, by contrast, can be recovered only through pragmatic inference. Below, I show how relevance theory's tripartite distinction between basic explicature, higher-level explicature, and implicature differs from the traditional Gricean distinction between *what is said* and *what is implicated* and why this makes relevance-theoretic analysis more appropriate for rhetorical questions.

4.5.1 Gricean Conversational Implicature

Grice's (1975) *what is said* is equivalent to the truth-conditional content of an utterance once subtasks like reference assignment and disambiguation are complete, whereas *what is implicated* is the pragmatic meaning of an utterance and is derived through inferential processing. Grice's inferential model is based on his well-known Cooperative Principle and four major maxims:

> *Cooperative Principle*:
>   Make your conversational contribution such as is required, at the stage at which it occurs, by the accepted purpose or direction of the talk exchange in which you are engaged.   (Grice, 1975, p. 45)

A. *Maxim of Quantity*
   1. Make your contribution as informative as is required (for the current purposes of the exchange).
   2. Do not make your contribution more informative than is required.
B. *Maxim of Quality*
   Supermaxim: Try to make your contribution one that is true.
   1. Do not say what you believe to be false.
   2. Do not say that for which you lack adequate evidence.
C. *Maxim of Relation*
   Be relevant.
D. *Maxim of Manner*
   Supermaxim: Be perspicuous.
   1. Avoid obscurity of expression.
   2. Avoid ambiguity.
   3. Be brief (avoid unnecessary prolixity).
   4. Be orderly.   (Grice, 1975, pp. 45–46)

Grice claims that, although the semantic meaning of *and* is equivalent to the truth-conditional content of the logical conjunction operator &, in conversation *and*-conjunction implicates temporal order or causal relationship of conjuncts based on conversational maxims. Grice calls this *conversational implicature*. For instance, consider (53a) and (53b):

(53) a. He took off his trousers and (then) he got into bed.
                                                          (Grice, 1981, p. 186)
   b. Ken hit Mary and (as a result) Mary cried.

The parenthetical temporal relationship in (53a) is implicated based on the fourth submaxim of the Maxim of Manner, *Be orderly*, whereas the causal relationship in (53b) is implicated based on the Maxim of Relation, *Be relevant*. Conjoining two events with the logical conjunction operator & is *pragmatically* understood as communicating that the events took place in the given order or are relevant to each other.

However, Carston (2002) argues from the standpoint of relevance theory that Grice's notion of *what is said* is flawed. Grice's view, she says, fails to distinguish at the level of *what is said* the utterance in (53a) from the utterance in (54):

(54) He got into bed and took off his trousers.   (Carston, 2002, p. 222)

If Grice's analysis were correct, Carston says, the two utterances would be "equivalent, truth-conditionally identical like their logical counterparts" (2002, p. 223), as shown in (55) below:

(55) P & Q = Q & P   (Carston, 2002, p. 222)

However, as pointed out by Itani (1995), this seems to be untrue. Consider the utterances in (56) below.

(56) a. If Ken hit Mary and Mary cried, I will report him.
    b. If Mary cried and Ken hit Mary, I will not report him.
                                                              (Itani 1995, p. 75)

As Itani explains, the fact that these utterances are not treated as contradictory means that the proposition embedded in the antecedent clause of (56a), *Ken hit Mary and Mary cried*, must be distinct from the one embedded in the antecedent clause of (56b), *Mary cried and Ken hit Mary* at the level of the "truth-conditional content of an utterance" (1995, p. 75): The causal implication falls under the scope of *if*-clause.

Moreover, even a temporal relationship between conjuncts can be more complex than simple sequentiality (Carston, 2002). Consider the following examples:

(57) a. He handed her the scalpel and she made the incision.
    b. We spent the day in town and I went to Harrods.
                                                            (Carston, 2002, p. 223)

The utterances in (57a) and (57b) communicate different types of temporal connotation. In (57b), the temporal relation could be paraphrased with *and then*, whereas in (57b) the event mentioned in the second conjunct (i.e., *I went to Harrods*) is contained within the time conveyed by the first conjunct (i.e., *the day*).

Carston argues that "pragmatically inferred relation could be a case of enrichment at the level of the proposition expressed (i.e. the truth-conditional content)" (2002, p. 223). The proposition expressed by the utterance in (57a) could be enriched as in (58a) below. The enrichment in (58b) is also possible, although it would be less usual.

(58) a. He handed her the scalpel and a second or two later she made the incision with that scalpel.
    b. He handed her the scalpel and simultaneously she made the incision

with her pocketknife.   (Carston, 2002, p. 226)

The reason why the interpretation in (58a) is more usual than (58b) can be explained in terms of "the accessing of contextual assumptions" (Carson, 2002, p. 226). Sequences of events are stored in memory in chunks, as frames or scripts. The hearer of the utterance in (57a) accesses a sort of surgical operation script, or perhaps a more general schema such as a person handing something to another and then the second person doing something with it. The hearer's interpretation process stops when the schema under consideration satisfies the expectation of relevance, so the most accessible valid schema is the one applied.

To recap, the temporal connotations in (57a) and (57b), although linguistically communicated, are not encoded in the utterances themselves because they cannot be recovered from the development of the logical operator &. In other words, the relevance-theoretic framework holds that not all the meaning linguistically communicated by an utterance is linguistically encoded.

4.5.2 Conventional Implicature

Grice (1975) also proposes what he calls *conventional implicature*, which is linguistically communicated but not truth-conditional. Consider:

(59) He is an Englishman; he is, therefore, brave.   (Grice, 1975, p. 25)
(60) *What is said*:
    a. X is an Englishman.
    b. X is brave.
(61) *What is conventionally implicated*: (60a) follows from (60b).

According to Grice, the utterance in (59) *says* the propositional contents in (60) and *conventionally implicates* the thought in (61). The conventional implicature in (61), linguistically communicated by the discourse connective *therefore*, does not, however, contribute to the truth-conditional meaning of the utterance, which is solely dependent on *what is said* in (60).

Grice regards discourse connectives such as *therefore, but, so* and *moreover* as communicating non-truth-conditional, conventional implicatures associated with the speech acts of *contrasting, explaining* and *adding*. Grice distinguishes such speech acts from other types of speech act like *asserting, ordering* and *asking*, which are linguistically encoded by mood indicators. He calls the speech acts performed by the connectives *higher-order* speech acts, in contrast to the *ground floor* or *lower-order* speech acts performed by mood indicators. Ground floor speech acts contribute to truth-conditional meaning whereas higher-order speech acts do not.

However, Blakemore (2002) points out that the Gricean notion of conventional implicature raises some questions. First, it is not clear what illocutionary forces are performed by the speech acts conventionally implicated by discourse connectives. For example, in Grice's analysis, the utterance P *but* Q (e.g., *He is home but he is busy*) would conventionally implicate a contrast between P *(he is home)* and Q *(he is busy)*. Blakemore argues against this view: "It cannot be the act of contrasting since the fact that there is a contrast is represented by the propositional content of the act" (2002, p. 48). Blakemore's argument is, in other words, that it is not clear why a conceptual representation like *There is a contrast between P and Q* or *P contrasts with Q* should not contribute to the truth-conditional content of the utterance as Grice claims.

Second, consider cases with no preceding linguistic information P (i.e., simply *But Q* rather than *P but Q*), like the following example:

(62) [A gives B, who has just received a shock, a glass of whisky. B utters:]
    But I don't drink.   (Blakemore, 2002, p. 105)

The utterance in (62) is nevertheless understood as contrasting the speaker's action, e.g., receiving a glass of whisky, with the thought *I don't drink*.

4.5.3 An Alternative Approach: Conceptual and Procedural Meanings

Blakemore (1987; also 1992, 1998, 2002) offers a reanalysis of discourse connectives that resolves these problems. She argues that *but* doesn't contribute to the conceptual representation *P contrasts with Q*, but instead constrains the hearer's inference from that representation. This section outlines her binary semantic concepts of *conceptual meaning* and *procedural meaning*.

According to Blakemore (1992), if a linguistic expression has a conceptual meaning, it contributes to the logical-form representation of an utterance, whereas if it has a procedural meaning, it constrains the hearer's inference from that representation. Consider the following example:

(63) Nigel is home but he's busy.   (Blakemore, 1992, p. 203)

In (63), constituents such as *home* and *busy* encode *concepts*, whereas the pronoun *he* and the discourse connective *but* encode not concepts but *procedures*. The pronoun *he* encodes a procedure which enables the hearer to derive the person who is referred to by the speaker, whereas *but* encodes a procedure which enables the hearer to interpret the utterance in terms of the contrast between the two sentences that *but* connects.

Blakemore's distinction between conceptual and procedural encodings is not parallel to the distinction between truth-conditional and non-truth-conditional meanings. The two distinctions are not co-extensive. Consider:

(64) a. Conceptual and truth-conditional
    b. Conceptual and non-truth-conditional
    c. Procedural and truth-conditional
    d. Procedural and non-truth-conditional

Whether a linguistic expression encodes procedural constraints is orthogonal to whether it contributes to the truth-conditional content of an utterance. For example, any pronoun encodes a procedural constraint which contributes the truth-conditional content of an utterance, but the discourse connective *but* does not contribute to the truth-conditional content at all. Consider another set of utterances:

(65) a. Nigel is home but he's busy.
    b. Nigel is home and he is busy.   (Blakemore, 1992, p. 147)

Unlike *but* in (65a), the connective *and* in (65b) does contribute to the truth-conditional content of the utterances. As Blakemore (1992, p. 147) points out, even if the two conjuncts (i.e., *Nigel is home*, *He is busy*) are presented in the opposite order, the truth-conditional contents of the utterances are not affected, but the implicature communicated by *but* may change. The meaning of *but* might be to *deny* an expectation that the first conjunct creates in the hearer's mind.

Consider another set of examples where linguistically encoded concepts do and do not contribute the truth-conditional content of an utterance:

(66) a. *Seriously*, your argument is fallacious.   (Ifantidou-Trouki, 1993, p. 70)
    b. Your argument is *seriously* fallacious.

As Ifantidou-Trouki observes, the semantics of sentential adverbials such as the *seriously* in (66a) are conceptual and non-truth conditional, whereas non-sentential adverbials such as the *seriously* in (66b) are conceptual and truth-conditional. That is, the utterance in (66a) is true if and only if the hearer's argument is fallacious — *seriousness* plays no role in its truth conditions — whereas the utterance in (66b) is true if and only if the hearer's argument is *seriously* fallacious.

To recap, procedural encodings impose constraints on the hearer's inferring process, whereas conceptual encodings contribute to the conceptual representations of utterances. Let us now reconsider the discourse connective *but*.

Blakemore (1992) suggests that *but* can be reanalyzed as encoding a procedural meaning to manipulate the hearer's inferential process towards contradiction or elimination of the thought preceding *but*. Hall (2004) develops this into a more concrete analysis according to which the procedural meaning of *but* constrains an implicature inferred from the thought preceding *but* and foregrounds the contradiction or elimination of that thought.

For example, given the utterance *He is home but he is busy*, the implicature recovered from the first conjunct (*Busy people are not at home*), is eliminated by the following *but*. According to this view, utterances with no first conjunct such as *But I don't drink* in (62) can also be explained: The implicature that is contradicted or eliminated is recovered from a relevant *act*, such as *The speaker will drink (a glass of whiskey)* recovered from the speaker's act of being given (i.e., receiving) the glass.

The advantage of Blakemore's procedural analysis is that it can be successfully applied not only to pronouns and discourse connectives but also to many other linguistic phenomena such as modality, intonation, and so forth. In studies of Japanese language, *modality* has been a major concern that sometimes inspires procedural analysis. For example, Itani (1993, 1995) argues in her relevance-theoretic analysis of sentence-final *ka* that *ka* contributes to the interpretation of a desirable representation (i.e., interrogative and exclamative utterances), manipulating the hearer to interpret the (relevant) thought as desirable. We will return to *ka* and other Japanese sentence-final particles in Chapters 6, 7, and 8, discussing their functions and meaning in order to investigate how they constrain the hearer's inferential process, particularly with respect to the interpretation of rhetorical questions.

4.6 Conclusion

The concept of desirability contributes to the interpretation of interrogative utterances. Interrogative utterances may be interpreted in terms of *to whom* the thought is desirable: rhetorical questions and expository questions communicate a thought which is desirable to the hearer whereas information-seeking questions, guess questions, and so on communicate a thought which is desirable to the speaker.

In addition to desirability, however, the attribution of the thought expressed by an utterance is another important factor in interpretation: the interpreter must think in terms of not only *to whom the thought is desirable* but also *who regards the thought as desirable*. This view seems to accommodate every type of rhetorical question, as the thought that conveys the rhetoricity may be more or less attributive (echoic). The true advantage of the relevance-theoretic notion of interpretive resemblance may lie in this multilayered approach to interpretation.

The next chapter contains further discussion of whether rhetorical questions can be interpreted as attributive representations. As the conception of *irony* varies among linguists, we must first explore how the relevance-theoretic analysis of irony in terms of echoic use illuminates the interpretation of interrogative utterances. The next step is to attempt a generalization of the processes involved.

Notes

1 Wilson and Carston (2006, p. 411) admit that metaphorical interpretations often involve the process of both narrowing and broadening. For example, in the utterance *Caroline is a princess*, the word *princess* communicates a broadened ad hoc concept PRINCESS* (who is not an actual princess) as well as the narrowed concept *spoiled or indulged girl*.

CHAPTER 5

Rhetorical Questions and Irony: The Echoic Hypothesis

This chapter uses the relevance-theoretic echoic hypothesis (Sperber & Wilson, 1995, 1998) to explain rhetoricity in interrogative utterances. The echoic hypothesis has successfully been applied not only to the most commonly invoked type of irony, which communicates the opposite of what is said (Grice, 1975), but also to many other types including *understatement* (Wilson & Sperber, 1992; Wilson, 2006). I argue that rhetoricity and ironicalness are causally interrelated in interrogative utterances, offering as evidence the fact that at least two distinct features of irony can also be seen in rhetorical interrogative utterances.

Some authors do admit a certain interrelation between irony and rhetorical questions, seeing ironicalness as a feature of rhetorical questions (Ilie, 1994) or classifying rhetorical questions as a subtype of irony (Leggit & Gibbs, 2000). In most studies, though, including relevance-theoretic works, rhetorical questions and verbal irony are treated separately and the interrelation between rhetoricity and ironicalness left unaddressed.

However, the relevance-theoretic analysis of verbal irony can fruitfully be applied not only to polarity-reversed rhetorical question such as (1a) below but also non-polarity-reversed questions such as (2).

(1) [A school teacher finds that Billy, a student in the class, is crying, and utters to the other students:]
 a. Teacher: Who hit Billy?
 b. Student: [sarcastically] *Who knows?*
(2) [On a rainy day, the speaker sees her co-worker, who usually wears sunglasses, in the office and utters:]
 Did you bring your sunglasses?

Throughout this chapter, I discuss the advantage of relevance-theoretic analysis in relation to irony. The chief concepts in the relevance-theoretic interpretation of utterances, i.e., *desirability* in interrogative utterances and *dissociative speaker's attitude* in verbal irony, permit a successfully blended analysis of rhetoricity and ironicalness in interrogative utterances.

Recall the framework of relevance-theoretic interpretation, particularly of interrogative utterances, outlined in Chapter 4. Under the relevance-theoretic view, an utterance is understood in terms of two relationships: one between its propositional form and the speaker's thought and one between that thought and what it represents (Sperber & Wilson, 1995). Regarding the relationship between the thought and what it represents, Sperber and Wilson say:

> Irony involves an interpretive relation between the speaker's thought and attributed thoughts or utterances;…interrogatives and exclamatives involve an interpretive relation between the speaker's thought and desirable thoughts (p. 231).

In other words, the thought that is optimally relevant to the process of understanding an interrogative utterance is a *desirable* thought, whereas for an ironical utterance it is an *attributed* thought.

The next section revisits the continuum of rhetoricity based on this relevance-theoretic view of interrogative utterances. This is followed by a review of some traditional accounts of verbal irony and the cognitive approach Kawakami (1984) offers as a criticism of these accounts. Next, some of the latest echoic theories of verbal irony are introduced, including the relevance-theoretic echoic hypothesis. In the following, the relevance-theoretic concept of echoic interpretation is used to develop an account of the process of understanding ironicalness and rhetoricity in interrogative utterances.

5.1 The Continuum of Rhetoricity Revisited

In Chapter 2, we observed that the dichotomy of direct and indirect requests in Searle's (1975) speech act theory assumes that ordinary interrogative utterances (i.e., direct requests for information) and other types of interrogative utterances (e.g., indirect requests, rhetorical questions) are processed differently by the hearer. In other words, speech act theory implies that the hearer of an interrogative utterance must determine whether an utterance is purely a request for information or not before processing it.

Relevance theory criticizes this account, arguing that hearers do not need to distinguish between ordinary and non-ordinary interrogative utterances during the understanding process. Instead, hearers simply search for the optimal relevance of an utterance. This view assumes no clear border between *information-seeking* and rhetorical interrogative utterances: Information-seeking and rhetorical ratings are not dichotomic features but might be located on a bipolar continuum. In other words, we should speak of these features in terms of degree.

According to Wilson and Sperber (1988/2012), in understanding interrogative utterances, the hearer accesses not only a thought with optimal relevance but also an assumption about to whom that thought is relevant. Regarding the relevant thought of an interrogative utterance, they say:

> How does the hearer decide what answer the speaker would regard as relevant? In the case of *yes–no* questions, the solution is straightforward. A positive question expresses a positive proposition, [and] a negative question expresses a negative proposition…The easiest assumption for the hearer to make, and thus the assumption favored by considerations of relevance, is that the speaker has chosen to express the very proposition she would regard as relevant if true. That is, a positive [*yes–no*] question…indicates that a positive answer would be, if anything, more relevant than a negative one, [whereas] a negative [*yes–no*] question suggests that a negative answer would be, if anything, more relevant than a positive one…
>
> Although *wh*-questions do not express complete propositions but merely incomplete logical forms, we claim that they are interpretively used to represent complete propositions that they resemble. Which complete propositions? The natural assumption…is that they represent completions of the incomplete logical forms they express. (p. 225)

In other words, the relevant assumption of an interrogative utterance is:

(3) a. (For yes-no questions) For positive interrogative utterances, an assumption equivalent to a positive proposition; for negative interrogative utterances, an assumption equivalent to a negative proposition
   b. (For *wh*-questions) An assumption developed from an incomplete logical form by adding a certain value to a variable X

The assumptions in (3) are desirable from either the speaker's or the hearer's viewpoint (Wilson & Sperber, 1988/2012, p. 226). If the speaker of an utterance wants to confirm the truthfulness of the thought or proposition it expresses, the thought is desirable from the speaker's viewpoint (see Chapter 3 regarding such *confirmation questions*). By contrast, if the speaker already has a strong belief that the thought is true, the thought is desirable from the hearer's viewpoint. In example (4) below, the relevant thought of (4a) is equivalent to the proposition in (4b). By uttering (4a), the speaker intends to remind the hearer of the thought in (4b).

(4) a. When did you say you were going to give up smoking?
   b. proposition (as desirable thought):
   The hearer said that she was going to give up smoking at t.

(Sperber & Wilson, 1995, p. 251)

As shown in Chapter 3, the distinction between confirmatory and rhetorical use of an interrogative utterance like *Aren't you going to the Bahamas?* (Gutiérrez-Rexach, 1998; see Chapter 3) depends on how confident the speaker is in the truthfulness of the proposition expressed by the utterance. If the speaker is less confident in the truthfulness of the proposition, the utterance may be used as a confirmation question to confirm that truthfulness. On the other hand, if the speaker is already confident in the proposition's truthfulness and wishes to make that truthfulness manifest to the hearer, the utterance may be used as a rhetorical question.

In other words, the rhetoricity of a given utterance depends on both the speaker's confidence in the relevant thought or proposition and to whom that thought or proposition is relevant.

Recall the literal–rhetorical continuum introduced in Chapter 3 (reproduced here as Figure 1 for convenience):

Information-seeking reading	Ambiguous reading	Rhetorical reading
Literal	Literally biased	Ambiguous	Rhetorically biased	Rhetorical

Figure 1. Literal–Rhetorical Continuum

Relevance theory holds that any interrogative utterance can be understood in terms of the desirability of the thought expressed by the utterance. In other words, the hearer's assessment of an utterance's place on this continuum might lead to an assumption about to whom the thought expressed by that utterance is relevant. Figure 2 below depicts this expanded model.

P relevant to speaker	P's relevance ambiguous	P relevant to hearer
Literal	Literally biased	Ambiguous	Rhetorically biased	Rhetorical

Figure 2. Relevance-Theoretic Information-Seeking–Rhetorical Continuum

As shown in Figure 2, if an interrogative utterance is understood as an information-seeking question, the thought or proposition it expresses is recognized as relevant to the speaker. On the other hand, if the hearer recognizes some degree of rhetoricity, the utterance is interpreted based on the assessment that the thought or proposition it expresses is relevant to the hearer. In other words, information seeking/rhetorical ratings, although not strictly calculated, can be used as clues by hearers to identify relevance.

What other aspects of an utterance can function as clues to optimal relevance? At least two distinct assumptions must be recovered during the cognitive process of understanding an interrogative utterance: (a) the speaker's propositional attitude (involving an assumption recoverable as a higher-level schema); and (b) the speaker's confidence in the truthfulness of the expressed proposition.

In particular, a *dissociative attitude* on the part of the speaker plays an important role in the understanding of rhetorical questions, just as it does in the understanding of verbal irony. Rhetorical questions cannot simply be subcategorized under ironical utterances in the relevance-theoretic framework, but the process of understanding rhetoricity in interrogative utterances does share two distinct features with the process of understanding irony, one of which can be seen in any rhetorically biased question.

5.2 Ironical Questions

5.2.1 Traditional Accounts of Verbal Irony

In classical rhetoric, irony is a trope where figurative meaning is the opposite of the literal meaning. Grice's (1975, p. 54) reassessment was that the opposite of what is literally said in irony is not a figurative meaning but a figurative *implication/implicature*. For example, *He is a fine friend* uttered ironically implies/implicates He is not a fine friend; the utterance can be understood as flouting the Maxim of Quantity. Similarly, Searle (1979) also claims that the speaker of an ironical utterance, "means the opposite of what he says" (p. 115). In another traditional example, *It's lovely weather* implying *It's awful weather*, the ironicalness can be recognized as a *violation* of felicity conditions on speech acts.

However, as some authors (Kawakami, 1984; Fogelin, 1988) point out, Searle's (1979) example means the *opposite* of the proposition it expresses, whereas Grice's example means the *contradiction* of that proposition. Fogelin (1988) says:

> These views are close, but not identical. Grice says that the intended meaning is the contradictory of the one the person purports to be putting forward, whereas Searle makes the seemingly stronger claim that

the speaker intends the opposite of what he actually says. This seems stronger, for by the opposite we usually mean something that lies at the other end of some scale — for example, big rather than small, none rather than all, bright rather than dark, and so forth. (p. 6)

Fogelin argues that neither of Grice's nor Searle's view is fully correct, and that irony implies "something *incompatible* with what we say" (p. 10). According to Fogelin, this incompatibility is a stronger concept than contradiction or opposition because it covers not only both of these two concepts but also a wide variety of other types of irony.

Kawakami (1984, p. 195) points out, however, that, in Grice's example *He is a fine friend*, the speaker implies the *contrary* assumption *He is a mean friend* rather than the *contradictory* assumption *He is not a friend*. Kawakami claims that his own account of verbal irony, based on a cognitive approach to the *contrary* relationship between two cognitions, can cover not only blame-by-praise types of verbal irony like Grice's example but also a range of peripheral cases. The next section outlines Kawakami's approach.

5.2.2 Kawakami's Cognitive Theory of Irony

According to Kawakami's (1984) cognitive approach to verbal irony, the ironicalness of utterances is recognized as a *discrepancy* between *outward appearance* (linguistic expression) and *reality* (context). Put more specifically, the discrepancy is between the speaker's *prior expectation or cognition* and *posterior recognition* (pp. 217–218). For example, in understanding Grice's blame-by-praise irony, suppose that the prior expectation or cognition *He is a fine friend* is symbolized as p and the posterior recognition *He is a mean friend* as $-p$. Then Kawakami's cognitive model, in which p and $-p$ are in contrary relation, can be constructed as follows:

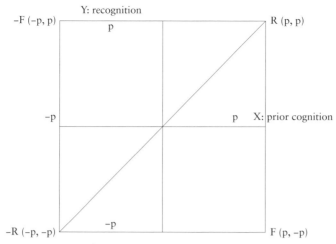

Figure 3. Kawakami's Cognitive Model (Kawakami, 1984)

In Kawakami's model, the polarity of the prior cognition lies on the X axis, and the polarity of the posterior recognition on the Y axis. R and $-R$ are linguistic expressions of positive and negative polarity respectively. Points on the diagonal line from R to $-R$ represent no discrepancy (i.e., an absence of irony), whereas the discrepancy is greatest at the points F and $-F$. Let us consider the next example in this context.

(5) [A driver cuts off the speaker without signaling. The speaker utters to his fellow passenger:]
I love people who signal. (Roy, 1978)

If the prior cognition of the utterance in (5) is symbolized as p and the posterior recognition as $-p$, then the linguistic expression (outward appearance) and context (reality) can be described as sets of contrary assumptions:

(6) *linguistic expression*
 a. I love people who signal. [= p]
 b. I hate people who don't signal. [= $-p$]
(7) *context*
 a. The driver that cut off the speaker signaled. [= p]
 b. The driver that cut off the speaker didn't signal. [= $-p$]
(Kawakami, 1984, p. 235)

The expressions in (6) and contexts in (7) can combine in four possible ways as shown in (8), each of which can be mapped onto one of the corners of the diagram, as shown in Figure 4:

(8) A. (6a) and (7a) = R
 B. (6a) and (7b) = F
 C. (6b) and (7a) = –F
 D. (6b) and (7b) = –R

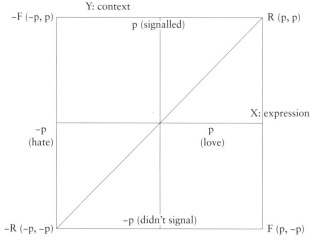

Figure 4. Mapping of Utterances (6a) and (6b) vs. Contexts (7a) and (7b)

According to Kawakami (1984, p. 236), (8A) and (8D) express the actual state of affairs, whereas (8B) and (8C) express a discrepancy between the expression and the actual state of affairs. The discrepancy of (8B) involves irony, but that of (8C) does not. Rather, (8C) indirectly involves the actual state of affairs, as it can be interpreted as implying that (6a).

Kawakami claims that his cognitive account can also be applied to interrogative uses of irony such as (9), an example from Roy's (1978) doctoral dissertation from the University of Michigan, in which there is a certain discrepancy between the linguistic form and context.

(9) [A and B are discussing volleyball rotation]
 A: Don't make it too complicated.
 B: It's like a circle. *Think you can handle a circle?* [emphasis added]
 (Roy, 1978, p. 20)

Because volleyball rotation, as everyone knows, is not complicated, the speaker of (9B) is understood to be sarcastic towards the thought expressed by the preceding utterance in (9A). The ironicalness of (9B) is understood based on the hearer's recognition of the discrepancy between what the preceding linguistic expression (9A) implied, i.e., The rotation is complicated, *and the context, i.e.,* Rotations are simple. This discrepancy lies at point F in the following diagram.

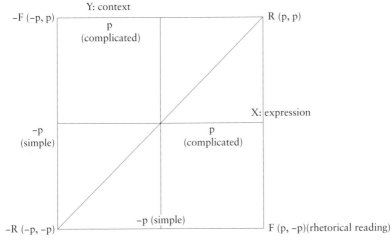

Figure 5. Mapping of Utterance in (9A)

Kawakami claims that the ironicalness of (9B) is caused by the speaker's *pretense* that (s)he believes *The rotation is complicated*. In other words, the ironicalness lies in the fact that the linguistic expression, i.e., *questioning whether the hearer can handle a circle*, presupposes the meaning expressed in (9A), i.e., *The rotation is complicated*.

Kawakami defines the felicitous conditions for questioning via interrogative utterance as: (a) the speaker does not know the answer; and (b) the speaker wants to know the answer. In other words, an interrogative utterance can be interpreted as an information-seeking question if and only if these two conditions are satisfied. Hence, the cognitive model of the interpretation of (9B) can be depicted as in the following diagram.

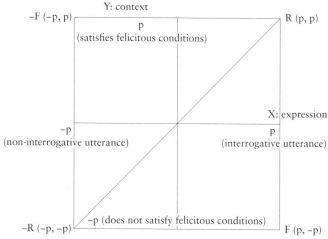

Figure 6. Mapping of Utterance in (9B)

Consider the sets of contrary assumptions that describe the linguistic expression (outward appearance) and the context (reality) in Figure 6:

(10) *linguistic expression*
   a. the speaker is questioning whether the hearer can handle a circle. [= p]
   b. the speaker is not questioning whether the hearer can handle a circle. [= -p]
(11) *context*
   a. The felicitous conditions of questioning are satisfied. [= p]
   b. The felicitous conditions of questioning are not satisfied. [= -p]

Each of the four possible combinations of these sets can be mapped onto one of the points of the diagram in Figure 6 as shown below:

(12) A. (10a) and (11a) = R [= (9B) uttered with information-seeking reading]
   B. (10a) and (11b) = F [= (9B) uttered with ironical reading]
   C. (10b) and (11a) = -F [Question in non-interrogative mood, e.g., declarative question]
   D. (10b) and (11b) = -R [Non-question in non-interrogative mood, e.g., ordinary declarative utterance]

It is implied in Kawakami (1984) that -p of the linguistic expression in (9B) is the case in which the speaker either does not produce any utterance or produces a non-interrogative one. Therefore, R and F involve the interpretation of the utterance in (9B) whereas -F and -R do not.

Note that the ironicalness expressed at the point F directly involves the recognition of an infelicitous use of an interrogative form. This makes the utterance in (9B) seem to be a rhetorical question: Not satisfying the felicitous conditions of questioning is directly linked to a lessened information-seeking rating for interrogative utterances. In my continuum model, the lower the recognized degree of information-seeking, the more a rhetorical reading is preferred.

Does this mean that any ironical utterance should be considered rhetorical? If we assume that any kind of interrogative utterances can be mapped onto Kawakami's cognitive model as shown in Figure 6, the recognition of ironicalness at the point F should necessarily lead to a rhetorical reading. Does Kawakami's model, then, imply that some ironical aspect in interrogative utterances provides a crucial clue to their rhetorical readings? I argue that this is the case, but nevertheless only a secondary process in understanding irony. For example, the cognition of the ironicalness of example (9B) involves two distinct processes. The recognition of its position at point F in Figure 6 is the primary process, whereas the recognition of its position at point F in Figure 7 is secondary. In my view, it is the secondary process that permits assessment of rhetoricity in interrogative utterances.

The crucial problems, then, are (a) whether these two distinct processes apply to any type of rhetorical questions; and (b) how the two distinct mappings in Figure 6 and Figure 7 are linked. The rest of this section explores the first question by applying the processes to two distinct types of rhetorical questions: *polarity-reversed* and non-polarity-reversed. Section 4 takes up the second question, offering a solution based on Wilson and Sperber's (1992) echoic interpretation of ironical utterances.

5.2.3 Polarity-Reversed Assumptions in Rhetorical Questions

As we saw in Chapter 2, polarity-reversed rhetorical questions such as those in (13) below are traditionally considered ironical because they imply assumptions of reverse polarity to the proposition expressed by the utterance, such as those in (14).

(13) [= (20a), (20b), (21a) and (21b) in Chapter 2]
    a. Is that a reason for despair?
    b. Isn't the answer obvious?
    c. Who knows?
    d. Who doesn't know?   (Quirk et al., 1985, p. 826)
(14) [= Speaker's assertions in (20a), (20b), (21a) and (21b) in Chapter 2]
    a. Surely that isn't a reason for despair.

b. Surely the answer is obvious.
c. Nobody knows.
d. Everybody knows. (Quirk et al., 1985, p. 826)

Hashimoto (1982) offers a similar account of rhetorical questions, claiming that rhetorical questions can be interpreted in terms of two distinct negative assumptions. Consider:

(15) a. Who knows?
    b. presupposition of (15a): *somebody knows*
    c. negation of presupposition: It is not the fact that somebody knows.
    d. focus of (15a): *who*
    e. negation of focus: It is not the fact that there is somebody.
(16) a. Am I my brother's keeper?
    b. presupposition of (16a): *the speaker is or is not his brother's keeper*
    c. negation of presupposition: It is false that the speaker is his brother's keeper.
    d. focus: *Am I my brother's keeper?*
    e. negation of focus: The speaker is not his brother's keeper.

According to Hashimoto (pp. 34–36), rhetorical questions assume the negation of both the *presupposition* and the *focus* of the utterance. In a *wh*-question, the focus is a *wh*-word and the presupposition is a proposition completed by substituting an existential quantifier *some*; in a yes-no question, the focus is the sentence itself and the presupposition is that the proposition is either true or false. Thus, a *wh*-rhetorical question like (15a) can be interpreted as assuming the negation of both the presupposition and the focus, as in (15c) and (15e). As for the yes-no rhetorical question in (16a), the negation of the presupposition is that the expressed proposition is false, as in (16c), whereas the negation of the focus involves the negation of the declarative equivalent (Hashimoto, 1982, p. 36) as in (16e).

(Hashimoto does not explain why the false option is adopted in (16c) as the negation of the presupposition in (16b). If it is adopted because of the positive polarity of the proposition expressed by the utterance in (16a), then presumably if the utterance were *Am I not my brother's keeper?* the negation of its presupposition would be It is *true* that the speaker is his brother's keeper.)

In my view, the negation of the presupposition in the case of both (15a) and (16a) explains the polarity-reversal aspect of their rhetoricity, which in turn is susceptible to Kawakami's cognitive theory of irony: it is easy to capture the discrepancy between *appearance* (the propositions expressed by the utterances), and *reality* (the polarity-reversed assumptions). The recognition of this discrepancy is the *primary process* when understanding the ironicalness of those utterances, and leads to the secondary process of assessing their rhetoricity. On this view, polarity-reversed rhetorical questions can be interpreted as a form of irony.

Kawakami's example in (9B), *Can you handle a circle?*, can also be interpreted as communicating the polarity-reversed assumption *You cannot (even) handle a circle*, which is implicated as a result of the hearer's recognition of the discrepancy between this and the preceding utterance in (9A) as depicted in Figure 7. The utterance in (9A) presupposes that the rotation is complicated, and the speaker of (9B) pretends to believe this thought.

5.2.4 Non-Polarity-Reversed Rhetorical Questions: Recognizing Discrepancies

Is Kawakami's theory also applicable to non-polarity-reversed rhetorical questions? Consider example (2) again:

(2) [On a rainy day, the speaker sees her co-worker, who usually wears sunglasses, in the office and utters:]
Did you bring your sunglasses?

The utterance in (2) does not seem to communicate a polarity-reversal assumption: It involves neither the thought *The hearer did not bring her sunglasses* as the negation of the focus nor the thought *It is false that the hearer brought her sunglasses* as the negation of the presupposition. However, the utterance is ironical; it is easy to capture a certain discrepancy, which might involve the act of *bringing sunglasses on a rainy day*.

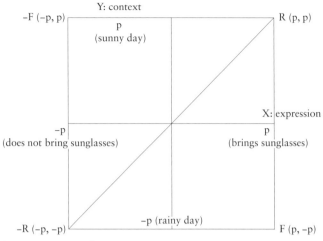

Figure 7. Mapping of Utterance in (2)

As depicted in Figure 7, the ironicalness of the utterance in (2) can be explained in terms of the socially inappropriate act of bringing sunglasses on a rainy day: the utterance is located at point F. The recognition of the discrepancy in Figure 7 is the primary process of understanding the utterance in (2). Based on this, the secondary mapping, which involves the recognition of rhetoricity, can occur.

However, is it necessary to recognize a cognitive mapping like that in Figure 7? Does the hearer need to recognize all four thoughts mapped onto the corners? I argue based on the relevance-theoretic view that human cognition is driven by searching for relevance that this is not the case: the understanding process of the hearer stops when a thought mapped to the point F is accessed. The hearer may or may not access the other three thoughts mapped to $-F$, R, and $-R$ beforehand, but this is irrelevant.

In other words, although Kawakami's cognitive model might depict the full range of thoughts accessible by the hearer of an interrogative utterance, it does not describe the *process* by which the hearer accesses those thoughts. Below, I attempt to address this lack based on the relevance-theoretic echoic hypothesis of Wilson and Sperber (1992).

5.3 Echoic Interpretation

5.3.1 Wilson and Sperber's Echoic Hypothesis

The relevance-theoretic account of verbal irony (Sperber & Wilson, 1981; Wilson & Sperber, 1992) departs from Grice's view that irony is a contradiction of what the speaker says (Grice, 1975, p. 53). Wilson and Sperber (1992) show that Grice's account cannot explain any of the cases of verbal irony in (17) below:

(17) a. *Ironical understatement*:
[You come upon a customer complaining in a shop, blind with rage and making a public exhibition of him. You turn to your companion and say:]
You can tell he's upset.
b. *Ironical quotation*:
[In a rainy rush-hour traffic jam in London, you say:]
When a man is tired of London, he is tired of life. (Boswell, *Life of Johnson*)
c. *Ironical interjection*:
[Your friend invites you to Tuscany in May, saying it is the most beautiful place on earth. You arrive, however, in a freak cold spell, wind howling, rain lashing down. You say:]
Ah, Tuscany in May!
d. *Non-ironical falsehood*:
[You are out for a stroll, and pass a car with a broken window. You turn to your companion and say:]
Look, that car has all its windows intact.
(Wilson & Sperber, 1992, pp. 54–56)

According to Wilson and Sperber, none of the utterances in (17) are understood as *saying the opposite of what is meant*.

For example, *understatements* like (17a) consist of "saying merely less than what is meant" (Wilson & Sperber, 1992, p. 54). Thus, the ironicalness of the utterance in (17a) lies in the understatement but does not communicate either of (18a) or (18b):

(18) a. You can't tell he's upset.
b. You can tell he's not upset. (Wilson & Sperber, 1992, pp. 54–56)

Similar analyses apply to the utterances in (17b)–(17d). Rather than saying the opposite of what is said, they variously consist of a quotation in (17b), an interjection in (17c), and a device for drawing the hearer's attention in (17d).

Wilson and Sperber claim that an ironical utterance has the following three features. First, it is a variety of interpretive use: the proposition it expresses represents a thought attributed to someone other than the speaker at the time of the utterance. Second, it is echoic. Third, its speaker expresses a dissociative attitude towards the echoed source. Wilson and Sperber describe irony as follows:

> A variety of echoic interpretive use, in which the communicator dissociates herself from the opinion echoed with accompanying ridicule or scorn. The recognition of verbal irony, and of what it communicates, depends on an interaction between the linguistic form of the utterance, the shared cognitive environment of communicator and audience, and the criterion of consistency with the principle of relevance. (pp. 75–76)

The most significant component of this description is the concept of *echoic interpretation*, which can encompass a wide range of emotional attitudes on the part of the speaker towards an echoed thought or utterance. In ironical utterances, the attitude expressed is dissociative. Compare (19) and (20):

(19) A: The Joneses aren't coming to the party.
    B: They aren't coming, hum. If that's true, we might invite the Smiths.
(20) A: It's a lovely day for a picnic.
    [They go for a picnic and it rains]
    B: (sarcastically) It's a lovely day for a picnic, indeed.
              (Sperber & Wilson, 1995, pp. 238–239)

Both (19B) and (20B) are echoic utterances: the proposition expressed is attributed not to the speaker herself but to the speaker of the preceding utterance. Sperber and Wilson claim that they are more than just a "reporting" (p. 238) of what the previous speaker said; the speaker of (19B) has "paid attention to [A's] utterance and is weighing up its reliability and implications" (p. 238), whereas the speaker of (20B) expresses disapproval or rejection of (i.e., a dissociative attitude towards) (20A).

In other words, the utterance in (19B) is a reconfirmation, whereas the utterance in (20B) is verbal irony. In the case of (20B), the following assumptions explicitly and implicitly communicated by the speaker might be accessed by the hearer:

(21) a. proposition expressed: It's a lovely day for a picnic.

b. propositional attitude: The speaker is disapproving of the thought ___.
c. The speaker has a dissociative attitude towards the thought *It's a lovely day for a picnic.*
d. implicated premise 1: If it rains, it's not a lovely day for a picnic.
e. implicated premise 2: It is raining.
f. implicated conclusion (21d + 21e): It's not a lovely day for a picnic.
g. other implicature (20A + 21f): The utterance in (20B) is of no use.

5.3.2 Universal Desires and Echoing

The relevance-theoretic notion of *echoing* is broad, and ironical utterances may echo a variety of sources. This broadness is controversial. Hamamoto (1997) raises the problem of identifying the echoed source in utterances like those in (22), whereas Seto (1997) provides examples of non-echoic verbal irony such as (23).

(22) a. [The speaker has slipped on the step]
    Oh, great. That's nice!
  b. [On a windy day, Junko, seeing her classmate Tomoko rush into the classroom with windblown hair, says to her:]
    You look perfect in your new hair style.   (Hamamoto, 1997, p. 260)
(23) A: Bob has just borrowed your car.
    B: Well, I like that!   (Seto, 1997, p. 242)

According to Hamamoto, the utterances in (22a) and (22b) sound ironical, but it is difficult to "trace the echoed source" (p. 260). Similarly, Seto argues that the utterance in (23) does not have any antecedent — not even any possible remote source (p. 242).

As a possible solution to his objection, Hamamoto refers to Kreuz and Glucksberg's (1989) *echoic reminder theory*, according to which any ironical utterance reminds the hearer of some antecedent event. Hamamoto claims that echoic interpretation might be explained as a "special case of reminders" (1997, p. 260), such that not all antecedent events need be actual or even implied utterances.

However, in replying to Hamamoto's and Seto's arguments, Sperber and Wilson (1998) argue that the range of possible echoed sources for utterances includes not only actual utterances or thoughts implied by utterances but also universal desires, norms and expectations. All of the utterances in (22) and (23), they claim, can be reanalyzed as dissociative echoing of universal desire: in other words, the utterances echo what is generally desired.

Blakemore (1992) offers a clear-cut example capturing the notion of universal desire or expectation as an echoed source. Consider:

(24) [The speaker and her friend are looking at a shop window displaying what she believes to be some particularly ugly china ornaments. She says to her friend:]
I simply must have one of those. (Blakemore, 1992, p. 167)

According to Blakemore, the echoed source of (24) is not an utterance but a thought that the speaker believes somebody else must have had. This can be explained as a case of what Sperber and Wilson (1998) call the echoing of *universal desire*: the thought echoed is attributed not to any speaker in the *real world*, but rather to one in a *possible world*.

Note that Blakemore (1992) argues that this sort of echoic interpretation involves taking a risk — the speaker might be misunderstood. Why would the speaker take this risk? Blakemore answers this question as follows:

> A hearer who is not particularly well acquainted with the speaker's tastes may not recognize the utterance as echoic, and may assume, mistakenly, that the speaker admires the ornament. On the other hand, if such a hearer does recognize the irony, the utterance will have the effect of increasing the degree of intimacy between them — the hearer will know, for example, that she can join in the joke by making fun of some other object in the window. It is this — the increase in intimacy — that makes the risk of misinterpretation worth taking. (Blakemore, 1992, p. 170)

The utterance in (25A) is another risky case. It, too, can be explained in terms of an increase in intimacy because it echoes a *desired thought* or an utterance in a possible world.

(25) [= (36) in Chapter 3]
[On a rainy day, the speaker sees her co-worker, who usually wears sunglasses, in the office and utters:]
A: Did you bring your sunglasses?
B: (i) [smiling] Yeah, why not?!
(ii) [pretending to be sad] No, I totally forgot.

The relevance-theoretic echoic hypothesis appears capable of accommodating any ironical aspect of a rhetorical question. Before attempting to verify this, however, let us review other theories of echo or allusion in verbal irony.

5.3.3 Other Echoic Approaches: Allusional Pretense and Implicit Display

As well as the relevance-theoretic echoic hypothesis, other studies of verbal irony shed light on the echoic or allusional aspects of utterances. Among them are Kumon-Nakamura, Glucksberg, and Brown's (1995) *allusional pretense theory* and Utsumi's (2000) *implicit display theory*.

The allusional pretense theory stipulates the two distinct recognitions of *pragmatic insincerity* and *echoic allusion* as prerequisites for understanding ironical utterances (Kumon-Nakamura et al, 1995). All ironical utterances violate at least one of speech act theory's felicity conditions for well-formed speech-acts (see Chapter 2 for more on this topic), and pragmatic insincerity is the result of this violation. Ironical utterances must also allude to some prior expectation, norm, or convention that has been violated in one way or another, giving the second prerequisite.

This notion of allusion seems to be compatible with the relevance-theoretic notion of echoing. However, as Wilson (2006) points out, it is in fact an allusional pretense involving a pragmatically insincere case of *saying*, i.e., *making as if to say*. Relevance theory does not require the recognition of pragmatic insincerity in the process of understanding utterances.

Utsumi (2000) agrees, saying that the allusional pretense theory "cannot explain the fact that hearers interpret ironic utterances without recognizing their violations" (pp. 1781–1782). In Utsumi's implicit display theory, verbal irony implicitly displays the three components of ironical environments listed in (26) under the conditions in (27) below:

(26) *Ironic environments*
   a. The speaker has a certain expectation E at time t_0.
   b. The speaker's expectation E fails (i.e., E is incongruous with reality) at time t_1.
   c. The speaker has a negative emotional attitude (e.g., disappointment, anger, reproach, envy) toward the incongruity between what is expected and what actually is the case.
   (temporal location t_0 and t_1 temporally precede the time of an utterance)
   (Utsumi, 2000, p. 1783)

(27) *Conditions of implicit display*
   a. An utterance U alludes to the speaker's expectation E.
   b. U includes pragmatic insincerity by intentionally violating one of the pragmatic principles, and
   c. U expresses indirectly the speaker's negative attitude toward the failure of E.
   (Utsumi, 2000, pp. 1784–1785)

Utsumi's implicit display theory is a prototype-based theory: although typical ironical utterances satisfy the three conditions, many do not. He suggests that the degree to which each of the three conditions in (27) is met can be measured on a scale from 0 to 1 in terms of the similarity between the utterance and the prototype, as described in (28).

(28) Calculation of the degree based on three conditions:
$d(U) = d_a + d_i + d_e$
d_a: the degree of allusion of U
d_i: the degree of pragmatic insincerity of U
d_e: the degree of indirect expression of negative attitude of U
(Utsumi, 2000, p. 1789)

In contrast to Kumon-Nakamura et al.'s allusional pretense theory and the relevance-theoretic echoic hypothesis, which permit allusion to or echoing of various sources, Utsumi insists that "only the speaker's expectation is assumed to trigger irony" (2000, p. 1794) in implicit display theory.

Utsumi also argues that the relevance-theoretic notion of dissociation does not sufficiently clarify the relationship between utterance and echoed source. By contrast, Utsumi's notion of allusion involves four distinct coherence relationships: *volitional-cause*, *non-volitional-cause*, *enable*, and *prevent*. An ironical utterance alludes to the speaker's expectation if and only if a certain coherence relationship is present. Consider:

(29) [Candy had baked a pizza to satisfy her hunger. When she was dishing it up, her husband entered the kitchen and gobbled up the whole pizza. Candy said to her husband:]
    a. I'm not hungry at all.
    b. I'm really happy to eat the pizza.
    c. Have you seen my pizza on the table? (Utsumi, 2000, p. 1786)

The coherence relationships in the utterances in (29a)–(29c) can be described as follows:

(30) *Coherence relationships*
    a. in (29a): $P = Q$
    b. in (29b): $P_i = A$ (i.e., P_i volitionally causes Q)
    c. in (29c): $P_i = X$ (i.e., P_i enables A ∧ A volitionally causes Q)
    Where:
        P = Propositional content of an utterance
        P_i = constituents of P

Q = [Candy is not hungry] (speaker expectation) A = [Candy eats a pizza] (action that volitionally causes Q)
X = [Candy's pizza is on the table] (state that enables A)

(Adapted from Utsumi, 2000, p. 1786)

Utsumi's implicit theory seems well adapted to declarative utterances as in the case of (29a). However, the cases of (29b) and (29c) raise questions. First, although Utsumi claims that the alluded-to/echoed source or speaker expectation is the thought *The speaker is not hungry*, implicit display theory does not provide any clear account of how the hearer of (29b) or (29c) accesses this thought.

For example, (31) and (32) below are thoughts describing the coherence relationships in (29b) and (29c) respectively.

(31) [= (30b)] If the speaker eats pizza, she is not hungry.
(32) [= (30c)] a. The fact that the speaker's pizza is on the table enables her to eat it.
        b. If the speaker eats pizza, she is not hungry.

If the utterances in (29b) and (29c) do communicate the thought *The speaker is not hungry*, then that thought might be deducted from the assumptions in (31) and (32) respectively. Intuitively, however, it is not clear why such a deduction should be necessary in understanding (29b) or (29c). Moreover, there seems to be no clear distinction between uttering an interrogative sentence and a declarative sentence with the same proposition. For example, there is no clear distinction between the utterance in (29c) and its declarative equivalent *You have seen my pizza on the table*.

5.3.4 What Do Borderline Cases of Verbal Irony Refer To?

If verbal irony can be understood in terms of the speaker's attitude, ironicalness depends on the strength of that attitude. This implies that there is no clear boundary between ironical and non-ironical utterances. This view is compatible to Utsumi's prototype-based account described in the preceding section, in which the ironicalness of an utterance is based on the degrees to which his three conditions are true.

In the relevance-theoretic echoic hypothesis, however, ironicalness is understood in terms of the speaker's (dissociative) attitude. In the hearer's cognitive process, ironicalness is assessed based on the strength of the speaker's dissociative attitude, possibly combined with other types of attitude as illustrated by the case of Mark Antony's repetition of Brutus is an honorable man *in* Julius

Caesar (3.2), which gradually comes to express disapproval as well (Sperber & Wilson, 1998; Yamanashi, 1998).

Yamanashi (1998) offers an example from Lewis Carroll that, he claims, "cannot be taken to be a hundred percent ironic" (p. 276):

(33) "You seem very clever at explaining words, Sir," said Alice. "Would you kindly tell me the meaning of the poem called 'Jabberwocky'?"
(Carroll, 1871/2000, p. 189)

Sperber and Wilson (1998) grant that Alice's utterance *You seem very clever...* is not entirely ironical, but observe that there is still a touch of irony because of a double echo of an earlier passage:

(34) Humpty Dumpty took the book, and looked it carefully. "That seems to be done right — " he began.
"You're holding it upside down!" Alice interrupted.
"To be sure, I was!" Humpty Dumpty said gaily, as she turned it round for him. "I thought it looked a little queer. As I was saying, that *seems* to be done right..."
(Carroll, 1871/2000, p. 188)

Alice's remark in (33), argue Sperber and Wilson, can be understood as echoing Humpty Dumpty's thought represented by his repeated use of the word *seem*, i.e., the thought that hardly any evidence is needed for something to *seem* to be the case. They point out that the echo in Alice's remark brings about not just a touch of irony but also other attitudes such as awe and bafflement.

To review, on the relevance-theoretic view, the speaker's attitude towards the proposition expressed by an ironical utterance is at least partly dissociative. Combination of dissociation with other attitudes might cause a positive or negative effect; the other attitude might strengthen or weaken the dissociation. In the process of understanding interrogative utterances, multiple attitudes — for example, a speech-act theoretic attitude and an ironical (i.e., echoic and dissociative) attitude — might function as clues towards the utterance's degree of rhetoricity.

5.4 Echo in Rhetorical Questions

We have confirmed the existence of borderline cases both between information-seeking and rhetorical interrogative utterances and between ironical and non-ironical utterances, and also confirmed that ironicalness in interrogative utterances directly affects rhetoricity. But how exactly does ironicalness have this effect? To answer this question, let us consider some more examples of rhetorical questions.

5.4.1 Echo in Polarity-Reversed Rhetorical Questions

Recall that the cognitive process of recognizing ironicalness in rhetorical questions can be explained in terms of the relevance-theoretic notions of *desirability* and *dissociation*. This view is comprehensive: it can cover any type of ironical (and therefore rhetorical) question, including borderline cases. For our first example, we will reanalyze polarity-reversed rhetorical questions.

As discussed above, the polarity-reversal aspect of a rhetorical question can be ironical. For example, recall utterance (1):

(1) a. Teacher: Who hit Billy?
 b. Student: [sarcastically] Who knows?

The proposition expressed by the utterance in (1b) can be completed by replacing the variable X in an incomplete proposition (35a) with a value, as shown in (35b) below.

(35) a. logical form: X knows.
 b. proposition expressed by the utterance: a particular person knows who hit Billy.
 c. higher-level explicature: The speaker has a sarcastic (i.e., dissociative) attitude towards the thought that a particular person knows who hit Billy.
 d. implicated premise: If the speaker has a sarcastic (i.e., dissociative) attitude to the thought that there is a person who knows who hit Billy (i.e., the existential presupposition of a variable X), then the empty value *nobody* is substituted.
 e. implicated conclusion 1 (35c + 35d): Nobody knows. / I don't know.
 f. implicated conclusion 2 (weaker implicatures than 35e): I don't care who. /
 It's a silly question (because nobody knows who).

Although Sperber and Wilson (1988) claim that the relevant (and therefore desirable) thought of an interrogative utterance is equivalent to the proposition it expresses, the thought in (35b) is not relevant enough to bring about certain cognitive effects because it is only an *attributed* thought: the point of uttering (1b) lies in communicating this attribution. The true relevant thought of (1b) might be equivalent to a higher-level explicature such as (35c) involving the utterance's ironicalness. In other words, the relevant thought of a rhetorical interrogative utterance is *not* the proposition it expresses.

In order for the hearer to understand the rhetoricity of the polarity-reversed *wh*-question in (1b), the higher-level explicature in (35c) must first be recovered. This communicates that the desirable thought or proposition of the utterance is attributed not to the speaker but to someone else. What is important is the speaker's sarcastic (dissociative) attitude towards the echoed thought or proposition.

It is easy to recognize the echo in (1b), given that it is uttered as a retort to the preceding information-seeking question: the echoed thought or the proposition of (1b) is what is implied by the preceding utterance in (1a). The speaker of (1b) exhibits a dissociative attitude towards the higher-level representation of (1a) involving the speech act *asking*. In other words, the speaker of (1b) communicates the assumption that (1a) is a silly question and not worth asking.

The process of understanding a polarity-reversed *yes-no* rhetorical question can be analyzed the same way. Consider utterance (36) [= (20a) in Chapter 2] and the assumptions in (37) below. In order for the hearer to recognize the rhetoricity of the polarity-reversed (36), it is necessary to recover the higher-level assumption as in (37c).

(36) Is that a reason for despair?
(37) a. logical form: [That is a reason for despair] or ¬ [That is a reason for despair]
   b. proposition expressed by the utterance: That is a reason for despair.
   c. higher-level explicature: The speaker has a dissociative attitude towards the thought *That is a reason for despair*.
   d. implicated premise: If the speaker has a dissociative attitude towards the thought *That is a reason for despair*, then the negative element *not* is embedded.
   e. implicated conclusion 1 (37c + 37d): That is not a reason for despair.
   f. implicated conclusion 2 (weaker implicature than 37e): The question itself is silly (because *surely* that is not a reason for despair).

Here, too, the recognition of rhetoricity involves the recognition of ironicalness, i.e., the speaker's dissociative attitude. The echo in the utterance in (36) can be explained in the same way as that of (1b): typically, it would be a response to a preceding utterance rather than the first utterance in an exchange. Therefore, the relevant thought allowing the hearer to recognize the rhetoricity of (36) is not the thought or proposition it expresses, as in (37b), but rather the higher-level explicature in (37c).

This view, however, does not seem to fit Wilson and Sperber's (1988/2012) claim that the relevant thought of an interrogative utterance is equivalent to the proposition expressed by the utterance, for the following three reasons: (a) relevance-theoretic analyses of interrogative utterances (Wilson & Sperber, 1988/2012; Sperber & Wilson, 1995) have mainly discussed non-polarity-reversed rhetorical questions such as *When did you say you were going to give up smoking?* rather than polarity-reversed rhetorical questions; (b) ironicalness has not been an issue in these analyses; and (c) discussion of the echoic hypothesis has mainly treated declarative rather than interrogative examples of verbal irony. By blending existing analyses of interrogative utterances and the echoic hypothesis, however, the causal interrelation of rhetoricity and ironicalness of interrogative utterances can be explained. The idea of such blending has already been introduced as *triple interpretation* by Sperber and Wilson (see Chapter 4), but I suggest that the concept can also be used to explain rhetoricity as an ironical aspect of interrogative utterances.

5.4.2 Echo in Non-Polarity-Reversed Rhetorical Questions: Possible Worlds as Echoed Source

Unlike the ironicalness of polarity-reversed rhetorical questions, the ironicalness of non-polarity-reversed rhetorical questions such as (25) and (29c) does not lie in the speaker's dissociative attitude towards the proposition expressed. Recall:

(25) [On a rainy day, the speaker sees her co-worker, who usually wears sunglasses, in the office and utters:]
   A: Did you bring your sunglasses?
   B: (i) [smiling] Yeah, why not?!
      (ii) [pretending to be sad] No, I totally forgot.
(29) [Candy had baked a pizza to satisfy her hunger. When she was dishing it up, her husband entered the kitchen and gobbled up the whole pizza. Candy said to her husband:]
   c. Have you seen my pizza on the table?

In the interaction in (25), the participants seem to be role-playing a scenario based on the mutually manifest assumption that *A always wears sunglasses*, given which the question in (25A) should be a request for information. If this scenario is mutually manifest between speaker and hearer, then the hearer will recognize that the speaker does not seek information, i.e., that the point of the utterance in (25A) does not lie in confirming the truthfulness of the proposition it expresses. In other words, it is mutually manifest that, although the speaker might or might not know whether the hearer has brought her sunglasses, the speaker does not in fact want to pursue which is true.

Some might see in the view that the participants are role-playing a scenario described by the literal meaning of an ironical utterance similarity to the staged communicative acts that Clark (1996, p. 372) developed from Clark and Gerrig's (1984) pretense theory. Clark's staged communicative acts are achieved by two layers of the assumption of verbal irony, one involving Speaker A and Hearer B, and the other involving their implied counterparts Ai and Bi:

> Layer 2: Ai is performing a serious communicative act for Bi.
> Layer 1: A and B jointly pretend that the event in Layer 2 is taking place.

However, Clark's concept of staged communicative acts is insufficient for our purposes. As Wilson (2006) argues in response to Clark and Gerrig (1984), Clark's analysis cannot accommodate cases of irony in the form of parody, which cannot be analyzed as pretense. Furthermore, Clark's view, being based on the concept of *joint pretense* presupposing common-ground information, is totally incompatible with the relevance-theoretic concept of mutual manifestness (see Chapter 2).

On the contrary, I argue that the interaction in (25) can be analyzed as a case of irony under echoic interpretation. The utterance in (25A) is echoic and expresses the speaker's attitude towards the echoed source. The echoed source might be an utterance identical to (25A) but made in a different situation (e.g., on a sunny day). In other words, the echoed source is not the proposition expressed by (25A), nor a universal desire such as the thought that one wears sunglasses on a sunny day, but rather an utterance in a *possible world*.

That is, if an utterance identical to (25A) were made on a sunny day, it could be interpreted as a confirmation question. The truthfulness of its propositional content would be understood as relevant to the speaker and its information-seeking rating as rather high. Uttering (25A) on a rainy day echoes this possible confirmatory use, and the ironicalness of the utterance is recognized when the contrastive two situations become manifest to the hearer. In other words, the ironicalness of the utterance in (25A) lies in the contrast between two possible situations: one in which (25A) is uttered in the sun, and another in which it is uttered in the rain. The differences between the two situations are summarized in Table 1 below:

	(a) Echoed source	(b) Echoic utterance [= (25A)]
(1) Utterance	Did you bring your sunglasses? (Utterance in *possible world*)	Did you bring your sunglasses? (Utterance in *real world*)
(2) Situation	Sunny day	Rainy day
(3) Proposition expressed by the utterance	Hearer brought her sunglasses.	Hearer brought her sunglasses.
(4) Attribution of the utterance	Speaker (general individual)	Speaker of the echoed utterance

Table 1. Comparison of Utterance in (25A) and Echoed Source

As seen in Table 1, the echoed source of (25A) is an identical interrogative utterance rather than the proposition expressed by the utterance. This means that the echoed utterance is not attributed to anyone in the real world. In other words, the echoed source is an utterance in a possible world where it is hot and the sun is shining, i.e., what (the speaker believes) is generally uttered in the hot sun. The assumption or proposition expressed by the echoed utterance might therefore be sort of a universal desire such as *Everybody should bring their sunglasses*.

On this view, the ironicalness of the utterance in (25A) arises from the speaker's dissociative attitude towards the echoed source. In the hearer's cognitive process, the echoed source might be represented as the thought of the information-seeking reading of the utterance in a *possible world* as shown in (38c-ii) below. The ironicalness become manifest as a result of the recognition of the contrast between the situations of the echoic utterance in (25A) and the echoed utterance itself. The set of assumptions which becomes manifest in the hearer's cognitive environment over the course of understanding the utterance in (25A) might be:

(38) a. proposition (25A) expresses: The hearer brought her sunglasses.
    b. higher-level explicatures 1 (assessment of information-seeking rating):
        (i) The thought in (38a) is desirable to either the speaker or the hearer.
        (ii) The speaker wants to confirm (with the hearer) to whom (38a) is desirable.
    c. contextual assumptions 1:
        (i) premise: People bring sunglasses only on sunny days and therefore it is natural to confirm whether someone has brought sunglasses on a sunny day.
        (ii) conclusion (higher-level explicature of the echoed utterance): (38a)

is desirable to the speaker.
  d. contextual assumptions 2:
     (i) premise 1: People do not bring sunglasses on rainy days, and therefore it is not natural to confirm whether (38a) on a rainy day.
     (ii) premise 2: The hearer brings sunglasses at any time and therefore it is natural to confirm whether (38a) even on a rainy day.
     (iii) conclusion: (38d-i) contrasts (38d-ii).
  e. higher-level explicature 2: The speaker has a dissociative attitude towards the thought that (38c-ii).
  f. (i) implicated premise: If (38e) is true, then (38a) is desirable to the hearer.
     (ii) implicated conclusion (= 38e + 38f-i) (based on result of assessment of information-seeking rating): (38a) is desirable to the hearer.

Note that two distinct sets of higher-level explicatures can be made manifest in this process. One involves the assessment of the information-seeking rating, as described in (38b), and the other involves the speaker's attitude towards that assessment, as described in (38e). I argue that one solution to the question of how ironical questions are understood can be given in terms of the causal interrelation between rhetoricity and ironicalness.

For example, in understanding the utterance in (25A), the thoughts in (38b) and other contextual assumptions result in the thought in (38e). Hence, it is assumed that the relevant thought of the utterance in (25A) is the thought that leads the hearer to recognize the ironicalness of the utterance: not the proposition expressed by the utterance (i.e., desirable thought), but the thought in (38e). Therefore, the following formulation can be applied not only to polarity-reversed rhetorical questions but also to non-polarity-reversal ironical questions such as (25A):

(39) the desirable thought or proposition expressed by a rhetorical interrogative utterance ≠ the relevant thought of an utterance

A similar analysis applies to the utterance in (29c), summarized in Table 2 below:

	(a) Echoed source	(b) Echoic utterance [= (29c)]
(1) Utterance	Have you seen my pizza on the table? (=utterance in *possible world*)	Have you seen my pizza on the table? (=utterance in *real world*)
(2) Situation	Speaker does not know that the hearer has eaten the pizza.	Speaker knows that the hearer has eaten the pizza.
(3) Thought or proposition expressed by the utterance	Hearer has seen the pizza on the table.	Hearer has seen the pizza on the table.
(4) Attribution of the utterance	Speaker in possible world	Actual speaker of echo

Table 2. Comparison of Utterance in (29c) and Echoed Source

If Candy, the speaker, is aware that the hearer has eaten up the pizza, the information-seeking rating of the utterance in (29c) is obviously low. Thus, the ironicalness of (29c), too, can be explained in terms of the speaker's attitude towards a higher-level explicature involving the speech act of asking. The echoed source of (29c), like that of (25A), is not the proposition expressed by the utterance but an utterance identical to (29c) itself. This echoed utterance is attributed to a different Candy in a possible world — what she might have uttered had she not known that her husband had eaten the pizza. In this possible world, the utterance would be interpreted as a pure confirmation question: Candy would be seeking to confirm whether the proposition it expresses, *The hearer has seen the pizza on the table*, was true.

In other words, the echoed utterance is identical to a confirmation question, and the ironicalness of (29c) can be explained in terms of the speaker's attitude to this confirmatory use of the utterance. The set of assumptions communicated by the utterance in (29c) might be as follows:

(40) a. proposition (29c) expresses: The hearer has seen the pizza on the table.
  b. higher-level explicature 1:
     (i) The thought in (40a) is desirable to either the speaker or the hearer.
     (ii) The speaker wants to confirm (with the hearer) to whom (40a) is desirable.
  c. contextual assumptions:
     (i) premise: In the context where the speaker does not know whether (40a) is true, it is natural to confirm it.
     (ii) conclusion (higher-level explicature of the echoed utterance): (40a) is desirable to the speaker.
  d. higher-level explicature 2: The speaker has a strong belief that the

hearer has seen the pizza on the table.
- e. contextual assumption 2: If (40d) is true, then the speaker has a dissociative attitude to the thought that (40c-ii).
- f. higher-level explicature 3 (40d + 40e): The speaker has a dissociative attitude to the thought that (40c-ii).
- g. implicated premise: If the speaker has a dissociative attitude to the thought that (40c-ii), then (40a) is desirable to the hearer.
- h. implicated conclusion (40f + 40g): (40a) is desirable to the hearer.

Note that whereas the assumptions of the utterance in (25A), given in (38), contain two higher-level explicatures, the assumptions of the utterance in (29c), given in (40), contain three: one for the assessment of desirability, one for the speaker's confidence in the proposition expressed by the utterance, and one for the recognition of the speaker's dissociative, ironical attitude. The distinction between the utterances in (25A) and (29c), therefore, lies in the speaker's confidence in the proposition expressed by each utterance: The speaker of (29c) knows that the hearer has seen the pizza on the table, whereas the speaker of (25A) does not know whether the hearer has brought her sunglasses or not.

If all other things are equal, the utterance in (29c) should require more processing effort than the utterance in (25A) because the speaker's confidence rating directly affects the assessment of the utterance's information-seeking rating. (Of course, as many things are not equal in the real world, it is not reasonable to compare the processing efforts of these utterances.)

Note that the formulation in (39) can also be applied to the understanding process of (29c). The relevant thoughts for the utterance in (29c) can be understood in terms of the recognition of the speaker's ironical attitude and the assessment of its information-seeking rating. In other words, the thoughts relevant enough to bring about cognitive effects and justify the speaker's uttering of (29c) might be the assumption described in (40f) along with the an assumption in (40h) resulting from (40f).

5.5 Conclusion

Interrogative utterances with a certain ironical flavor may be considered rhetorical questions to the extent that two distinct ironical aspects become manifest in the hearer's cognitive process: a discrepancy between the linguistic expression and the context of the utterance and another discrepancy between interrogative mood and the speaker's attitude towards the proposition expressed by the utterance. During the hearer's cognitive process, a variety of contextual clues lead to ironical readings.

For example, polarity-reversed assumptions like the assumption *Nobody knows* in the utterance *Who knows?* can be recovered as a result of the hearer's recognition of the discrepancy between the proposition expressed by the utterance and a preceding thought. On the other hand, non-polarity reversed rhetorical questions such as Have you seen the pizza on the table? *or* Did you bring your sunglasses? involve a discrepancy between the linguistic information in a given situation and that in an echoed (possible-world) situation.

Discrepancies of this sort also function as effective clues leading the hearer to recognize the other discrepancy: that between the interrogative mood and the speaker's attitude towards the speech act of asking. As Kawakami (1984) claims, the recognition of this secondary discrepancy involves assessment of the rhetoricity of the utterance. In the relevance-theoretic framework, the echoic hypothesis of irony accommodates these two distinct discrepancies.

Regarding the ironicalness of interrogative mood, Kawakami's cognitive model of ironical utterances, depicted in Figure 7 above, plausibly maps four possible hearer interpretations onto the four points F, $-F$, R, and $-R$, with the rhetorical reading of interrogative utterances associated with the point F. However, it does not seem necessary for the hearer of an utterance to metarepresent all possible interpretations: on the relevance-theoretic view, the hearer may simply access one relevant interpretation and stop the interpretation process if that interpretation achieves some cognitive effects. In other words, although the diagram may be held in a human's cognitive environment as a cognitive model, the hearer of an interrogative utterance does not necessarily need to access it except in borderline cases requiring more effort than typical information-seeking or rhetorical questions.

The recognition of the secondary discrepancy in ironical questions is fundamental for interpreting any type of rhetorical question. In non-ironical cases, such as Who do you think is my favorite team? (*answer:* The Dallas Cowboys!) *and* What company do I work for? (*answer:* I work for Apple), hearers may become aware of the discrepancy between the interrogative mood and the speaker's *dissociative* attitude towards the speech act of asking by using clues such as contextual information: visual information such as the speaker's wearing of the team's uniform, the inanity of the speaker questioning the hearer about information that the speaker already knows, etc.

Given that this discrepancy is ironical (i.e., dissociative in the relevance-theoretic sense), any rhetorical question can also be understood as ironical. Indeed, in my relevance-theoretic analysis, I argue that rhetoricity lies within the irony of the discrepancy between interrogative mood and the speaker's ironical (dissociative) attitude towards the higher-level explicature involving the speech act of asking.

* * * * * * * * * *

In my continuum model based on relevance theory, the assessment of an interrogative utterance's information-seeking vs. rhetorical rating plays an important role in understanding that utterance. However, it is not a prerequisite, as it is held to be in speech act theory. In my view, *any* interrogative utterance, including ambiguous cases, involves a metarepresentation of the higher-level embedding schema *The speaker is asking* P, and the speaker's attitude towards the thought embedded in the schema is assessed by the hearer. The hearer may be aware of the speaker's attitude towards the thought *The speaker is asking* P, which can function as a clue to examining the confidence rating of the answer or expressed proposition.

The view that any interrogative utterance leads the hearer to the higher-level explicature *The speaker is asking* P implies that the speaker expects the hearer to accessing the answer to the question or the proposition expressed by the utterance (P). This expectation might appear related to the concept of an indirect request for an answer in speech act theory. However, the relevance-theoretic continuum model is more useful than speech act theory here because it accommodates borderline cases that speech act theory cannot.

In daily interactions, there seem to be as many borderline cases (including ambiguous questions) as there are clear information-seeking or rhetorical questions. However, in my model, understanding an interrogative utterance does not require the hearer to assess the speaker's confidence in the proposition expressed by the utterance in advance, i.e., determine whether the question is highly information-seeking, highly rhetorical, or a borderline case. Instead, the hearer can collect clues to a relevant interpretation that brings about some cognitive effect. This search for relevance may or may not lead the hearer to the thought the speaker intended to communicate.

Nevertheless, in my continuum model, the speaker's confidence rating does play a central role in the process of interpreting interrogative utterances. This confidence rating is deeply related to the speaker's attitudinal higher-level schema, typically given as:

(41) a. The speaker wonders whether *P*. (purely information-seeking or confirmatory reading)
   b. The speaker is doubtful that *P*. (rhetorical [polarity-reversed] reading)
   c. The speaker believes that *P*. (rhetorical [non-polarity-reversed] reading)

If the speaker is asking *P* sincerely, and *P* is relevant to the speaker, i.e., the case of (41a) above, an information-seeking or confirmatory reading is strongly preferred: P is relevant enough to have the cognitive effect of confirming the speaker's existing assumption. On the other hand, in the cases of (41b) and (41c), the speaker has doubts about and strong confidence in P respectively; thus, the speaker is dissociative towards the thought *The speaker is asking* P and rhetorical readings are strongly preferred.

In other words, according to the relevance-theoretic echoic hypothesis, rhetoricity in interrogative utterances can be explained in terms of the speaker's dissociative (i.e., ironical) attitude towards the thought *The speaker is asking* P. The level of dissociativity can be described using a continuum model, presupposing borderline cases. If an interrogative utterance is neither clearly ironical nor clearly not, then the level of dissociativity, and therefore rhetoricity, is unclear too.

* * * * * * * * *

The next three chapters consider some examples of rhetorical questions in Japanese based on my relevance-theoretic cognitive-pragmatic model of a continuum of rhetoricity. In particular, the semantic and pragmatic properties of two elements will be examined: the hearsay (or echoic) construction *to iu* in Chapter 7, and the formal noun *mono* in the *mono ka* construction in Chapter 8. It is argued that these elements commonly appear in (McGloin, 1976) or even mark (Maynard, 1997) rhetorical questions. In fact, however, they occur not only in rhetorical questions but also in other types of questions. They, too, can be explained in the framework of relevance theory in terms of their contribution to the interpretation of desirable thoughts and attributed thoughts.

CHAPTER 6

Rhetorical Questions in Japanese

The Japanese language has a vast number of sentence-final particles, many of which involve modality or attitudinal representation (Uyeno, 1971; Maynard, 1993, 1995, 1997; Itani, 1993, 1995). The sentence-final particle *ka* in interrogative utterances is one example. Some particles, including *ka*, can also be combined into sentence-final expressions. SFEs can convey a rich variety of speaker attitudes and strongly affect the interpretation of rhetorical bias in Japanese interrogative utterances.

Whereas interrogative utterances in English are typically marked by syntactic features such as subject-auxiliary inversion and *wh*-fronting, interrogative utterances in Japanese are typically marked by the sentence-final particle *ka* and question words such as *dare* 'who' and *doko* 'where' (Itani, 1995). Consider the example of a Japanese declarative in (1) and the corresponding yes-no/*wh*-interrogatives in (2) below:

(1) Watashi wa pātii ni ikimasu.
    I   TOP party to go
    'I (will) go to the party'.
(2) a. Anata wa   pātii ni ikimasu ka?
       you   TOP party to go   Q
       'Will you go to the party?'
    b. Anata wa   doko ni ikimasu ka?
       you   TOP where to go   Q
       'Where will you go?'
    c. Dare ga pātii ni ikimasu ka?
       who S party to go   Q
       'Who will go to the party?'

Itani (1995) points out that Japanese interrogatives do not have an interrogative mood: There are no syntactic properties such as *wh*-fronting — note that both (2b) and (2c) are possible — or subject-auxiliary inversion — as can be seen by comparing (1) and (2).

The particle *ka* appears frequently in both yes-no and *wh*-interrogatives in Japanese. However, *ka* itself does not encode the speech act of asking, because ka can also occur in exclamatives. Consider:

(3) Nante takai   n desu *ka*!
     how   expensive COP   Q
     'How expensive it is!'   (Itani, 1995, p. 143)

Itani (1993, 1995) claims that because *ka* is not only an interrogative marker but also an exclamative marker, making a categorical distinction between these types of sentence is not necessarily. Itani points out that *ka* can be nicely explained in the framework of relevance theory (Sperber & Wilson, 1995) using the concept of interpretive use, *which provides a general account of non-declarative utterances (see Chapter 7 for Itani's relevance-theoretic account of the sentence-final particle* ka as an interpretive use marker).

Like English interrogative utterances, Japanese interrogative utterances marked with the sentence-final particle *ka* are used not only as information-seeking questions but also as various kinds of non-information-seeking questions. Consider:

(4) a. Self-oriented question (pondering):
     [The speaker is suffering from serious illness, and wonders:]
     Itsu made watashi wa   shigoto o tsuzuke-rareru   darō   *ka*.
     when until I   TOP work   DO continue AUX-can   AUX-will Q
     'I wonder how long I will be able to continue working.'
     b. Expository question:
     [In a literature class, the lecturer utters:]
     Kono shosetsu ga kakareta   no   wa donna jidai
     this novel   S write-PASS COMP TOP what era
     datta   deshō   *ka*.
     COP-PAST   AUX-will   Q
     Mazu hajime ni...
     First beginning at...
     'What kind of era was it when this novel was written? First of all...'

In addition to self-oriented questions such as (4a) and expository questions such as (4b), *ka* can also mark many other non-information-seeking questions such as exam questions, guess questions, speculative questions and rhetorical questions. This is further evidence that, like the interrogative mood in English, *ka* does not encode the speech act of asking.

6.1 Sentence-Final Expressions (SFEs) in Japanese

When the sentence-final particle *ka* occurs in rhetorical questions, the utterance is usually marked by falling intonation. Information-seeking *wh*- and yes-no interrogatives in Japanese always have rising intonation, but rhetorical questions can have falling intonation. Thus, the following interrogative utterance can be interpreted as either an information-seeking question or a rhetorical question:

(5) Dare ga shitteiru *ka*.
     who S know   Q
     'Who knows?'

When *ka* has rising intonation, (5) is interpreted as an information-seeking question seeking *an individual who knows something*. On the other hand, when *ka* has falling intonation, the utterance is interpreted as a rhetorical question communicating that *nobody knows*.

Some might argue that (5) is not typical as either an information-seeking question or a rhetorical question. They might say that there are two possible distinct expressions that would be more typical:

(6) a. Dare ga shitteiru no (desu) ka.
        who S know   COP   Q
     b. Dare ga shitteiru mono (desu) ka.
        who S know   FN   (COP) Q

Most Japanese native speakers can easily distinguish the implications of these two expressions and would say that (6a) is more likely as an information-seeking question than (6b), which would preferably be used as a rhetorical question.

When an interrogative utterance is used rhetorically, it is often marked by other elements co-occurring with *ka*, usually preceding it. For instance, *to iu* as well as *mono* can occur with *ka* to make SFEs. Consider (7). Authors including McGloin (1976) and Maynard (1997) say that *mono ka* in (7a) and *to iu no ka* in (7b) are markers of rhetorical questions. McGloin argues that Japanese interrogatives marked by *mono ka* always communicate a negative assumption on the part of the speaker.

(7) a. Dare ga shiru *mono ka*.
    who S know FN Q
    'Who knows?'
   b. Dare ga shiru *to-iu* no *ka*.
    who S know QUO-say COP Q
    'Who do you say knows?'

Both utterances in (7) typically communicate the speaker's assumption that *nobody knows*. (Note: Although I gloss the *mono* of *mono ka* as a formal noun, my analysis holds that *mono* in this context essentially has the function of the *mono da* construction, and should not be confused with use of *mono* on its own. See Chapter 8 for details.)

According to McGloin, *mono ka* functions as a negative context (1976, p. 76) that allows negative polarity items. This is partially supported by examples like the following:

(8) Dare mo iku mono ka.
    who   go FN   Q
    'Nobody will go.'   (Adapted from McGloin, 1976, p. 76)

In (8), the construction *mono ka* is said to allows the occurrence of the negative polarity item *dare mo* 'nobody'. However, as I will show in Chapter 7, McGloin's argument is incorrect. Although the utterance in (7a) does not contain a negative polarity item, McGloin (1976) still argues that the *mono ka* SFE indicates only a negative assumption, i.e., *Nobody will know*.

Maynard (2005, p. 405) indicates that the hearsay construction *to iu* co-occurring with *ka* is rhetorical. In other words, an interrogative utterance marked by to iu (no) ka *can be often interpreted as a rhetorical question. In spite of the lexical meaning of* to iu *as a hearsay construction, the utterance in (7b) does not report or echo any previous utterance. Similarly to the *mono ka* interrogative in (7a), the utterance in (7b) communicates the speaker's negatively biased assumption that *nobody knows*.

As we have seen, both McGloin (1976) and Maynard (2005) claim that *mono ka* and *to iu (no) ka* are compound units marking rhetorical questions. I would argue, however, that they should not be considered compound units as such, but rather combinations of particles and other elements, each functioning individually. This is because ka *alone can indicate a rhetorical interpretation, and so it may be important to know the semantic/pragmatic properties of* mono *and* to iu *as well as those of* ka.

6.2 Conclusion

The variety of interrogative utterances in Japanese can be explained in the same way as that in English. No syntactic features in Japanese interrogatives encode the speech act of asking. Interrogatives marked by *ka* or question words such as *doko* 'where' are interpreted not only as information-seeking questions but also as other types of questions including guess questions, expository questions, and rhetorical questions. (Some utterances marked by *ka* can also be interpreted as exclamatives.) The relevance-theoretic concept of *interpretive use* enables us to explain the process of understanding the slight differences between these utterances. Moreover, a further relevance-theoretic concept, Blakemore's binary concept of conceptual/procedural encodings, can also provide an account of sentence-final particles indicating rhetoricity. The relevance-theoretic approach to the semantics of these particles will be explored in Chapters 7 and 8.

CHAPTER 7

SFEs in Japanese Interrogatives 1: The Case of *To Iu No Ka*

This chapter investigates the meanings of the interrogative or exclamative particle *ka* and the hearsay particle *tte*, both in isolation and when they co-occur, and the mechanism by which those meanings affect interpretation of both information-seeking and rhetorical questions. Japanese sentence-final particles represent the speaker's attitude towards the proposition expressed by an utterance (See Maynard, 1995, 1997, for *yo* and *ne*; Itani, 1995, for *yo*; Itani, 1994, for the hearsay particle *tte*; and Itani, 1993, for the interrogative particle *ka*). As Itani (1993) points out, although sentence-final particles and other elements can be combined into sentence-final expressions (SFEs), the combined expression does not have a single complex meaning but still conveys the separate meanings communicated by each element. Consider the following examples:

(1) a. He is a student *ka tte*?
    'Is he a student, you say?'
   b. He is a student *ka tte ka*?
    'Are you asking me whether he is a student?' (Itani, 1993, p. 145)

According to Itani's (1993, 1994, 1995) account, the utterance in (1a) is an echoic use of an immediately preceding utterance *He is a student* ka? 'Is he a student?' whereas the utterance in (1b) is a question asking whether the hearer asked the question *He is a student* ka? In other words, these particles could be added again and again, as in *He is a student* ka tte ka tte? Doing so might communicate additional cognitive effects, such as the speaker's sarcastic attitude, but no matter how many times *ka* and *tte* are added, *ka* always functions as an interrogative marker and *tte* always functions as an echoic marker.

Typically, information-seeking questions contain one of the following two distinct sentence-final expressions: (a) the interrogative particle *ka* alone, or (b) a combination of *ka* and a copular construction (e.g., *da, desu, no desu*), as in examples (2a) and (2b) below respectively. The hearsay marker *to iu* commonly co-occurs with the second case to form a common interrogative expression *to iu no (desu) ka* as in (2c) below.

(2) a. Pātii ni ikimasu *ka*?
    party   go   Q
    'Will you go to the party?'
  b. Pātii ni iku *no desu ka*?
    party   go   COP   Q
    'Are you really going to the party?'
  c. Pātii ni iku *to iu   no desu ka*?
    party   go QUO-say COP   Q
    'Do you mean that you are going to the party?'

The utterances in (2a), (2b), and (2c) can all be used as information-seeking questions regarding the truthfulness of the propositions they include, i.e. The hearer is going to the party. Each sentence-final expression indicates a particular attitude on the part of the speaker towards the proposition of the utterance.

It is known that in declarative utterances, the copula *da* is often used to *emphasize* or *highlight* the speaker's thoughts or the proposition expressed by the utterance (Maynard, 1997), and this is also true of interrogative utterances. In particular, the copula is often used in confirmation questions to emphasize the speaker's confirmatory intent. In utterance (2b), the copula *desu* suggests that the speaker has a presupposition like *The hearer will not go to the party* that they seek to confirm.

In utterance (2c), *ka* co-occurs with *to iu* and the copula *da*. Maynard (1997) claims that the combined interrogative sentence-final expression that results (*to iu no desu ka*) often indicates a rhetorical reading. It is true that the utterance in (2c) can be interpreted as a rhetorical question. Suppose that the speaker has reason to believe that the hearer will not go to the party, such as the hearer's having been sick in bed and suffering from a fever. The utterance is interpreted as a rhetorical question if the speaker's belief is strong enough to imply that it should be impossible for the hearer to go out. In this case, the speaker does not seek information but rather intends to communicate the thought *The hearer will not go to the party*.

In fact, *to iu* is often used in rhetorical questions. But why should a quotative element lead to rhetorical readings of interrogative utterances? Intuitively, it cannot be caused by the quotative element alone. The reason must lie in the combined expression *to iu no desu ka*.

This chapter investigates whether the meanings and functions of the combined sentence-final interrogative expression *to iu no desu ka*, which seems to mark rhetorical questions, can be adequately explained by the relevance-theoretic framework. The chapter begins with a discussion of the meaning of *ka* based on Itani's relevance-theoretic approach to its use as an interrogative marker. The next section compares the meanings of *to iu* in declarative utterances to those in interrogative utterances. The two sections after that focus on the echoic function of *to iu* interrogative utterances and discuss the distinction between *tte* and *to iu/tte iu*. The concept of *echoic reformulation*, which functions as a clue to the rhetorical reading of an interrogative utterance to which *to iu* or *tte* is appended, is then proposed. The final section explores *to iu* in *wh*-interrogative utterances, which can be analyzed in a similar way to their yes-no equivalents.

7.1 *Ka* As Interpretive Use Marker

In some accounts by Japanese grammarians (Uyeno, 1971), *ka* is an interrogative marker. It encodes an illocutionary force conveying that *the speaker is asking* P (where P is the proposition of the utterance). In other words, their account treats *ka* as linguistically encoding the following conceptual representation:

(3) The speaker is asking P (P = proposition of the utterance)

According to this view, a yes-no interrogative like (4a) and a *wh*-interrogative like (4b) encode the information in (5a) and (5b) respectively:

(4) a. Is Tokyo the capital of Japan?
    b. Where is the capital of Japan?
(5) a. *The speaker is asking* whether Tokyo is the capital of Japan.
    b. *The speaker is asking* where the capital of Japan is.

Although Itani (1993) accepts part of this approach, agreeing that the sentence-final *ka* can be an interrogative marker, she argues against speech act theoretic accounts of *ka*, providing many examples of interrogative utterances ending in *ka* that they cannot explain. One such example is given below:

(6) [Hearer has claimed that he would give up smoking, but later the speaker sees the hearer smoking, and utters:]
    Tabako wa yameru to itsu iimashita ka?
    cigarettes TOP stop QUO when say-PAST Q
    'When did you say that you would stop smoking?'

The utterance in (6) is not an information-seeking question but a rhetorical question. The speaker knows the answer and intends to remind the hearer that he claimed he would give up smoking at a certain time in the past. *Ka* in (6) does not encode the schema of conceptual representation in (3), and therefore the utterance does *not* encode (7) below:

(7) *The speaker is asking* when the hearer said that he would stop smoking.

Itani (1993, 1995) also argues that *ka* can be an exclamative marker as well as an interrogative marker. Consider (8) below:

(8) Nante takai   n desu ka!
    how expensive COP Q
    'How expensive it is!, isn't it?' / 'How expensive it is!, eh?'
                                    (Adapted from Itani, 1995, p. 225)

Itani claims that the dual interrogative and exclamative function of *ka* can be adequately explained by Sperber and Wilson's relevance-theoretic accounts of interrogatives and exclamatives in which both are analyzed in terms of the notion of *interpretive use* (Sperber & Wilson, 1995; Wilson & Sperber, 1988/2012; see also Chapter 4). According to Itani (1993, p. 143), although *ka* can be either an interrogative marker or an exclamative marker, the process through which the hearer interprets utterances ending in *ka* does not require specifying which of these the speaker intends to communicate, because they can both be explained in terms of the interpretation of a desirable representation. Consider the following example, which is the original version of Itani's example in (6):

(9) [Hearer has claimed that he would give up smoking, but later the speaker sees the hearer smoking, and utters:]
    When did you say you were going to give up smoking?
                                    (Sperber & Wilson, 1995, p. 251)

In (9), the interrogative mood leads the hearer to an interpretation in which the thought (i.e., the answer) that *The hearer said he was going to give up smoking at* t *(*t=a certain time in the past) should be desirable from the hearer's viewpoint, not from the speaker's. The desirable thought is relevant, giving rise to cognitive effects as a "reminder" (Sperber & Wilson, 1995, p. 252; Wilson & Sperber, 1988/2012, p. 227). Itani claims that sentence-final *ka* is an interpretive use marker like sentential mood.

Itani (1993) also argues against the speech act theoretic analysis of the sentence-final *ka* positing that it encodes a non-truth-conditional *conceptual* meaning as a part of a higher-level representation as in (7). She argues that *ka* encodes "*procedural* constraints on the inferential construction of higher level explicatures" (Itani, 1995, pp. 229–230). In other words, the encoded meaning of *ka* is procedural, not truth-conditional: *Ka* encodes a procedure to constrain the construction of the higher-level representation that "expresses the speaker's attitudes of desire" (Itani, 1995, p. 230).

Itani claims that when an utterance ending in *ka* is recognized as an information-seeking question, the higher-level representation of (10a) below is recovered, whereas if it the utterance is recognized as a rhetorical question, (10b) is recovered instead.

(10) a. The speaker is asking P.
     b. The speaker is reminding the hearer of P.

Itani's view as outlined above seems to agree with my argument that the interpretation of interrogative utterances can be examined with respect to a continuum between information-seeking and rhetoricity. The encoded meaning of *ka* may be formulated in terms of a desirable interpretation, as in:

(11) The proposition represented by an utterance U is desirable to a participant X if it is relevant to X.

I argue that the interpretation of the particle *ka* is primarily processed based on the formulation in (11), which can be developed to replace X with a definite value by pragmatic inference — that is, to examine to whom the proposition represented by an utterance is relevant.

7.2 The Meaning of *To Iu No (Desu) Ka*

Maynard (1997, pp. 156–158) claims that the sentence-final expressions *to iu no desu ka* and its less formal variant *tte iu no desu ka* are often used for rhetorical questions, and appear frequently in detective novels to communicate the speaker's doubt or disbelief regarding the propositional content. Consider:

(12) [There has been a murder in a mansion. A detective says something indicating that the murderer is an insider. A maid responds to the detective, uttering:]
    Maid: Anata wa hannin ga o-yashiki no hito da *to iu*
          you TOP murderer S HON-mansion GEN person COP QUO-say

> *n-desu ka.*
> COP Q
> 'Do you mean that the murderer is an insider?'
> (Utano, 1992, p. 200; cited in Maynard, 1997, p. 157; my translation)

Maynard points out that, despite the use of the hearsay construction *to iu*, the utterance in (12) does not report any preceding utterance: There *is* no preceding utterance whose propositional content is simply *the murderer is an insider*. Maynard argues that the rhetoricity of (12) is clear because it does not permit an answer. Consider:

(13) A: Anata wa hannin ga o-yashiki no hito da *to iu n desu ka.*
> 'Do you say that the murderer is an insider?'
> B: *Hai, sō desu. / *Iie, sō de wa arimasen.
> *'Yes, I do.' / * 'No, I don't.'   (Maynard, 1997, p. 157; my translation)

According to Maynard, the utterance in (12) [= (13A)] is a rhetorical question because it expresses the speaker's doubt about the thought that *the murderer is an insider*. If this is so, the unacceptability of both responses in (13B) could arise from the fact that the doubt expressed by the utterance in (13A) is strong enough to prevent the hearer from providing an answer.

A speaker who truly intended to seek information or confirm *whether the hearer said that the murderer is an insider*, would usually use *to itta*, the past tense of to iu. Consider the following information-seeking equivalent:

(14) [There has been a murder in a mansion. A detective says that the murderer is an insider. But a maid is not sure she heard clearly and responds to the detective, uttering:]
> Anata wa hannin ga o-yashiki no hito da *to itta n desu ka.*
> 'Did you say that the murderer is an insider?'

Indeed, *to itta* as in (14) typically appears in information-seeking questions, whereas *to iu* as in (12) typically appears in rhetorically biased questions. Nevertheless, some information-seeking interrogatives do contain *to iu or tte iu*, such as (2c) above.

7.2.1 *To Iu/Tte Iu* in Declarative Utterances

The hearsay construction *to iu* or *tte iu* consists of *to/tte* (a quotative particle used as a predicate complementizer) and *iu* 'say,' making it equivalent to say that…*in English*. There is a slight distinction between the uses of *to* iu *and* tte *iu*: Tte iu *is more colloquial than* to iu, although both can be used in spoken Japanese. Itani (1994) introduced (15) below as a typical use of *to iu* at the end of a sentence:

(15) Hitobito wa   Mary wa   kashikoi *to iu*.
     people   TOP   Mary TOP   smart   QUO-say
     'People say that Mary is smart.'
                                                                     (Itani, 1994, p. 390)

The utterance in (15), however, becomes less natural if *to iu* is replaced by *tte iu* as in (16) below:

(16) ?? Hitobito wa Mary wa kashikoi *tte iu*.

The lower acceptability of (16) may derive from the combination of colloquial *tte* and the word *hitobito* 'people,' which is rather formal and typically used in written texts or prepared speeches. If the word *hitobito* is replaced by a more colloquial word such as *minna* 'everybody,' *to iu* and *tte iu* are equally acceptable:

(17) Minna   ga Mary wa   kashikoi *to iu/tte iu*.
     (all) people S   Mary TOP   smart   QUO-say
     'Everyone says that Mary is smart.'

Another difference between *to* and *tte* lies in the fact that *tte* in (17) can be used alone as in (18a) below, giving the same meaning as (17), whereas *to* cannot (Yamazaki, 1996).

(18) a. Minna ga Mary wa kashikoi *tte*.
     b. Minna ga Mary wa kashikoi **to*.

Maynard (1997, p. 184) claims that *to iu/tte iu* in declarative utterances typically co-occurs with a copular construction, *no da* or *no desu*. The four possible combinations — *to iu no da, to iu no desu, tte iu no da,* and *tte iu no desu* — are all equally acceptable in declarative utterances. A bare sentence-final *to/tte iu* without a copular construction is typical of narrative and less acceptable in conversation. Consider:

(19) a. [preferred in narrative speech or written text]
        Sensei   ga Mary wa   kashikoi *to iu/tte iu*.
        teacher S   Mary TOP   smart   QUO-say
        'Our teacher says that Mary is smart.'

b. [preferred in conversation]
   Sensei ga Mary wa   kashikoi *to iu/tte iu   no da/desu*.
   teacher S Mary TOP smart   QUO-say   COP
   'Our teacher says that Mary is smart.'

Consider the following monologue extracted from a novel, which shows the contrast between sentences with or without the copula *da*:

(20) [The speaker is a shop owner suffering from a decrease in sales]
   Ore wa   komiageru sabishisa o   koraete jibun ni iikikaseta.
   I   TOP overcome loneliness DO hold   oneself tell-PAST
   'I said this to myself, enduring my rising loneliness:'
   Mō   chūmon sarenakutatte   kamaya shinai no *da*.
   anymore order   give-PASS-NEG-CON care-NEG   COP
   'I won't care even if nobody places an order *no da*.'
                                    (Maynard, 1997, p. 184; my translation)

The two sentences in (20) are part of a long monologue. The first sentence, a narrative part of the monologue, contains no copula. This contrasts with the second sentence, a self-quotation containing *no da*. Maynard (1997) claims that when *no da* or *no desu* is used in a monologue it emphasizes the speaker's thought.

However, it is not clear from Maynard's account what thought is emphasized in the second sentence. In other words, what would it mean for *no da* to emphasize the thought *I won't care even if nobody places an order*? Uchida (1998, 2011, 2013) argues in his relevance-theoretic analysis of *(no) da* that it encodes procedural information to constrain the recovery of higher-level explicature. For example, from the utterance in (21) below, the hearer will recover a basic explicature like (22a) and a higher-level explicature such as (23a), (23b) or (23c) (all emphasis added):

(21) Gokiburi *da*.
    'Cockroach *da*.'
(22) There's a cockroach at a certain place at a certain time.
(23) a. *I say that* it is a cockroach.
    b. *I believe that* it is a cockroach.
    c. *I find that* it is a cockroach.   (Uchida, 2011, p. 107)

The assumptions in (23) represent possible propositional attitudes of the speaker: the thought in (23a) involves the speech act of saying; the thought in (23b) the speaker's belief that there is a cockroach (rather than a cricket); and the thought in (23c) the speaker's conclusion (rather than anyone else's) that there is a cockroach. The sentence-final expression (consisting of a copular construction) *(no) da* constrains the process that leads the hearer to a relevant interpretation. According to this view, the effect of (no) da in the second sentence in (20) is to place constraints on the recovery of a higher-level explicature, such as:

(24) The speaker *says/believes/finds (etc.)* that he won't care even if nobody places an order.

(No) da/(no) desu represent the speaker's attitudinal thought not only in monologues but also in utterances. Moreover, some utterances communicate speaker attitudes involving modality. Kiefer (1994, p. 2516a) defines modality as "the speaker's cognitive, emotive, or volitive attitude toward a state of affairs." In the following examples, volitive speaker attitudes such as *will* or *wish* can be seen:

(25) a. I do my assignment *no da/no desu*.
    'I *will* do my assignment.'
    Higher-level explicature:
        The speaker is determined to do their assignment.
  b. You do your assignment *no da/no desu*.
    'You *must* do your assignment.'
    Higher-level explicature:
        The speaker wishes that the hearer would do their assignment.

What about cases where *no da/no desu* and *to iu/tte iu* co-occur? Will they represent thoughts directly or constrain the recovery of the represented thought? Consider the following example:

(26) [The hearer, a schoolgirl, has been sick in bed and absent from school. The speaker, her classmate, visits the hearer and utters:]
  Kinō,   Mari ga machi de   anata o   mita   to iu   no desu.
  yesterday Mari S town LOC   you   DO see-PAST QUO-say COP
  'Mari says that she saw you in town yesterday.'

In my view, the speaker's attitude expressed by the utterance in (26) is likely to be surprise or doubt, directed not the bare propositional content *Mari saw the hearer* (= P) but rather at the representation *Mari said that P*. The hearer may recover a higher-level representation like the following:

(27) The speaker *is surprised/doubts* that Mari *says* she saw the hearer.

Note that the *to iu* in (26) is in the non-past form, equivalent to the present tense ('*says* that') in English. The fact that the speaker of (26) could have but did not use the past tense *to itta* ('*said* that') or *to itteita* ('*was saying* that') may imply that the use of the non-past *to iu* conveys rhetoricity. I argue that it is the combination of *no da/no desu* with *to iu/tte iu* and *no da/no desu* that affects the recovery of an attitudinal higher-level explicature like the one in (27).

The hearsay particle *tte*, as the short form of *to iu*, *tte iu*, *to itta*, and *tte itta*, can substitute for *to iu no desu* as seen in (28) below:

(28) Kinō,   Mari ga machi de   anata o   mita   *tte*.
      yesterday Mari S town LOC you   DO see-PAST QUO
      'Mari said that she saw you in town yesterday.'

However, for a sentence like (28) a literal past-tense interpretation is preferred: *Mari said that she saw you in town yesterday*. The utterance does not convey an attitude such as surprise or doubt; it merely conveys the fact that the speaker heard from Mary that she saw the hearer.

Can this distinction between *tte* and *to iu/tte iu* be explained by the meaning of *tte*? The next section explores this question.

7.2.2 The Meaning of *Tte*

There appears to be a significant difference between *to iu/tte iu* and plain *tte* (*to* is not used alone in utterances like [28] above). Itani (1994) points out that tte *has a procedural meaning*, arguing that "*what* tte *itself encodes is that the utterance it is attached to is based on another utterance*" (p. 385). Itani also *claims that* tte can be used to report only actual utterances, not thoughts (Itani, 1994, p. 396). According to Itani, there are two distinct uses of *tte*. Consider:

(29) According to her teacher, Mary is smart *tte*. I always knew it.
(30) A: Our teacher said that Mary is smart.
      B: Mary wa   kashikoi *tte*?!
         Mary TOP   smart   QUO
         'Mary is smart?! *Did she say that?* Goodness!'   (Itani, 1994, p. 381)

The standard use of *tte* can be seen in (29), in which the speaker reports her teacher's actual utterance *Mary is smart*. On the other hand, *tte* in (30B) is not *reporting* but *echoing* an utterance attributed to someone else. In the relevance-theoretic account (Wilson & Sperber, 1992), this is echoic use: the

speaker dissociates herself from the utterance that she echoes.
However, consider the following example:

(31) [With a bored tone of voice]
   This is a lovely party *tte*. * [*sic*]

According to Itani (1994), *tte* is not acceptable in (31) because the echoed source is a thought rather than an actual utterance. Itani's view contrasts with Maynard's (1997, p. 408) argument that both *tte* and *tte iu (no desu ka)* can be appended to utterances whose propositional forms are attributed to an utterance *or* a thought. Recall that *tte* can be a shortened form of both non-past *tte iu* 'say that' and past *tte itta* 'said that.' That Maynard's analysis treats the echoic functions of *tte* and tte iu (no desu ka) *in the same way may imply that she regards* tte *as a shortened form of* tte iu (no desu ka) *only*. Maynard's analysis seems correct in the sense that *tte* can be not only a shortened form of a declarative *tte iu* or *tte itta* but also a shortened form of an interrogative *tte iu no (desu) ka* or *tte itta no (desu) ka*, because *tte* itself does not refer to any sentential mood. In fact, some of my examples of *tte* (marked as having an interrogative mood) may echo an attributed thought, and support her argument. The following two sections in this chapter investigate such echoic use in interrogative utterances of *tte iu no (desu) ka* and *tte* respectively.

7.3 *Tte* and *Tte-Iu No (Desu) Ka* in Interrogative Utterances

Similarly to the declarative case, interrogative *tte* and *to iu/tte iu* are both acceptable. However, *to iu/tte iu* is typically accompanied by *no (desu) ka*, as in the following examples:

(32) a. Sensei   ga Mary wa   kashikoi *tte*?
       teacher S   Mary TOP   smart   QUO
       'Did/does your teacher say that Mary is smart?'
     b. Sensei   ga Mary wa   kashikoi *to iu/tte iu no desu ka*?
       teacher S   Mary TOP   smart   QUO-say COP   Q
       'Does your teacher say that Mary is smart?'

Both *tte* in (32a) and *to iu/tte iu* in (32b) communicate that the proposition expressed by the utterance, *Mary is smart*, is attributed to an actual utterance. In other words, both (32a) and (32b) can be produced to confirm the teacher's speech act of *saying* P (where P = *Mary is smart*).

However, *tte* and *to iu/tte iu no desu ka* are not interchangeable. Consider the following interaction, in which (33A2) is uttered as a confirmation question (note that *tte* can be abbreviated to *te* following /n/):

(33) [A mother asks her child, who is named Mary, about what her teacher said]
    A1: Sensei wa nan *te*?
        teacher TOP what QUO
            'What does/did your teacher say?'
    B: Mary wa kashikoi *tte*.
        Mary TOP smart QUO
            'He says/said that Mary is (= I am) smart.'
    A2: *Hontō? Sensei ga Mary wa kashikoi tte?*
        really teacher S Mary TOP smart QUO
            'Really? Your teacher says/said that Mary is (= you are) smart?'

In every utterance in (33), *tte* can be regarded as a shortened form of either *tte iu* 'says that' or *tte itta* 'said that.' Consider a more formal version of the interaction in (33):

(34) A1: Sensei wa nan *te iimashita ka*?
        teacher TOP what QUO-say-PAST Q
            'What did your teacher say?'
    B: Mary wa kashikoi *tte iimashita.* / ... *tte itta no desu.*
        Mary TOP smart QUO-say-PAST QUO-say-PAST COP
            'He said that Mary is smart.'
    A2: *Hontō? Sensei ga Mary wa kashikoi tte itta no desu ka?*
        really teacher S Mary TOP smart QUO-say-PAST COP Q
            'Really? Your teacher said that Mary is smart?'

The interrogative utterance in (34A1), in which a copula does not appear, can be interpreted as a non-biased information-seeking question. *Iimashita* is simply a more formal version of *itta* 'said' and does not convey any particular attitudinal implication. The declarative utterance in (34B) can be interpreted as either reporting or echoing. The combination of *tte itta* and *no desu* as in (34B) can mark the echoic use of a preceding utterance, encouraging the recovery of an attitudinal higher-level explicature, whereas the use of *(t)te iimashita* without *no desu* as in (34A1) simply reports a preceding utterance. The interrogative utterance in (34A2), by contrast, can be interpreted as a confirmation question with which the speaker intends to confirm whether or not the teacher said that Mary is smart at a certain time in the past (e.g., yesterday or this morning). From the utterance in (34A2), two distinct higher-level explicatures can be recovered:

(35) a. The speaker *is wondering whether it is true that* the teacher said that Mary is smart.
b. The speaker *is surprised that* the teacher said that Mary is smart.

Note that whereas *tte iu no desu ka* can replace *tte itta no desu ka*, in its reporting use it must co-occur with a word or phrase permitting this use of the present tense. For example, the use of *itsumo* 'always' in (36A2) below implies that the speaker regards the teacher's utterance as a habit:

(36) A1: Itsumo sensei wa nan te iimasu ka?
always teacher TOP what QUO-say Q
'What does your teacher (always) say?'
B: Mary is smart *tte iimasu*. /...*tte iu no desu.*
'He says that Mary is smart.'
A2: *Hontō? Itsumo sensei ga Mary wa kashikoi tte iu no desu ka?*
really always teacher S Mary TOP smart QUO-say COP Q
'Really? Does your teacher (always) say that Mary is smart?'

The utterance in (36A2) conveys not only that the speaker wishes to confirm whether it is true that the teacher always says Mary is smart, but also a range of possible attitudinal higher-level explicatures, including:

(37) a. *The speaker is wondering whether it is true that* the teacher always says that Mary is smart.
b. *The speaker is surprised that* the teacher always says that Mary is smart.
c. *The speaker is doubtful that* the teacher always says that Mary is smart.

This means that attitudinal higher-revel schemas of representation like the ones italicized in (37) are communicated by the sentence-final *no desu ka* rather than the hearsay construction *tte iu*.

As noted above, the use of *to iu/tte iu* in interrogative utterances can report or echo a thought as well as an utterance. In other words, the proposition expressed by an interrogative utterance to which *to iu/tte iu* is appended may be attributed to the speaker's thoughts and not necessarily an actual utterance. This view fits the relevance-theoretic echoic hypothesis of verbal irony (see Chapters 4 and 5 for the hypothesis in detail), because the speaker's attitude in an interrogative utterance including to iu/tte iu is often dissociative (i.e., sarcastic) with respect to the thought expressed by the utterance. Such echoic dissociation is presumably attributable to rhetorical (non-literal) use of *to iu/tte iu.*

Consider the following interaction:

(38) [Mary is a female lab monkey who is always doing something silly. Tom, A, and B all work at the laboratory]
    A1 [*laughing*] Mary is really stupid.
    B: [*seriously*] But Tom said that Mary acts like that intentionally.
    A2: [*with surprise/scorn*]
        Tom wa   Mary ga kashikoi tte iu   no desu ka?
        Tom TOP Mary S   smart   QUO-say COP   Q
        'Does Tom say that Mary is smart?'

In the utterance in (38A2), it is clear that the propositional content *Mary is smart* was not previously uttered. However, the thought *Mary is smart* can be derived from (38B), which reports Tom's utterance that Mary acts the way she does intentionally. In other words, the thought *Mary is smart* can be regarded as a restatement of the thought implicated by the immediately preceding utterance. Consider another example:

(39) [In the same context as the interaction in (38)]
    A1 [*laughing*] Mary is really stupid.
    B: [*seriously*] But it looks like she acts like that intentionally.
    A2: [*with surprise/scorn*]
        Anata wa Mary ga kashikoi tte iu   no desu ka?
        you   TOP Mary S   smart   QUO-say COP   Q
        'Are you saying that Mary is smart?'

Similarly to the interaction in (38), the propositional content of (39A2), *Mary is smart*, was not previously uttered. However, because the thought *Mary is smart* can be derived from the immediately preceding utterance (39B), the propositional content of (39A2) can be viewed as a restatement of that of of (39B).

    Why do the speakers of (38A2) and (39A2) restate the preceding utterance? In other words, what thought is desirable in these interrogative utterances and to whom is that thought relevant? As one solution, I propose that the thoughts which are desirable in (38A2) and (39A2) are echoic and that this sort of echoing is ironical: The speaker dissociates from the thought expressed (i.e., the thought is not attributed to the speaker but to the speaker of the preceding utterance). This dissociative attitude may imply an emotional attitude such as surprise or doubt, leading the hearer to understand why the speaker used the interrogative mood: If the utterance simply expresses the speaker's surprise, it is interpreted as a confirmation question; if it also expresses doubt, it is interpreted as a rhetorical question. In the framework of relevance theory, it might be said that in both (38A2) and (39A2) *tte iu* is used to echo the thought implicated in the preceding utterance.

Let us consider the thoughts communicated by the utterances in (38B) and (39B). The basic explicatures recovered from the propositions these utterances express are:

(40) a. Tom said that Mary intentionally behaves in a stupid way.
 b. Mary looks as if she intentionally behaves in a stupid way.

The explicit information in (40a) and (40b) can be developed into a higher-level representation as follows:

(41) a. *The speaker is saying that* Tom said that Mary intentionally behaves in a stupid way.
 b. *The speaker believes that* Mary looks as if she intentionally behaves in a stupid way.

Furthermore, the hearer may access an implicated premise as contextual information, as in (42a) below. From the thought in (42a) and the explicit information in (41a) and (41b), the thought in (42b) can be derived as an implicated conclusion of the utterances in (38B) and (39B):

(42) a. If Mary intentionally behaves in a stupid way, Mary is not really stupid but rather smart.
 b. Mary is not really stupid but rather smart.

Therefore, the proposition expressed by (38A2) and (39A2), *Mary is smart*, corresponds exactly to the implicated conclusion of their preceding utterances in (42b). In the relevance-theoretic analysis, which accommodates a variety of echoed sources, both (38A2) and (39A2) are echoic utterances because both communicate the speaker's attitude towards the echoed thought (See Chapter 5 for more on Sperber and Wilson's [1995, 1998] echoic hypothesis).

The relevance-theoretic view outlined above is consistent with Maynard's (1997) analysis of *to iu/tte iu* in interrogatives. I argue that the use of *tte iu no desu ka* in (39A2) is similar to that found in Maynard's example of a rhetorical question in (12). Recall:

(12) [There has been a murder in a mansion. A detective says something indicating that the murderer is an insider. A maid responds to the detective, uttering:]

Maid: Anata wa hannin ga o-yashiki no hito da *to iu n desu ka.*
'Do you say that the murderer is an insider?'

According to Maynard (1997, pp. 156–158), utterances such as (12) are "manipulating a hearer's voice." The propositional content of the utterance in (12) is attributed not to an actual utterance that has been previously made, but rather a fictional utterance or thought representing what the speaker assumes the hearer must have uttered. In other words, the speaker treats the fictional utterance, a thought created by the speaker, as if it had actually been uttered. Maynard calls this sort of utterance *sōtei in'yō,* 'fictional quotation,' and claims that fictional quotation in interrogative utterances indicates rhetoricity.

However, *to iu/tte iu* also seems to be used in information-seeking (confirmation) questions. Consider the following example:

(43) [A princess is weeping for her golden ball, which has fallen into a well. A frog appears and utters:]
    A1 (Frog): Mō   nakanaide. Watashi ga ii yō ni shite agemasu kara...
                    anymore cry-NEG   I   S   well   do for you   CON
                'Don't cry. (Because) I will make sure things go well for you.'
    B (Princess): Mari o   mitsukete kureru *tte iu*   no desu ka.
                    ball   DO find for me   QUO-say COP   Q
                'Do you say that you will find the ball for me?'
    A2 (Frog): Ē,   mitsukete agemashō.
                Yes, find for you
                'Yes, I will find it for you.'
                                      (Grimm & Grimm, 1812/1949, p. 5)

The utterance in (43B) does not report any actual utterance: The proposition expressed by the frog in his immediately preceding utterance, that he will make sure things go well for the princess, does not correspond to that in (43B), that he will find the ball. Instead, the thought or proposition reported by the utterance in (43B) was implicated by the frog's utterance in (43A1). In other words, the utterance in (43B), just like (38A2) and (39A2), echoes the implicature communicated by (43A1) and expresses the speaker's emotional attitude towards the implicated thought — in this case, surprise.

The utterance in (43B) seems to be a confirmation (surprise) question rather than a rhetorical question, because it is answerable. Indeed, the frog's answering the question with (43A2) shows that he interpreted the utterance as an information-seeking question. Intuitively, however, the utterance in (43B) also has an element of rhetoricity, implicitly communicating the speaker's strong doubt regarding the proposition the utterance expresses, as if she believed the task itself to be difficult or impossible. A strong clue to this interpretation may therefore be found in the speaker's attitude towards the thought in (43B).

If *tte iu* is omitted from (43B), the acceptability of the utterance becomes rather low, as in (44B) below. The low acceptability of (44B) shows that *to iu* and *tte iu* in interrogative utterances function as connectives indicating that the utterance restates a proposition expressed by a preceding utterance. Thus, to render the utterance in (44B) acceptable again, another linguistic marker with similar function must replace *tte iu*, as seen in (45) with the word *tsumari* 'in other words.'

(44) A: I will make sure things go well for you.
    B: ?? Mari o mitsukete kureru *no desu ka*?
       'Will you find the ball for me?'
(45) A: I will make sure things go well for you.
    B: *Tsumari*, mari o mitsukete kureru no desu ka?
       '*In other words*, will you find the ball for me?'

In relevance theory, linguistic expressions such as *in other words, namely, that is*, and *in short* are called reformulation markers (RMs) (Sperber & Wilson, 1986, 1995; Blakemore, 1996, 2002). Blakemore (1996, p. 329) distinguishes two types of RMs, one involving discourse sequence and the other nominal apposition. *Tsumari* in Japanese has characteristics of both types (Sasamoto, 2006; Nagano, 1986). According to Blakemore (p. 340), RMs such as *in other words* have a conceptual and non-truth conditional meaning, which leads the hearer to recover a higher-level explicature such as:

(46) The speaker believes that P is a faithful representation of a thought Q.

Blakemore (1996) explains (46), saying:

> A speaker who produces an utterance which is a representation of another utterance cannot be taken to be creating expectations of truthfulness. She can only be taken to be creating expectations of FAITHFULNESS. The degree of faithfulness attempted will vary from situation to situation, as with any other aspect of utterance interpretation, it will be constrained by the criterion of consistency with the principle of relevance (p. 338).

I claim that *to iu/tte iu* in interrogative utterances has a similar function to RMs such as *tsumari* or *in other words*: it contributes to the recovery of the higher-level explicature described in (46). What is expressed (P) in an interrogative utterance including *to iu/tte iu* is understood to be a faithful representation of a thought (Q) implicated by the preceding utterance in combination with the echoic representation of the hearsay construction *to iu/tte iu*. Hence, I call *to iu/tte iu* in interrogative utterances an *echoic reformulation marker*, classifying it as a type of echoic use marker.

7.4 Does *Tte* Alone Function as an Echoic Reformulation Marker?

Maynard (1997, p. 166) introduces several cases of *tte* as fictional quotation or, in my terminology, an echoic reformulation marker. This section investigates whether tte *alone functions as an echoic reformulation marker in the same way as* tte iu no desu in interrogative utterances. Consider the following examples excerpted from a Japanese comic book. Maynard argues that the use of *tte* in the utterances in (47) and (48b) below is quite similar to the use of *to iu/tte iu no desu ka* in her example (12).

(47) Demo, yappari komaru. Ima sara, donna kao de   Mitchan ni ae   *tte*...!?
    but   DM   worry   now   what face   with Mitchan   see QUO
    'But...after all, I can't. How can I dare to face Mitchan...!?'
(Maynard, 1997)

(48) A (Man): Sukoshi wa matomo ni   natta   no   ka.
          a little   right   become-PAST COP Q
          'Have you become a better person even a little?'
    B (Woman): [in a thought balloon]
    Kono taido   no   doko ga atashi o   ki ni itteru *tte*!?
    this   attitude GEN where S   me   DO like   QUO
    'Where in this attitude does it show that he likes me?'
(Maynard, 1997)

There is, however, at least one fundamental problem with each example. The utterance in (47) is not a complete utterance: the periods after *tte* indicate that something is missing. Intuitively, to make the utterance in (47) a complete sentence, something like *iu no desu ka* is required after *tte*, making it an unsatisfying example of bare tte.

In comic books, a sentence appearing in a thought balloon, as (48B) does, is generally regarded as a thought rather than an utterance. Nevertheless, Maynard claims that (48B) can be treated as an utterance in the sense that there are hidden hearers (i.e., the readers of the comic).

Clearly, the utterance in (48B) does not echo any thought implicated by the immediately preceding utterance. Instead, it echoes a past thought of the speaker herself. The story might be as follows. The speaker had believed, with good reason, that the man loved her (e.g., after hearing it through the grapevine or observing the man's behavior). However, when the man uttered (48A) to her, even though he intended it as a joke, the woman started to wonder if her existing belief was true. In such a possible interpretation, it is manifest between the man and the woman that the man's utterance is not purely information-seeking: It is a rhetorical question to indicate his ironical attitude. The point of the woman's utterance in (48B) may lie in the contrast between the speaker's existing belief, i.e., *He loves me*, and the thought communicated by the immediately preceding utterance in (48A). In this case, the utterance in (48B) would echo this past belief and communicates her dissociative (ironical) attitude towards it. The use of *tte* in (48B) does not indicate echoic reformulation of the immediately preceding utterance, but may be closer to the typical echoic use of *tte* described by Itani (1994, p. 381), such as:

(49) A: Our teacher said that Mary is smart.
    B: Mary wa kashikoi *tte*!
(50) Mary is smart, *did I say that?* Goodness!

In Itani's view, the echoed source of *tte*-appended utterance in (49B) is not necessarily the immediately preceding utterance as in (49A). As shown in the English translation (50), "*tte* can be used when echoing a past utterance of the speaker herself" (p. 381).

Therefore, neither of Maynard's examples is a satisfying example of *tte* as an echoic reformulation marker. However, I am able to offer some better examples. Consider the following exchange from a television show:

(51) [Nodame is a student at music academy. She is currently in a slump, and spends all her time absent-mindedly practicing piano. Her boyfriend Chiaki, another student at the academy, is worried about her, and utters:]
    A (Chiaki): [sadly] Mō   ii   kara yamero.
                      now good CON stop
                'That's enough. Stop it.'
    B (Nodame): [irritatedly]
                Watashi no   piano ga kikenai   tte iu   n desu ka?
                me   GEN piano S   listen-NEG QUO-say COP   Q
                'Do you say that you can't (bear to) listen to my playing piano?'
                                        (Adapted from Etō, Ninomiya, & Takeuchi, 2008)

Clearly, *tte iu no desu ka* in (51B) can be interpreted as an echoic reformulation marker: The propositional content of (51B) is not attributed to any preceding utterance but instead is equivalent to the implicature derived from the preceding utterance (51A). The implicature of (51A) can be inferred as a conclusion of the following set of thoughts:

(52) Thoughts communicated by the utterance in (51A):
    a. The two propositions expressed by the utterance:
       i. The hearer has played the piano enough.
       ii. The hearer should stop playing the piano.
    b. The higher-level representations:
       i. *The speaker is saying that* the hearer has played the piano enough.
       ii. *The speaker is saying that* the hearer should stop playing the piano.
    c. The implicated premise:
    If the speaker is saying that the hearer should stop playing the piano, the speaker does not want to listen to the hearer play piano.
    d. The implicated conclusion [(51c) + (51b-ii)]:
    The speaker does not want to listen to the hearer play piano.

The implicated conclusion in (52d) is equivalent to the thought echoed in the utterance in (51B).

The utterance in (51B) can be interpreted as a rhetorical question, which does not expect an answer from the hearer but rather communicates the speaker's thoughts. The speaker's thoughts can be recovered as a higher-level representation involving the speaker's emotional attitude towards the proposition expressed by the utterance. For example:

(53) a. *The speaker is irritated that* the hearer says that he doesn't want to listen to her play piano.
    b. *The speaker is disappointed that* the hearer says that he doesn't want to listen to her play piano.
    c. *The speaker is surprised that* the hearer says that he doesn't want to listen to her play piano.

Now let us consider what happens if *tte iu no desu ka* in (51B) is replaced by *tte*:

(54) A: That's enough. Stop it.
    B: [irritated]
       Watashi no piano ga kikenai   *tte*?!
       I   GEN piano S listen-NEG QUO

'You can't (bear to) listen to my playing piano?'

The use of *tte* in (54B) is acceptable. The sentence is intuitively interpreted similarly to (51B). The utterance neither reports nor echoes any preceding utterance, but rather echoes a thought implicated by the preceding utterance. This view, however, clashes with Itani's (1994) account of *tte*, according to which *tte* can reports or echoes *only* an utterance, i.e.:

(55) A: Chiaki ga anata no piano wa kikenai *tte*.
    Chiaki S you GEN piano TOP listen-NEG QUO
    'Chiaki can't (bear to) listen to your playing piano.'
  B: Watashi no piano ga kikenai *tte*?!
    my GEN piano S listen-NEG QUO
    'He can't (bear to) listen to my playing piano?!'

In (55), A uses *tte* to report an actual utterance and B uses it to echo the immediately preceding (actual) utterance.

Note that, as Ōta (1980, p. 624) claims, negative polarity in an interrogative utterance indicates the speaker's existing belief/expectation that the proposition expressed by the utterance is false. Consider the following case:

(56) A: That's enough. Stop it.
  B: [irritated]
    Watashi no piano ga kike*nai* n desu ka?
    me GEN piano S listen-NEG COP Q
    'You cannot (bear to) listen to my playing piano?'

The utterance in (56B) can be interpreted as a rhetorical question or a confirmatory surprise question, communicating in either case the speaker's emotional attitude towards the thought or proposition it expresses. The attitude itself may derive from an interpretation similar to that in (51B), but the utterance itself does not communicate echoic reformulation. Two distinct types of higher-level explicatures can be recovered from (56B): one explicature involving the speech act of asking (57a below), and multiple others about speaker's emotional attitude (57b and 57c):

(57) a. The speaker is asking whether the hearer cannot (bear to) listen to the speaker play piano.
  b. The speaker is surprised that the hearer cannot (bear to) listen to the speaker play piano.
  c. The speaker is disappointed that the hearer cannot (bear to) listen to the

speaker play piano.

The distinction between two interpretations may lie in the strength of the speaker's existing belief that the hearer will (can bear to) listen to the speaker's piano. In an information-seeking (confirmation) reading, appropriate in a context where the speaker's belief is strong enough to be preserved, the interpreter will recover the thoughts in (57a) and (57b) and regard them as equally important. In a rhetorically biased reading, by contrast, the thought that the speaker intends to make manifest between participants may be an attitudinal thought like (57b) or (57c) rather than a thought involving the speech act of asking like (57a). If the rhetorical bias is extreme enough, the only thought made manifest may be (57c).

7.5 Strong and Weak Implicatures

We have observed that both *tte iu* and *tte* in interrogative utterances can be used for echoic reformulation. Does this mean that *tte* and *to iu/tte iu no desu ka* are interchangeable as echoic reformulation markers? No: I argue that their linguistically encoded meanings differ and, therefore, their echoic function too.

For instance, *to iu no desu ka* in Maynard's detective example in (12) cannot be replaced by *tte* as in (58) below:

(58) [There has been a murder in a mansion. A detective says something indicating that the murderer is an insider. A maid responds to the detective, uttering:]
  Maid: ?? The murderer is an insider *tte*!?

Tte is not acceptable in (58).
  Recall from above that *tte iu no desu ka* in (51B) can replace *tte* as in (54B):

(51/54) A (Chiaki): Mō ii kara   yamero.
               'That's enough. Stop it.'
(51) B (Nodame): Watashi no piano ga kikenai *tte iu n desu ka*?
               'Do you say that you can't (bear to) listen to my playing piano?'
(54) B: Watashi no piano ga kikenai   *tte*?!
               'Do you mean you can't (bear to) listen to my playing piano?'

There is, nevertheless, a slight distinction in meaning between (51B) and (54B). The non-acceptability of *tte* in the detective example in (58) may be related to the acceptability of *tte* in the following echoic use.

(59) A: It turns out that the murderer is an insider.
    B: The murderer is an insider *tte*?! / ??…*tte iu no desu ka*!?

In (59), the utterance in (59B) echoes the immediately preceding utterance in (59A). Thus, *tte* is acceptable and *tte iu no desu ka* is not. If utterance (51) is similarly rewritten, the same can be observed in that exchange:

(60) A (Chiaki): I can't bear to listen to your playing piano.
    B (Nodame): You can't bear to listen to my playing piano *tte*?! / ?? *tte iu n desu ka*!?

To summarize, *tte* alone can echo an utterance as in (59) and (60) or a thought as in (54B), but it cannot echo a thought in (58). The logical conclusion is that this derives from a difference in the echoed source of (54B) and in (58). The distinction may be explained in terms of implicature strength. The attributed thought echoed by the utterance in (54B), i.e., *The hearer cannot bear to listen to the speaker's playing piano*, is strongly implicated by the immediately preceding utterance in (54A) as a conclusion of the union of two premises as described in (52). I recall them here for the sake of convenience:

(52) b-ii. Higher-level explicature (premise 2):
        The speaker is saying that the hearer should stop playing the piano.
    c. The implicated premise (premise 1):
        If the speaker is saying that the hearer should stop playing the piano, the speaker does not want to listen to the hearer play piano.
    d. The implicated conclusion [(52c) + (52b-ii)]:
        The speaker does not want to listen to the hearer play piano.

The implicature in (52d) is relevant enough to bring about some cognitive effect; there is no other implicature to compete with it.

On the other hand, the echoed source of (12) is not relevant (i.e., strong) enough to bring about a cognitive effect. This may lead us to an explanation for the non-acceptability of *tte* in (58). Consider the original text of Maynard's example (12), in which a few of (12)'s preceding utterances that Maynard did not cite are included:

(61) [There has been a murder in a mansion. The mansion's owner's daughter Shizuka was killed. The discourse participants are Shizuka's tutor, a detective, and a maid called Tamami. Tamami told the detective that she was

choked while she was sleeping a few days before Shizuka was killed. The tutor had been informed of this fact by Tamami earlier]

A1 (Tutor): The murderer intended to choke Shizuka, but discovered it was Tamami, not Shizuka. Then he ran away.

B1 (Detective): [to Tutor] So, the murderer must have been the person who choked Tamami. But why didn't you tell me about such a serious incident? It's a significant clue to the murderer's identity.

A2 (Tutor): I thought that the incident had nothing to do with the murder, because Tamami is not a member of their family.

B2 (Detective): Anyway, I think that the murderer is —

C (Tamami): Anata wa hannin ga o-yashiki no hito da *to iu n desu ka*? [= (12)]

'Do you say that the murderer is an insider?'

(Utano, 1992, pp. 199–200; my translation)

As discussed earlier, an utterance is an echoic reformulation if the echoed source is the implicature of the preceding utterance. Is the utterance in (12) [= (61C)] truly an echoic reformulation in this sense? Note that the utterance in (61B2), the utterance preceding (61C), is not a complete utterance — the utterance in (61C) interrupted (61B2). Moreover, none of the earlier utterances strongly implicate the thought *The murderer is an insider*. Consider the explicit information communicated by (61A1), (61B1), and (61A2):

(62) a. Explicature of (61A1):
The speaker has a belief that the murderer intended to choke Shizuka.
b. Explicature of (61B1):
The speaker has a belief that the fact that the murderer is the person who tried to choke Tamami is a significant clue to the murderer's identity.
c. Explicature of (61A2):
The speaker had a belief that the incident had nothing to do with the murder because Tamami is not a member of the family.

An important clue may be the thought communicated by (61A2), *Tamami is not a member of the family*. Not being a member of the family can be interpreted as not being an insider. The thought in (62c) implicates that the speaker now has a new belief that Tamami being choked had something to do with the murder. The shared thought by the speakers A and B may be *The murderer is the choker*, but this is not directly related to the thought *The murderer is an insider*. What, then, do the thoughts above have to do with the thought *The mur-

derer is an insider?

In other words, the thought that (61C) echoes is only weakly implicated by the earlier utterances. Consider a set of weak implicatures that may be derived from those utterances:

(63) a. The choker easily gained access through the bedroom where Tamami was sleeping.
   b. The murder has something to do with the incident of Tamami being choked.
   c. The murderer may be the person who choked Tamami, if he intended to choke Shizuka but mistook Tamami for her.
   d. If the murderer and the choker are one and the same, he has been in the house at least twice.
   e. A person who has been in the house at least twice must have easy access to the house.
   f. [From (63a) to (63e)] The murderer is possibly the choker, and *he is an insider* because he has easy access to the house.

Thus, although both *tte* and *to iu/tte iu no desu ka* can be used for echoic reformulation, *tte* is only acceptable in cases where the utterance echoes a thought strongly implicated by the preceding utterance. By contrast, *to iu/tte iu no desu ka* can be used to echo any thought implicated by the preceding utterance or contextual information, no matter how strongly or weakly.

Moreover, this distinction between *tte* and *to iu/tte iu no desu ka* may influence the utterance's level of rhetoricity. When *tte* is used to report or echoes an utterance, the result can be interpreted as both information-seeking (confirmation) and rhetorical. However, in cases of echoic reformulation like (51B) and (54B), the possibility that the utterance is information-seeking is very remote; indeed, the utterance in (54B) is no doubt an extremely rhetorical question. This may be because *tte* is always interpreted as if it echoed an actual utterance, even when it actually echoes a thought. In other words, it implies that the speaker has a strong belief that the hearer believes the thought is true and that must have produced an utterance expressing that thought at some point.

Some might object that it is not clear whether *tte*-using utterances such as (54B) are in fact interrogative. However, this can be indicated by intonation. If spoken with rising intonation to indicate an interrogative mood, an utterance using *tte* can be interpreted as interrogative.

7.6 *To Iu/Tte Iu* in *Wh*-Interrogatives

The previous examples have all been yes-no interrogatives, but *to iu no desu / tte iu no desu ka* can also be used in *wh*-interrogatives:

(64) [It is midnight and the speaker sees the hearer walking towards the door. The speaker utters:]
 Doko e iku *to iu* no desu ka?
 where LOC go QUO-say COP Q
 'Where are you going *to iu no desu ka*?'
 Implicature: There is nowhere you can go (at this time of night).

(65) A: It's your fault. You should go back to her and apologize.
 B. Watashi ga nani o shita *to iu* no desu ka?
 I S what DO do-PAST QUO-say COP Q
 'What did I do *to iu no desu ka*?'
 Implicature: I didn't do anything wrong. / It's not my fault. / It's not my concern.

What thought or utterance is echoed in these cases? Just as in yes-no interrogatives, the echoed sources of *wh*-interrogatives are the thoughts implicated by preceding utterances and/or contextual information.

 In (64), although there is no preceding utterance, the thought *The hearer is going out* is implicated by the contextual information (i.e., the hearer's act of approaching the door). In (65B), the preceding utterance implicates the thought *You did something wrong*.

 Note that the construction *to iu no desu ka* in (64) and (65B) cannot be replaced by *tte* alone:

(66) [It is midnight and the speaker sees the hearer walking towards the door. The speaker utters:]
 ?? Doko e iku *tte*?

(67) A: It's your fault. You should go back to her and apologize.
 B. ?? Watashi ga nani o shita *tte*?

However, the utterance in (66) would be permissible if it echoed an utterance as in (68) below. In this case, it would be interpreted as communicating a strong emotion like surprise or resentment.

(68) [A mother sees her daughter walking towards the door at midnight. The daughter utters:]

Daughter: I'm just going to get something to drink.
Mother: [furiously] Doko e iku *tte*?!

The speaker's emotion in (68) can be recovered as a dissociative attitude to the proposition expressed by the utterance. The distinction of acceptability between (66) and (68) may lie in the value substituted for the variable X in the logical form *The hearer is going to* X. The proposition expressed by (66) is simply The hearer is going somewhere *(X is an arbitrary place), whereas in (68)* X *can be replaced by a particular value* (e.g., a pub). This distinction, too, supports our previous hypothesis that *tte* is preferably used to echoing an utterance rather than a thought.

7.7 Conclusion

This chapter has investigated the similarities and differences between the functions of two distinct sentence-final expressions found in interrogative utterances: to/tte iu no desu ka *and* tte. In the framework of relevance theory, both particles function as echoic use markers. One advantage the relevance-theoretic approach to echoic utterances contributes to our analysis is the concept of strong and weak implicatures, which enables us to explain the slight distinction between echoed sources of *tte*-appended utterances and *to/tte iu no desu*-appended interrogative utterances.

The relevance theoretic approach to echoic utterances fruitfully explains how sentence-final particles affect the derivation of rhetorical readings for interrogative utterances. The dissociative attitude to the echoed source appears to play an important role in the interpreting process. This dissociation is associated with varying degrees of speaker emotion, and the emotional (propositional) attitude may affect the rhetoricity level. The difference between a confirmatory surprise question and a rhetorical question comes down to the relevant thought of the utterance. The conceptual representation of sentence-final expressions such as *tte* or *tte iu no desu ka* leads the hearer to access information relevant to a rhetorical reading, i.e., that an attitudinal (higher-level) representation rather than a confirmatory speech act representation is relevant enough to bring about a certain cognitive effect.

I have introduced a new concept I call *echoic reformulation* which is based on Blakemore's (1996) analysis of RMs. In this relevance-theoretic approach, Maynard's detective-novel example in (12) can be reanalysed as echoic reformulation. Although Maynard regards the echoed source of this sort of utterance as fictionalan utterance imagined by the speaker — I disagree to an extent. The thought is not entirely fictional, but is derived from previous utterances or the context in some way. The concept of echoic reformulation offers a more accurate explanation of the semantic/pragmatic functions of sentence-final *to/tte iu no desu (ka)* than Maynard's (1997) concept of fictional quotation can.

CHAPTER 8

SFEs in Japanese Interrogatives 2: The Case of *Mono Ka*

In Japanese, formal nouns such as *mono*, *koto*, and *tokoro* can be combined with other elements to form sentence-final expressions (SFEs). For example, they appear combined with the copula *da* (*mono da*, *koto da*, *tokoro da*) in declarative utterances and with the interrogative marker *ka* (*mono ka*, *koto ka*, *tokoro ka*) in interrogative utterances. (See Fujii, 2000, and Tamaji, 2007, for *mono*; see Josephs, 1976, for *koto* and *tokoro*.)

Lexically, *mono*, *koto*, and *tokoro* are ambiguous between their meanings as nouns and their meanings as formal nouns. As nouns, *mono*, *koto*, and *tokoro* literally mean 'thing,' 'fact,' and 'place' respectively. For example: *Ii **mono** moratta* 'I've received a good *thing*,' *Kuwashii **koto** o shiritai* 'I want to know the *facts* in detail,' and *Tōi **tokoro** kara kita* 'I came from a distant *place*.' However, when they are used in SFEs, these meanings disappear and they function as formal nouns. For example: *Kodomo wa soto de asobu **mono** da* 'Children should play outside,' *Tsukareta nara hayaku neru koto da* 'If you are tired, go to bed early,' and *Ima iku **tokoro** da* 'I'm just about to go.' In other words, each has two distinct uses associated with different meanings.

Authors including McGloin (1976), Horn (1989), and Josephs (1976) have argued that the construction *mono ka*, combining the formal noun *mono* and the sentence-final particle *ka*, functions like a fixed expression that always expresses strong denial on the part of the speaker of the proposition expressed by the utterance. McGloin and Horn say that *mono ka* functions as a *negative context* that licenses negative polarity items (NPIs). This, McGloin says, can be seen in the following example of *mono ka* licensing the occurrence of NPIs such as *kesshite* 'definitely' and *dare mo* 'nobody':

(1) a. Kesshite   iku   *mono   ka*.
      definitely   go   FN   Q
      'I will never go.'

b. Dare mo   iku *mono ka*.
who   go FN   Q
'Nobody will go.'   (Adapted from McGloin, 1976, p. 76)

The fact that (1a) and (1b) communicate the speaker's objection to the proposition expressed by the utterance suggests that in these utterances *ka* is not being used as an interrogative marker (Uyeno, 1971; Itani, 1993). It seems these utterances are not made as questions but declaratives.

Note that Japanese NPIs generally require an overt negative element such as the negative verb ending *-nai*. Furthermore, they are not licensed in positive declaratives:

(2) a. Kesshite   ika*nai*.
    definitely go-NEG
    'I will never go.'
  b. Kesshite *iku.
    certainly go
(3) a. Dare mo   ika*nai*.
    who NPM go-NEG
    'Nobody will go.'
  b. Dare mo   *iku.
    who NPM go

Moreover, Japanese NPIs are not licensed in any utterances with positive polarity, including not only positive declaratives but also some weaker negative contexts, such as (information-seeking) positive questions and positive precedent clauses of *if*-conditionals. Consider the following examples:

(4) a. Kesshite   iku ka. (Rhetorical reading only)
    definitely go Q
    Speaker's assumption: I will never go.
  b. *Kesshite   iku nara...
    definitely go   CON
(5) a. Dare mo   iku ka. (Rhetorical reading only)
    who NPM go Q
    Speaker's assumption: Nobody will go.
  b. *Dare mo   iku nara...
    who NPM go   CON

Kesshite and *dare mo* can occur in positive interrogatives as in (4a) and (5a) only if these utterances convey negative speaker assumptions: in other words, only if they are (polarity-reversed) rhetorical questions. On the other hand, neither of them are licensed in the precedent clauses of *if*-conditionals as in (4b) and (5b).

This contrasts with NPIs in English, many of which can be licensed by a wide range of environments including questions and *if*-conditionals, as authors including Borkin (1971), Horn (1989), and van der Wouden (1997) have observed. Consider the following examples:

(6) a. He didn't help *anybody*.
    b. No one has *ever* been to Japan.
    c. If you *ever* come to Tokyo, visit me.
    d. Did *anybody* help Mary?

In examples (6a) through (6d), the NPIs *anybody* and *ever* are licensed by NPI licensors (i.e., negative contexts) such as sentential negation (6a), negative element (6b), *if*-clause (6c) and interrogative form (6d).

It seems that the NPIs *kesshite* and *dare mo* might be similar (although not equivalent) to English *ever* and *anybody* in the sense that *kesshite...-nai* and *dare mo...-nai* are equivalent to *never* and *nobody* respectively. *Kesshite* and *dare mo*, however, can only be licensed by an explicit *-nai* (as in negative declaratives) or an implicit *-nai* (as in the speaker assumptions for a rhetorical question), not *the* variety of environments as seen in (6).

Van der Wouden (1997) classifies NPIs into three types based on their distribution: strong, medium, and weak. Strong NPIs are only licensed by negative declaratives, medium NPIs can also be licensed by weaker contexts like *if*-clauses, and weak NPIs are licensed by the weakest negative contexts, like *at most* N). According to this classification, many Japanese NPIs, including *kesshite* and *dare mo*, can be considered strong NPIs.[1]

Does this mean that *mono ka* functions as a negative context, as McGloin (1976, 1986) argues? I argue that the answer is no for two main reasons: (a) *mono ka* is not a fixed expression but a combined expression which consists of two different elements: *mono* and *ka*; and (b) therefore, it is not the whole of *mono ka* but the interrogative particle *ka* that licenses NPIs such as *kesshite* and *dare mo*.

Dictionaries of Japanese typically define the collocational *mono ka* construction as consisting of the formal noun *mono* and the particle *ka* and describe it as representing the speaker's surprise at or negative attitude towards the propositional content of the utterance (Matsumura, 1995; Nihon Kokugo Daijiten Dai Nihan Henshū Iinkai, 2000–2002). This implies that sentence-final *mono ka* does not always mark rhetorical questions and supports my argument in this chapter that *mono ka* is used not only for rhetorical questions but also for surprise (information-seeking) questions and exclamative utterances.

Some authors claim that when, in a declarative utterance, *mono* is combined with the copula *da* to make the *mono da* construction, this functions as a sentence-final marker representing the speaker's attitude towards the proposition expressed by the utterance (Fujii, 2000; Tamaji, 2007). I argue that *mono* functions the same way in *mono ka* interrogatives, indicating the speaker's attitude towards the proposition expressed by the utterance.

Another argument against an analysis of *mono ka* as a fixed expression providing a negative context is the fact that, as noted above, *mono ka* interrogatives can be information-seeking or speculative questions (i.e., pondering) as well as rhetorical questions. Consider the following examples:

(7) Kodomo ga oya no meirei ni shitagau *mono ka*.
    child S parent GEN order IO obey FN Q
    'Do children obey their parents' orders?'
(8) Kono koto o kodomo ni siraseta *mono ka*.
    this fact DO child IO inform-PAST FN Q
    'I wonder whether I should break this news to the child.'

The utterance in (7) might be either an information-seeking question or a rhetorical question. The interpretations are distinguished by intonation: When rhetorical, the utterance typically (but not necessarily) has a falling intonation. The utterance in (8) would typically be used as a speculative question or as a self-oriented question. In this case, the tense of a main verb tends to be the past tense (*shiraseta*) rather than non-past (i.e., *shiraseru*). The past tense in Japanese can imply the lower possibility of a future event, similar to the subjunctive mood in English.

In these cases, *mono ka* does not necessarily license NPIs. Recall (4a) and (5a), where NPIs are licensed. I argue that the utterances in (4a) and (5a) indicate rhetorical interpretations. Hence (7) licenses NPIs only if the utterance is made as a rhetorical question. If (7) is uttered as an information-seeking question, it does not license NPIs; neither does a speculative question such as (8), as shown in (9) and (10):

(9) Dare mo oya no meirei ni shitagau *mono ka*. (Rhetorical reading only)
    who NPM parent GEN order IO obey FN Q
(10) *Kesshite kono koto o kodomo ni siraseta *mono ka*.
    definitely this fact DO child IO inform-PAST FN Q

These examples show that *mono ka* itself does not license NPIs. The *mono ka* construction must be analyzed not as a fixed expression but as co-occurrence of the two distinct elements *mono* and *ka*.

If this is so, then what is communicated by *mono* and *ka*, respectively, in interrogative utterances? In this chapter, I argue first that *mono* in the *mono ka* construction is exactly the same as *mono* in the *mono da* construction, adopting Tamaji's (2007) monosemic approach to *mono* in the *mono da* construction. Tamaji argues that the semantics of *mono* are not ambiguous: It has a prototypical/core meaning from which either an epistemic or a deontic meaning is derived. Using Tamaji's framework, I argue that the two distinct meanings of *mono* (like deontic and epistemic *should* in English) are communicated not explicitly but implicitly.

Turning to *ka*, I adopt Itani's (1993) account of *ka* as an *interpretive use* marker. As we observed in the previous chapter, Itani argues against the speech act theoretic account holding that *ka* encodes an illocutionary act such as *The speaker is asking* P. Observing that *ka* is not only an interrogative marker but also an exclamative one, Itani argues that this can be explained without needing to make a categorical distinction using the relevance-theoretic concept of *interpretive use*, which provides a general account for non-declarative utterances.

8.1 The *Mono Da* Construction

8.1.1 Background Studies

It is generally argued that, although the lexical meaning of the noun *mono* is 'thing,' in sentence-final expressions *mono* means not a thing as such but rather a *type* of circumstance (Fujii, 1998, 2000). This latter *mono* has been recognized as a *keishiki meishi* 'formal noun,' which has experienced "the process of grammaticalization, change from content word to grammatical feature" (Tamaji, 2007, p. 16). When this *mono* appears sentence-finally, it should be followed by the copula *da*. Compare the following examples:

(11) a. Ii   *mono*   moratta.
      good thing   receive-PAST
      'I've received something good.'   (Fujii, 2000, p. 86)
   b. Hahaoya wa itsumo kodomo no tame ni gisee ni naru *mono da*.
      mother TOP always child   GEN sake IO sacrifice oneself FN   COP
      'A mother should sacrifice herself for the sake of her child.'
                                                            (Fujii, 2000, p. 86)

As Fujii (2000, p. 86) observes, the noun *mono* 'thing' often appears with a modifying element like the adjective *ii* 'good' in (11a), whereas the sentence-final (formal noun) *mono* in the *mono da* construction as seen in (11b) conveys the speaker's attitude to the proposition expressed. Some authors argue that sentence-final *mono* means *something natural or taken for granted* (Tamaji, 2007; Fujii, 1998), derived from its original meaning *thing*. In other words, the meaning of sentence-final *mono* is an extension of the original usage of *mono* "to describe certain situation [*sic*]" (Tamaji, 2007, p. 17) or "conventionally implicated" (Fujii, 2000, p. 92). Fujii's account is based on Grice's conventional implicature: The meaning of sentence-final *mono* is said to be conventional because it is not cancelable. The possible interpretations of (11b) are described as follows:

(12) a. 'A mother is something (someone) that sacrifice itself (herself) for the sake of her child.'
  b. (i) 'It is proper and/or natural that a mother sacrifices herself for the sake of her child. A mother should sacrifice herself for the sake of her child.'
  (ii) 'You should sacrifice yourself for the sake of your child.'
(Fujii, 2000, p. 89)

According to Fujii, although the literal interpretation of (11b) is (12a), the default interpretation is (12b-i). Fujii argues that, as seen in (12b-i), a *mono da* utterance conventionally implicates a deontic modality (obligation) regarding the proposition it expresses. Fujii further argues that in particular contexts a *mono da* utterance conversationally implicates a directive speech act of suggestion or command like the one in (12b-ii).

There are several problems with Fujii's argument. First, Fujii incorrectly claims that (12b-i) expresses only deontic (obligation) modality. However, Tamaji (2007) introduces some counter-examples showing that the utterance can be interpreted as either deontic or epistemic depending on context. Second, there is no clear account of how the first and the second interpretations in (12b-i) are related to each other.

Fujii also incorrectly claims that both interpretations in (12b-i) are conventional implicatures. I would argue that the first sentence in (12b-i) (i.e., *It is natural…*) is the explicit meaning communicated by the *mono da* construction, whereas the second sentence (*A mother should…*), which refers to either epistemic or deontic interpretation, is the implicit meaning. In other words, the deontic interpretation of (11b) is cancelable and therefore not conventionalized. Let us turn to discussion of the process whereby the interpreter or hearer reaches either a deontic or an epistemic interpretation.

8.1.2 Deontic and Epistemic Interpretations of *Mono Da*

What are the deontic and epistemic interpretations of (11b)? Tamaji (2007) provides examples that show a clear contrast. According to Tamaji, the use of *mono* in the *mono da* constructions in declaratives can be interpreted as communicating both epistemic and deontic modality. Tamaji's argument is based on Palmer's (2001, pp. 9–12) four semantic categories of modality — dynamic, deontic, epistemic, and evidential — according to which deontic modality refers to external conditioning factors such as obligation whereas epistemic modality deals with the speaker's judgment of the factual status of the proposition.

A single modal marker communicating both deontic and epistemic modality can be found across many typologically heterogeneous languages. For example, English has the modal verb *should*, and Chinese has a similar word, *yīnggāi* (Bybee, Perkins, & Pagliuca, 1994). By contrast, in Japanese, modal verbs communicate either deontic or epistemic modality — not both. For example, the Japanese equivalents of English *should* are *beki da* (deontic) and *hazu da* (epistemic; Tamaji, 2007). *Da* is the copula, *beki* is a modal marker encoding deontic modality, and *hazu* is a modal marker encoding epistemic modality. They are not interchangeable, as the following examples show:

(13) a. Renshū sureba   piano ga jōzu ni naru   *hazu da*/*beki da.
       practice do-CON piano S   become good   hazu COP/*beki COP
       'If you practice the piano, (it follows that) you should become good (at playing it).'

   b. Shiken ni gōkaku suru tame ni wa,
      exam IO pass   do sake IO TOP
      'In order to pass the exam,
      ichi nichi san jikan wa benkyō suru   *hazu da/*beki da*.
      1 day   3 hours   study   do   *hazu COP/beki COP
      'you should/need to study three hours a day.'
                                      (Adapted from Tamaji, 2007, p. 17)

Hazu in (13a) indicates a probable state as a result of the action described in the precedent *if*-clause, i.e., *practicing the piano*. There is a causal relation between the *if*-clause and the *hazu*-clause. In this case, *hazu* cannot be replaced by *beki*.

On the other hand, *beki* in (13b) indicates a state desirable to the speaker in which the hearer studies at least three hours a day in order to pass the exam. In this case, *beki* cannot be replaced by *hazu*.

Note that, as there is a causal relation between studying hard and passing the exam, in the following *if*-conditional with *studying three hours a day* in the precedent clause, *hazu da* is acceptable but *beki da* is not:

(13′)   ichi nichi san jikan benkyō sureba,
        1   day   3   hour   study   do-CON
       'If you study 3 hours a day,
         shiken ni gōkaku suru *hazu da/*beki da*.
         exam   IO pass   do   hazu COP/*beki COP
        (it follows that) you should pass the exam.'

Unlike these modal verbs, sentence-final *mono* implicitly communicates both deontic and epistemic modality. *Mono da* can replace both *hazu da* or (13a) and *beki da* in (13b), as seen in (14) below: Which modality is derived is contextually dependent. In other words, in a context such as (14a) where *hazu da* is acceptable but *beki da* is not, *mono* necessarily implicates epistemic modality, whereas in a context such as (14b) where *beki da* is acceptable but *hazu da* is not, *mono* necessarily implicates deontic modality.

(14) a. Renshū sureba   piano ga jōzu ni naru *mono da*.
        practice do-CON piano S become good FN   COP
        'If you practice the piano, you should become good (at playing it).'
    b. Shiken ni   gōkaku shitakattara,
        exam   IO pass   do-want-CON
        'If you want to pass the exam,
        ichi nichi san jikan wa benkyō suru *mono da*.
         1   day   3   hours   study do FN   COP
        'you should study three hours a day.'

Tamaji (2007, pp. 19–20) claims that the surface formal structure can help the hearer form inferences when interpreting *mono da* utterances. The connections between form and modality according to Tamaji are as shown in Table 1:

	Epistemic	Deontic
(thematic) subject	animate or inanimate	always animate (volitional)
predicate	verb, noun, adjective	action verb

Table 1. Connection Between Form and Modality for *Mono Da*

Examples (14a) and (14b) show a clear contrast in predicates. The sentence in (14a) contains the state verb *naru* 'become,' expressing the expected change in state after practicing the piano. The sentence in (14b) has the action verb *benkyoo suru* 'study,' expressing the recommended hearer action of studying.

8.1.3 Explicit and Implicit Meanings of *Mono Da*

Epistemic or deontic modality is clearly indicated for sentences like (14a) and (14b), but some utterances do not communicate modality as clearly. Consider the following example:

(15) Kodomo wa oya   no   meirei ni shitagau *mono da*.
    child   TOP parent GEN order IO obey   FN   COP
    'Children obey their parents' orders *mono da*.'

The surface form of example (15) contains the action verb *shitagau* 'obey'; therefore, according to Tamaji's (2007) account, the *mono da* construction should be interpreted as communicating deontic modality. However, (15) can also be interpreted with epistemic modality depending on the context, as seen in the following examples:

(16) a. Chanto   wake o   hanaseba,
      properly reason DO   tell-CON
      'If you properly tell them the reason why (they should do so),'
      kodomo wa oya   no   meirei ni shitagau *mono da*.
      child   TOP parent GEN order IO obey   FN   COP
      'children *should* obey their parents' orders.'
   b. Matomo na ningen ni naru   tame ni,
      upright   person become in order to
      'In order to become a good person,'
      kodomo wa oya   no   meirei ni shitagau *mono da*.
      child   TOP parent GEN order IO obey   FN   COP
      'children *should* obey their parents' orders.'

The speaker of (16a) expresses an epistemic belief or expectation that, if parents talk to their children correctly, they will obey their parents' orders, whereas the speaker of (16b) expresses a deontic belief that children must obey their parent's orders to become a good person. This is evidence against Fujii's account of the deontic modality of the *mono da* construction as conventional implicature.

Then what is encoded by the *mono da* construction? The encoded meaning of the abstract noun *mono* should be semantically distinguished from that of the general noun *mono* 'thing.' According to Fujii, the difference between the general noun *mono* and the formal noun *mono* in the *mono da* construction is that the former refers to a *token*, a visible and tangible representation of something abstract, whereas the latter refers to a *type* representing the overall class or world.

Fujii (2000) argues that the use of the *mono da* construction enables the speaker to present "the event, state, or situation referred to by the proposition as a general type representing the overall class or world" (p. 94). If this is the case, we might formulate the encoded meaning of *mono* in the *mono da* construction as follows:

(17) The encoded meaning of the *mono da* construction (i.e., P *mono da*) =
 '*P* is a type (representing the overall class/world)'
(P = proposition expressed by utterance)

But (17) is insufficient: It is not clear what *represent* and *overall class/world* mean. Does the proposition expressed by the utterance in (15), *Children obey their parents' orders*, for example, represent the overall class/world?

In addition, as seen earlier in this chapter, although some authors argue that the default interpretation of *mono* in the *mono da* construction is *something natural* (Tamaji, 2007), or an embedding schema such as *It is natural/proper that...*(Fujii, 2000), it is not at all clear how we should interpret *natural*. There are several meanings of the word that might apply, e.g., *found in nature* or *expected*. Can these proposed default interpretations (i.e., P *is natural/It is natural that* P) be linked to the encoded meaning of *mono* in the *mono da* construction?

Fujii's account of *P* as a type rather than a token does not seem entirely incorrect. However, it seems more reasonable to interpret *P* as a type representing what the speaker assumes about the (thematic) subject rather than a type representing some overall class/world. For example, in example (15), *P* is a type of what the speaker assumes is children's behavior.

However, Anno's (2003) semantic approach to the typical *mono da* sentence form X *wa* Y *mono da*, is closer to my intuition as a native speaker of Japanese. Anno explains that the X *wa* Y *mono da* form represents a conceptual assumption that the speaker empirically believes that the fact 'X → Y', i.e. *if X, then Y*, is true. The noun X represents a concept, whereas the predicate Y represents a general attribute. In other words, the speaker's belief that 'X → Y' is based on his/her cumulative experiences of events which are represented as '*x* (token of X) → *y* (token of Y)'. This explanation can be formulated as in Figure 1 below:

> Experience $x_1 \to y_1, x_2 \to y_2, ..., x_n \to y_n \Rightarrow$ X *wa* Y *mono da*
> X is the set $\{x_1, ..., x_n\}$, Y is the set $\{y_1, ..., y_n\}$.

Figure 1: Representation of X *Wa* Y *Mono Da* Construction (Anno 2003, p. 15)

Consider the following examples:

(18) a. A beautiful woman is expected by others to be just as smart as she is good-looking *mono da*.
 b. A baby cries every three hours *mono da*.

(Anno, 2003, p. 15)

The concept of a *beautiful woman* in (18a) has the general attribute *is expected by others to be just as smart as she is good-looking*, whereas the concept of a *baby* in (18b) has the general attribute *cries every three hours*.

Anno's analysis matches my intuition. Based on relevance theory, however, the semantic formulation in Figure 1 might be developed in terms of a set of assumptions in the speaker's cognitive environment. As explained in Chapter 4, relevance theory suggests that the intention of speakers is to modify the hearers' cognitive environment. The cognitive environment contains a set of logical forms representing assumptions. Hearers are led by new information (conveyed in utterances) to modify their cognitive environment by deleting old assumptions, adding new ones, or strengthening the confidence ratings of existing ones. For example, the speaker of (18b) may have strengthened the assumption X *(BABY)* $\to$ Y *(CRY)* after each experience with a crying baby until finally it was contained as a truth in that speaker's cognitive environment. Thus, among the set of assumptions which refer to X *wa* Y (i.e., X $\to$ Y) in the speaker's cognitive environment may be the logical form or assumption represented by an X *wa* Y construction. The set of assumptions for X *wa* Y may be depicted as in Figure 2 below:

> $x_1 \to \{y_{1a}, y_{1b}, y_{1c} ..., y_{1n}\}, x_2 \to \{y_{2a}, y_{2b}, y_{2c} ..., y_{2n}\}, ...,$
> $x_n \to \{y_{na}, y_{nb}, y_{nc} ..., y_{nn}\} \Rightarrow$ X *wa* Y
> X is the set $\{x_1, ..., x_n\}$, Y is the set $\{y_1, ..., y_n\}$.

Figure 2: Assumptions for the X *wa* Y Construction

The speaker of (18a) may have assumptions regarding *beautiful woman* other than *A beautiful woman is expected by others to be just as smart as she is good-looking*. The speaker's set of assumptions may also contain assumptions such as *A beautiful woman is expected by others as kind as she is good-looking*, or a superordinate assumption such as *A beautiful woman is expected by others to be perfect in every way*. Similarly, the speaker of (18b) may have assumptions for *baby* other than *A baby cries every three hours*: the set of assumptions of the speaker may contain assumptions such as *A baby wants milk often* or *A baby cries because it wants milk*.

Moreover, the concepts of the nominals *beautiful woman* and *baby* can be regarded as subordinate to superordinate concepts like *something which makes us feel a spiritual beauty* and *being at an early development phase* respectively. Although it is assumed in relevance theory that each person has different confidence ratings for each assumption, the sentence-final *mono da* in both (18a) and (18b) communicates that the speaker has strong confidence in the truthfulness of the proposition expressed by the utterance.

Let us consider the meaning encoded by X *wa* Y *mono da* sentences in the relevance-theoretic framework. Again, although I do not argue that Fujii's (2000) view of the *mono da* construction as representing P *is a type* is totally invalid, I nevertheless avoid the term *type* in order to avoid ambiguity.

Assume that the speaker of a *mono da* utterance has a cognitive environment containing a set of assumptions C_1. C_1 is the set of beliefs that the speaker has about the behavior or state of the subject of an utterance. P, a logical form or assumption, is therefore a member of C_1. The speaker has a belief that P is true because C_1 is actually the set of assumptions that the speaker believes to be true. The concept encoded by the *mono da* construction is, therefore, something like the following:

(19) Encoded meaning of P (= X *wa* Y) *mono da*
Speaker has a belief that P is a member of C_1.
$C_1 = x_1 \rightarrow \{y_{1a}, y_{1b}, y_{1c}, ..., y_{1n}\}$,
$x_2 \rightarrow \{y_{2a}, y_{2b}, y_{2c}, ..., y_{2n}\}$, ...,
$x_n \rightarrow \{y_{na}, y_{nb}, y_{nc}, ..., y_{nn}\}$
$P = X$ wa Y ($X \rightarrow Y$)
X is the set $\{x_1, ..., x_n\}$, Y is the set $\{y_1, ..., y_n\}$

How, then, can either of the two modal interpretations (epistemic and deontic) be derived? This information is recovered by pragmatically enriching the encoded meaning. If the contextual assumptions are simply assumptions about facts, an epistemic meaning will be derived; if the contextual assumptions include moral principles (about what people should do in general), a deontic meaning will be derived. In other words, if you restrict C_1 to deontic assumptions (moral principles), the interpretation is deontic. On the other hand, if C_1 includes only assumptions that are facts, then the interpretation is epistemic. Recall (16):

(16) a. Chanto wake o hanaseba,
'If you properly tell them the reason why (they should do so),'
kodomo wa oya no meirei ni shitagau *mono da*.
'children *should* obey their parents' orders.'
   b. Matomo na ningen ni naru tame ni,
'In order to become a good person,'
kodomo wa oya no meirei ni shitagau *mono da*.
'children *should* obey their parents' orders.'

The assumptions communicated by (16a) and (16b) are provided in (20a) and (20b) respectively:

(20) a. (epistemic *should*) Children *should* obey their parents' orders.
    b. (deontic *should*) Children *should* obey their parents' orders.

In (16a), the speaker's set of assumptions includes the assumption (20a), which is about a fact as the result of an action (i.e., telling children the reason why). As a result, the hearer arrives at the epistemic interpretation. On the other hand, in (16b), the speaker's set of assumptions includes the assumption (20b), a moral principle. The hearer of this utterance arrives at the deontic interpretation. In other words, the hearer accesses one or the other of the two interpretations by pragmatically enriching the explicit information.

How does the hearer know that the set of assumptions C_1 lead the hearer to either an epistemic or a deontic interpretation? What makes C_1 accessible (more so than anything else)? This can be explained in terms of optimal relevance. As seen in Chapter 4, according to the Principles of Relevance, the most accessible assumption that the hearer of (16a) or (16b) can infer might be that the speaker's set of assumptions in (16a) or (16b) includes an assumption about fact or about moral principle. Contextual information such as the relation between the antecedent and the conclusion of the *if*-clause will lead the hearer to either interpretation. The hearer's process of inference stops when it provides one interpretation that is more relevant than the other.

Moreover, in particular contexts, assumptions such as (21a) or (21b) might also be implicated by the utterance in (15):

(21) a. (epistemic *should*) You *should* obey your parents' orders.
    b. (deontic *should*) You *should* obey your parents' orders.

Consider the following examples:

(22) [Mother is worrying about her child Tom's cheeky attitude, and utters to

Father:]
a. Mother: Lately Tom does not listen to me.
b. Father: Chanto wake o hanaseba, kodomo wa oya no meirei ni shitagau *mono da*. [= (16a)]
'If you properly tell him the reason why he should do so, he *should* obey your orders.'

(23) [Father encourages his child to do his homework before watching TV, uttering:]
Do your homework first!
Matomo na ningen ni naru tame ni, kodomo wa oya no meirei ni shitagau *mono da*. [= (16b)]
'In order to become a good person, you *should* obey my orders.'

Note that whereas the word *kodomo* 'child' refers to a generic child in (16a) and (16b), it refers to *Tom* in (22) and *the hearer* in (23). In the latter cases, the hearer's inference process might require more effort than in (16a) and (16b), as the hearer is expected to access an assumption that the word *children* does not refer to children in general but rather a particular individual, i.e., the speaker's child. If the thought that the hearer accesses first is an assumption about children in general, the hearer might fail to obtain the relevance of the utterance.

As we have seen in this section, the concept that *mono* encodes is not a part of the proposition expressed by an utterance. By using the *mono da* construction, the speaker represents an attitude towards the proposition expressed by the *mono da* utterance. This attitude can be recovered as a higher-level attitudinal representation, given as in (19), in the hearer's cognitive process. Recall (19) for the sake of convenience:

(19) Encoded meaning of P (= X *wa* Y) *mono da*
Speaker has a belief that P is a member of C_1.
$C_1 = x_1 \rightarrow \{y_{1a}, y_{1b}, y_{1c}, ..., y_{1n}\}$,
$x_2 \rightarrow \{y_{2a}, y_{2b}, y_{2c}, ..., y_{2n}\}$, ...,
$x_n \rightarrow \{y_{na}, y_{nb}, y_{nc}, ..., y_{nn}\}$
$P = X$ wa Y ($X \rightarrow Y$)
X is the set $\{x_1, ..., x_n\}$, Y is the set $\{y_1, ..., y_n\}$

The concept encoded by the *mono da* construction is non-truth-conditional, i.e., not a part of the proposition expressed by an utterance. Thus, the encoded meaning of *mono* in the *mono da* construction is conceptual and non-truth-conditional, like the sentential adverbial *seriously* mentioned in Chapter 4. Recall:

(24) [= (66a) in Chapter 4] *Seriously*, your argument is fallacious.

Now consider (25) below. It shows that *mono (da)* falls within the scope of *if* in the *if*-conditional and is therefore non-truth-conditional.

(25) Kodomo ga oya   no   meirei ni shitagau *mono de* aru nara,
     children S parent GEN order IO obey   FN   COP CON
     'If children *should* obey their parents' orders,
     oya   wa nan no   shimpai mo nai.
     parent TOP what GEN anxiety   have-NEG
     'their parents would have no anxiety.'

Parents are said to have no anxiety if and only if children obey their parents' orders. In other words, the truth condition of the utterance is not affected by *mono da*. Compare the utterance in (25) with the following example:

(26) Kodomo ga oya   no   meirei ni shitagau nara,
     children S parent GEN order IO obey   CON
     'If children obey their parents' orders,
     oya   wa nan no   shimpai mo nai.
     parent TOP what GEN anxiety   have-NEG
     their parents have no anxiety.'

The distinction between (25) and (26) lies in the fact that the speaker of the utterance in (25) communicates that the assumption *Children obey their parents' orders* already exists in the speaker's cognitive environment regarding children's behavior, whereas the speaker of the utterance in (26) does not communicate this. In other words, the speaker of (25) communicates that *She has an existing belief* that children *should* obey their parents' orders. This, too, suggests that the sentence-final expression *mono da* in (25) is non-truth-conditional. In other words, we can safely conclude that the formal noun *mono* in the *mono da* construction encodes non-truth-conditional conceptual meaning.

    Intuitively, this encoded meaning of *mono* in the *mono da* construction should also apply to *mono* in the *mono ka* construction in interrogatives. As seen in (7) and (8) above, when *mono* appears in questions, it is typically combined with an interrogative particle *ka*. As Itani (1993) claims, the particle *ka* constrains higher-level representation. The next section examines how *mono* and *ka* are processed in interpreting interrogative utterances.

8.2 The *Mono Ka* Construction in Interrogatives

The *mono ka* construction in interrogatives consists of two elements, *mono* and *ka*. In my account of this construction, I adopt Itani's account of *ka* (see Chapter 7). Below, I provide evidence that the encoded meaning of *mono* in the *mono da* construction (as analyzed above) can also be applied to *mono* in the *mono ka* construction. It follows that both *mono* and *ka* in *mono ka* questions should be non-truth-conditional, and that *mono* is conceptual whereas *ka* is procedural.

8.2.1 *Mono* in the *Mono Ka* Construction

Recall (19) from above:

(19) Encoded meaning of P (= X *wa* Y) *mono da*
  Speaker has a belief that P is a member of C_1.
  $C_1 = x_1 \rightarrow \{y_{1a}, y_{1b}, y_{1c}, ..., y_{1n}\},$
  $\quad\quad x_2 \rightarrow \{y_{2a}, y_{2b}, y_{2c}, ..., y_{2n}\}, ...,$
  $\quad\quad x_n \rightarrow \{y_{na}, y_{nb}, y_{nc}, ..., y_{nn}\}$
  $\quad\quad\quad\quad P = X$ wa $Y (X \rightarrow Y)$
  $\quad\quad\quad\quad X$ is the set $\{x_1, ..., x_n\}$, Y is the set $\{y_1, ..., y_n\}$

The *mono da* construction encodes a non-truth-conditional conceptual schema as given in (19). I argue that the same conceptual schema is communicated by *mono* in *mono ka* interrogatives. It follows from this that *mono* and *ka* should be analyzed separately.

Generally speaking, two or more non-truth-conditional sentence-final particles can be combined (Maynard, 1995, 1997; Itani, 1995), but the combined expression does not form a unit with a single complex meaning. Itani (1993, 1995) further observes that the interpretive use markers *tte* and *ka* frequently co-occur, giving constructions like *ka tte* and *ka tte ka*. Recall the following examples:

(27) [≑ (1) in Chapter 7]
  a. He is a student *ka tte*?
    'Is he a student, you say?'
  b. He is a student ka_1 *tte*   (kiiteiru no) ka_2?
            COMP (asking COP)
    'Are you asking me whether he is a student?'   (Itani, 1995, p. 228)

As observed in Chapter 7, according to Itani (1995, p. 229), sentence-final *ka* and *tte* indicate subtypes of interpretive use: *ka* indicates desirable thoughts and *tte* indicates attributed thoughts. Itani claims that *ka* in (27a) has its scope over the logical form *He is a student*, and itself falls within the scope of *tte*. In (27b), *tte* functions not as a hearsay particle but as an echoic marker indicating that the speaker is echoing the *ka*-appended utterance in (27a). Similarly, ka_1 in (27b) also has scope over the logical form *He is a student*, but the non-final use of *tte* functions as a complementizer (although the verb of asking is implicit, as shown in the optional parenthetical expansion). Ka_2 then has scope over the whole preceding part of the utterance.

The combined sentence-final particles *mono ka* can be explained similarly. The difference is that whereas the semantics of both *mono* and *ka* are non-truth conditional, *mono* is conceptual whereas *ka* is procedural. Recall (7) and (8):

(7) Kodomo ga oya   no   meirei ni shitagau *mono ka*.
    child   S parent GEN order IO obey   FN   Q
    'Children have to obey their parents' orders *mono ka*'

(8) Kono koto o   kodomo ni shiraseta   *mono ka*.
    this fact DO child IO inform-PAST FN   Q
    'I broke this news to the child *mono ka*'

Mono in (7) and (8) has scope over the logical forms *Kodomo ga oya no meirei ni shitagau* 'Children obey their parents' orders' and *Kono koto o kodomo ni shiraseta* 'I broke this news to the child' respectively; *mono* itself falls within the scope of *ka*. In other words, *ka* has the conceptual representation of everything preceding it in the utterance, including the conceptual representation of *mono*, in its scope.

As seen in Chapter 7, the procedural encoding of *ka* constrains the recovery of a higher-level representation that *The proposition represented by* U *is desirable if it is relevant to* X. The desirable thought (i.e., the answer to the question) in (7) is equivalent to the conceptual representation of the *mono*-appended utterance, i.e., *The speaker has a belief that* C_1 *includes the idea that children should obey their parents' orders*. *Ka* indicates that the thought is desirable, either because relevant to the speaker (in an information-seeking reading) or because relevant to the hearer (in a rhetorical reading). In both cases, the utterances achieve relevance if they give rise to cognitive effects. In the former (information-seeking) case, the thought might lead the speaker (e.g., a parent) to relax their attitude towards their children, whereas in the latter (rhetorical) case, the thought might remind the hearer that children do not obey any of their parents' orders.

Note that the subjects in both (7) and (8), i.e., *kodomo* 'child' and the hidden subject *I* (the speaker) respectively, are not marked by the particle *wa*. This means that the subjects are not thematic subjects but actors of predicates.

The desirable thought of the speculative or self-addressed question (8) may be equivalent to the conceptual representation of the *mono*-appended sentence, i.e., *The speaker has a belief that* C_1 *includes the idea that the speaker should break the news to the child*. In the case of a speculative question, like that of an information-seeking question, *ka* indicates that the thought is desirable if it is relevant to the speaker. According to Wilson and Sperber (1988/2012, p. 227), the difference between speculative questions and information-seeking questions can be explained in terms of mutual manifestness. The speaker of an information-seeking question regards the thought (i.e., the answer) as desirable to themselves and manifestly expects it to be provided by the hearer. The speaker of a speculative question, however, manifestly regards the thought as desirable to themselves but does not manifestly expect it to be provided by the hearer. In this sense, self-addressed questions are similar to speculative questions.

We have ascertained so far that the explicit communication of *mono ka* in questions can be explained in terms of the combination of the separately encoded meanings of *mono* and *ka*. The fact that the combined expression *mono ka* can be used for three distinct types of questions (information-seeking, rhetorical, and speculative) is further evidence for Itani's (1993, 1995) account of *ka* as an interpretive use marker and against McGloin's (1976) and Horn's (1989) accounts of *mono ka* as an NPI licensor (i.e., negative context).

What about the implicit information communicated by *mono ka* interrogatives? As outlined above, Tamaji's (2007) account holds that *mono* in the *mono da* construction implicates either deontic or epistemic modality. *Mono* in *mono ka* interrogatives communicates the same implicit meaning. Recall (15):

(15) Kodomo wa oya no meirei ni shitagau *mono da*.
    'Children obey their parents' orders *mono da*.'

The explicit information (encoded conceptual meaning) communicated by (15) is shown in (28) below, whereas the implicit information might be one of the set of assumptions provided in (29):

(28) The speaker has a belief that C_1 includes *P* (*P* = children obey their parents' orders).
    (C_1 = the set of beliefs that the speaker has about children's behavior)
(29) a. (epistemic *should*) Children *should* obey their parents' orders.
    b. (deontic *should*) Children *should* obey their parents' orders.
    c. (epistemic *should*) You *should* obey your parents' orders.

d. (deontic *should*) You *should* obey your parents' orders.

The concept encoded by *mono*, as given in (28), and an implicit assumption like one of those in (29a)–(29d) are also communicated by the following *mono ka* interrogative:

(30) Kodomo ga oya no meirei ni shitagau *mono ka*.
'Children obey their parents' orders *mono ka*.'

Let us consider how context affects which of the assumptions in (29) is communicated by the utterance in (30):

(31) [Mother is worrying about her child Tom's cheeky attitude, and utters to Father:]
   a. Mother: Lately Tom does not listen to me at all.
   b. Father: Kodomo *ga* oya no meirei ni shitagau *mono ka*. [= (30)]
(32) [Father encourages his child to do his homework before watching TV, uttering:]
   a. Father: Do your homework first!
   b. Child: oya   no   meirei ni shitagau *mono ka*.
           parent GEN order IO obey   FN   Q
   'I obey my parents' orders *mono ka*.'

A *mono ka* question like (31b) could be used as an information-seeking question or a rhetorical question. The explicit content of the utterance indicates that one of the following positive or negative answers is relevant:

(33) a. Children obey their parents' orders *mono da*.
   'The speaker has a belief that C_1 includes P (P = children should obey their parents' orders).'
   b. Children obey their parents' orders *mono de wa nai* (COP-NEG).
   'It is not the case that the speaker has a belief that C_1 includes P.'

As the two distinct modalities implicitly communicated by *mono* function parallel to the polarities given in (33), there can be four possible answers to (31b):

(34) a. (i) (epistemic *should*) 'The speaker has a belief that children *should* obey their parents' orders.'
      (ii) (deontic *should*) 'The speaker has a belief that children *should* obey their parents' orders.'
   b. (i) (epistemic *should*) 'It is not the case that the speaker has a belief that

children *should* obey their parents' orders.'
(ii) (deontic *should*) 'It is not the case that the speaker has a belief that children *should* obey their parents' orders.'

However, in most cases, (31b) is interpreted as a rhetorical question indicating a negative answer with epistemic modality like (34b-i). In fact, it is hard to imagine a circumstance where the utterance in (31b) would be a non-biased information-seeking question. The speaker of (30b), Father, implicates the thought in (34b-i) to indicate that children's behavior is far from the parental ideal.

How, then, does this utterance achieve its relevance? The utterance of (31b) can be considered a response to the previous utterance (31a). The utterance of (31b) is a rhetorical question for which the thought (i.e., the answer) is relevant from the hearer's (i.e., Mother's) viewpoint. In other words, the thought is relevant when it achieves cognitive effects such as providing the hearer with relief from concern that her child's behavior is uncommonly bad.

The utterance in (32b) is also a rhetorical question and even less likely to be interpreted as an information-seeking question. However, instead of any of the four assumptions in (34), the speaker of (32b) conveys something developed from (34b-ii). In other words, the speaker indicates refusal of Father's suggestion. The thought considered desirable might be the negative assumption *It is not the case that the speaker believes that she should* (deontic) *obey his parents' orders*.

There is a syntactic difference between (31b) and (32b): The sentential subject *kodomo* 'child' and the nominal marker *ga* disappear in (32b). The utterance still has the implicit subject *kodomo* referring to the speaker; note that the following completion with an explicit *watashi ga* 'I (S)' is not acceptable as either an information-seeking question or a rhetorical question:

(35) Child: *Watashi ga oya   no   meirei ni shitagau mono ka.
           I   S   parent GEN order IO obey   FN   Q

In (32b), the desirable thought that *It is not the case that the speaker believes that the speaker should obey his parents' orders* is relevant from the hearer's viewpoint, giving rise to cognitive effects, i.e., leading the hearer to access the answer to (i.e., refusal of) the hearer's offer/command.

Let us consider another example. Recall (8):

(8) Kono koto o   kodomo ni shiraseta   *mono ka.*
     this fact DO   child IO inform-PAST   FN   Q
     'Should I break this news to the child?'

As seen above, the utterance in (8) can be interpreted as either a speculative or a self-addressed question. The past tense of the main verb (i.e., *shiraseta*) marks the uses of *mono ka* as indicating a speculative and self-addressed question. The use of the past tense indicates that the possibility of an event or action occurring is low. The past tense of the verb of Japanese is used not only for past events or state but also for the subjunctive mood, similarly to English. In the same context, the present tense, as in (36), is not acceptable:

(36) Kono koto o kodomo ni *shiraseru mono ka*.

The utterance in (36) is not marked with an asterisk because, although it could not be a speculative question/self-addressed question, it could be an information-seeking question or a rhetorical question indicating *I won't tell the news to the child*.

In (8), *mono* can be replaced by *beki*, equivalent to the deontic *should* in English, but not *hazu* equivalent to English's epistemic *should* (see above for the distinction between *beki* and *hazu*). Compare the following examples:

(37) a. Kono koto o   kodomo ni shiraseru beki ka.
       this fact DO child   IO inform   beki Q
       'Should I/must I break this news to the child?'
     b. Kono koto o kodomo ni shiraseru *hazu ka*.

(37a) can be uttered as a speculative or self-addressed question. The difference between (8) and (37a) lies in the fact that *beki* encodes the deontic modality of the speaker, whereas *mono* does not encode any modality but implicitly communicates either deontic or epistemic modality.

8.2.2 *Mono Ka* in *Wh*-Interrogatives

So far we have only considered examples of the *mono ka* construction in yes-no interrogatives, but *mono ka* also appears in *wh*-interrogatives. Consider the following example:

(38) Dare ga iku *mono ka*.
     who S go FN   Q
     'Who should go?'

The utterance in (38) could be an information-seeking question but would more typically be a rhetorical question. The two interpretations can be distinguished by intonation: If the utterance has falling intonation, it will be interpreted as a rhetorical question, whereas if it has rising intonation it will be interpreted as an information-seeking question. *Wh*-interrogatives in Japanese, like yes-no interrogatives, generally have rising intonation — unlike *wh*-interrogatives in English, which typically have falling intonation.

Wh-interrogatives, like yes-no interrogatives, can be interpreted in terms of a desirable thought. According to Sperber and Wilson (1995), the relevant answer to a *wh*-interrogative is the proposition obtained by supplying a value for a variable in the incomplete logical form. Consider the following example:

(39) Who would go?
(40) X would go.

The utterance in (39) expresses an incomplete logical form something like (40). *Wh*-interrogatives are interpretively used to represent complete propositions they resemble (Sperber & Wilson, 1995; Wilson & Sperber, 1998).

The variable X might have one of the possible answers in the answer set assigned to it. Suppose that the following three individuals can be possible values for the variable: Tom, Peter, and Mary. Then the answer set contains 8 possible answers:

(41) a. Tom
 b. Peter
 c. Mary
 d. Tom and Peter
 e. Peter and Mary
 f. Tom and Mary
 g. Everybody (Tom, Peter, and Mary)
 h. ∅ (nobody)

If the utterance in (39) is an information-seeking question, the thoughts that can be obtained by supplying values in (41) are equally relevant to the speaker, giving rise to cognitive effects such as leading the speaker to make a decision or arrange an appointment.

On the other hand, if the utterance (39) is a rhetorical question, the desirable thought might be the one that contains the empty set, i.e., *Nobody would go*. This thought would be relevant to the hearer and give rise to cognitive effects such as reminding the hearer of something. Consider the following example:

(42) [A woman is interested in a guided tour labeled "a survival tour of the jungles of Peru" and asks her boyfriend to join her. But her boyfriend responds with a strong refusal, uttering:]

I won't go. Who would go on such a tour?

In this case, the speaker indicates the thought *Nobody would go*, which is desirable from the hearer's viewpoint because it is relevant to her and gives rise to cognitive effects such as leading her to access the answer to her offer.

Wh-interrogatives in Japanese can be explained in the same way. The relevant thought is a proposition completed by supplying the variable in the incomplete logical form with a value. Recall (38):

(38) Dare ga iku *mono ka*.
 who S go FN Q
 'Who goes *mono ka*?'

The incomplete logical form of the *wh- mono ka* interrogative in (38) is (43) below:

(43) X would go.

As *mono* in the *mono ka* construction represents a higher-level schema such as the one that *the speaker has a belief that* C_1 *includes* P, the completed proposition obtained by supplying the variable X with a value should be embedded in this schema. If (38) is an information-seeking question, the thought will be relevant to the speaker; if it is a rhetorical question, the answer will be relevant to the hearer.

Authors including McGloin (1976) and Horn (1989) argue that the utterance in (38) communicates the assertion *Nobody will go*. There are three respects in which this claim is incorrect. First, *mono ka* utterances do not assert anything because the particle *ka* is an interrogative marker. The utterance in (38) can be interpreted as either an information-seeking question or a rhetorical one, but it cannot be said to assert that nobody will go.

Second, the variable X might be supplied with the empty value *nobody* during in the interpretation of (38) as a rhetorical question, but not necessarily. In fact, there are cases where the proposition can be obtained by supplying the variable X in the logical form of the utterance with the value *I* (i.e., the speaker). Consider the following example:

(44) [A woman talks to her boyfriend about an upcoming trip, but they have just had a petty quarrel and are in a bad mood]
 a. Woman: About that trip next month...
 b. Man: I won't go.
 c. Woman: Don't say that. Everybody will come with their partner.

d. Man: I will never go. *Dare ga iku mono ka.*

In this context, it is manifest that the speaker of (44d) does not mean that *nobody* will go, but rather that *I* (i.e., *the speaker*) won't go. To obtain this reading, it is necessary to supply the variable X with *I* (i.e., the speaker) rather than *nobody* in the logical form of the utterance given in (43).

Third, McGloin (1976) and Horn (1989) both ignore what is explicitly communicated by *mono*. *Mono* and *ka* function separately: Assumptions like *Nobody will go* or *I won't go* can be communicated without *mono*. Even if *mono* in (44d) is omitted, the utterance still indicates the speaker's refusal:

(45) Man: I will never go. *Dare ga iku ka.*

Dare ga iku ka in (45) can be interpreted as communicating *I won't go* if it replaces a *mono ka* interrogative in (44d). The assumption *I won't go* is relevant to the hearer, giving rise to the cognitive effect of providing a reply to the hearer's previous offer.

The utterance in (45) generally assumes that either *nobody will go* or *I won't go*. This means that in most cases it will be a rhetorical question (i.e., have a falling intonation). However, if the copular construction *no* is added, it could be an information-seeking question:

(46) Dare ga iku *no*   ka.
 who S go COP Q
 'Who will go?'

We need to be able to distinguish what is communicated by *ka* and what is communicated by *mono ka* in both *wh*-interrogatives and yes-no interrogatives. Compare the following examples:

(47) a. [= second utterance in (45)] Dare ga iku *ka.*
                  'Who goes *ka*'
  b. [= second utterance in (44d)] Dare ga iku *mono ka.*
                  'Who goes *mono ka*'

The difference between (47a) and (47b) is that the proposition expressed by (47b) is itself embedded in the higher-level representation encoded by *mono*, i.e., *The speaker has a belief that* C_1 *includes* P, as seen in (19). The desirable thoughts for utterances (47a) and (47b) are relevant completion of the logical forms (i.e., *X will go*). In particular contexts in which (47a) and (47b) are interpreted as rhetorical questions, the logical forms of both utterances are completed by supplying a value for the variable X.

The desirable thought for the *ka* interrogative utterance in (47a) is equivalent to the proposition expressed by the utterance (i.e., P), whereas the desirable thought for the *mono ka* interrogative utterance in (47b) is equivalent not to the proposition expressed by the utterance but to the higher-level representation *The speaker has a belief that* C_1 *includes* P. Therefore, the desirable thoughts for (47a) and (47b) are (48a) and (48b) below respectively:

(48) a. x_1 will go. (x_1 = a particular value for X).
     b. The speaker has a belief that C_1 includes the thought that x_1 will go.
        (C_1 = the set of beliefs that the speaker has about the behavior/state of the subject of an utterance, i.e., x_1)

Here, note that interrogative utterances communicate another higher-level representation that can be constrained by the encoded meaning of *ka*. One of two distinct interpretations of an interrogative utterance (the information-seeking reading or the rhetorical reading) can be brought about by the recognition of the speaker's attitude towards this higher-level speech-act representation. According to this view, the rhetorical reading of (47a) and (47b) should be preferred when the speakers attitudes are recognized as dissociative from the higher-level representations as in (48'a) and (48'b) below respectively:

(48') a. The speaker is asking whether x_1 will go.
      b. The speaker is asking whether the speaker has a belief that C_1 includes the thought that x_1 will go.

Thoughts such as *Nobody will go* and *I won't go* may be implicated as a result of the recovery of higher-level representations in (48'a) or (48'b).

Moreover, there are other *ka/mono ka wh*-interrogatives indicating that *nobody will go* or that *everybody will go*. The *wh*-words in those cases are marked by the negative or positive polarity marker *mo* or *demo* respectively. Consider the following examples:

(49) a. Dare *mo*   iku *ka*.
      who NPM go Q
      'Nobody will go.'
    b. Dare *mo*   iku *mono ka*.
      who NPM go FN   Q
      'Nobody will go.'
(50) a. Dare *demo* iku *ka*.
      who PPM go Q

'Will everybody go?'
b. Dare *demo* iku *mono ka*.
   who PPM go FN Q
   'Will everybody go?'

The particle *mo* is a strong negative polarity marker: *Dare mo* can be licensed by sentence negation, but *mo* cannot be licensed by a positive declarative or other weaker negative contexts (e.g., in an *if*-clause), as shown below:

(51) a. Dare *mo*   ika-nai.
        who NPM go-NEG
        'Nobody will go.'
     b. Dare *mo*   *iku.
        who PPM go

On the other hand, the particle *demo* in (50a) and (50b) seems to function as a positive polarity marker. (Whether *demo* is a polarity sensitive marker or not is still being debated, but will not be addressed in this thesis. See Nakanishi, 2006, and Yoshimura, 2007, for further discussion.) Consider these examples:

(52) a. Dare demo *ikanai.
        who PPM   go-NEG
     b. Dare demo iku.
        who PPM go
        'Everybody will go.'

Because *mo* in (49a) and (49b) requires a strong negative element, it strongly implicates *Nobody will go*. The interpretations of the utterances are in clear contrast to the interpretations of the *dare ga* interrogatives (47a) and (47b) because (47d) and (47b) can implicate *The speaker (=I) won't go* as well as *Nobody will go*, whereas (49a) and (49b) can only implicate the latter. Recall (44) and (45):

(44) [A woman talks to her boyfriend about an upcoming trip, but they have just had a petty quarrel and are in a bad mood]
     a. Woman: About that trip next month...
     b. Man: I won't go.
     c. Woman: Don't say that. Everybody will come with their partner.
     d. Man: I will never go. *Dare ga iku mono ka*.
(45) Man: I will never go. *Dare ga iku ka*.

In (44), it is mutually manifest among the discourse participants (i.e., between the speaker and the hearer) that everybody (except the participants) will come with their partner. It follows that the utterances in (44d) [= (47b)] and (45) [= (47a)] cannot be interpreted as implicating the assumption *Nobody will go*. Whereas the utterances in (49a) and (49b) are only acceptable in a context where it is assumed that *nobody will go*, the utterances in (44d) [=(47b)] and (45) [=(47a)] are acceptable whether it is assumed that nobody will go or that even if everybody else goes, the speaker won't.

To reiterate, *mono ka* interrogatives do not assert anything. The claims made by some authors that *mono ka* utterances assert negatively biased assumptions are incorrect. Such negatively biased assumptions are brought about by other factors, e.g., the existence of an NPI licensor such as *dare mo* or *kesshite* as in examples (1a) and (1b). The two elements *mono* and *ka* function as non-truth conditional markers and express the propositional attitude of the speaker of the utterance.

According to Itani's analysis, *ka* can be either an interrogative or an exclamative marker. The next section introduces some *mono ka* exclamatives and their interpretation in terms of the relevance-theoretic concept of desirable thoughts.

8.2.3 *Mono Ka* in Exclamatives

As we observed in the previous section, *mono ka* interrogatives can be used in various ways: information-seeking questions, rhetorical questions, and speculative/self-addressed questions. In all these cases, *ka* functions as an interpretive use marker, which fits Itani's (1993) account of *ka*.

According to Itani's account, *ka* also functions as an exclamative marker. Do *mono* and *ka* function in the same way in exclamatives as in interrogatives? Consider the following examples:

(53) A: How much is this?
    B: It's 10,000 yen.
    C: Sonna ni takai   no desu ka?!
        So   expensive COP   Q
        'Is it so expensive?!'   (Itani, 1993, p. 142)
(54) Nante takai   n desu ka!
     how   expensive COP   Q
     'How expensive it is!, isn't it?'   (Itani, 1993, p. 143)

As Itani (1993, p. 143) observes, there is a slight difference between (53C) and (54): (54) is clearly an exclamative utterance, whereas (53C) is ambiguous between a surprise question and an exclamative. Itani argues, however, that there is no need to distinguish the two cases: Both should be interpretable in terms of desirable thoughts, and *ka* encodes such procedural information.

As Sperber and Wilson (1995; see also Wilson & Sperber, 1988/2012) claim, exclamatives, like interrogatives, can be explained in terms of desirable thoughts. The difference between exclamatives and interrogatives is that the speaker of an exclamative utterance already has the completion of the propositional form (i.e., the desirable thought) in mind and that proposition is relevant to the speaker. For example, the speaker of (54) already has in mind the fact that it is expensive; furthermore, that the information is relevant to the speaker: It gives rise to surprise. On the other hand, the speaker of an interrogative utterance might or might not already have the thought in mind. If the utterance is an information-seeking question, the completion of the propositional form is relevant to the speaker, whereas if the utterance is a rhetorical question, the completion of the propositional form is relevant to the hearer. Whether the utterance in (53C) is interpreted as an exclamative or an interrogative, the sentence-final *ka* encodes the assumption that the proposition expressed by the utterance is desirable if it is relevant to the speaker or hearer.

Mono can appear in similar cases. Consider the following examples:

(55) A: How much is this?
B: It's 180,000 yen.
C: Natsu no Igirisu iki no kōkū-ken wa
summer GEN England bound GEN airline ticket TOP
sonna ni takai *mono ka*?!
so expensive FN Q
'*Should* an airline ticket to England in summer be so expensive!?'
(56) Natsu no Igirisu iki no kōkū-ken wa
summer GEN England bound GEN airline ticket TOP
nante takai *mono ka*!
how expensive FN Q
'How expensive an airline ticket to England in summer is! (It is the case that an airline ticket to England in summer *should* be so expensive, isn't it?)'

The utterance in (55C) can be analyzed either as a surprise question or an exclamative. Whether it is a surprise question or an exclamative utterance, the speaker expresses her surprise at the thought (i.e., expressed proposition) *An airline ticket to England in summer is so expensive*. This speaker's surprise at the price is communicated even without *mono*.

Like *mono* in interrogative utterances, *mono* in exclamative utterances encodes the conceptual representation *The proposition expressed (P) is a member of* C_1. In (55C) and (56) above, C_1 is the speaker's set of assumptions about the prices of airline tickets. In these utterances, the speaker expresses not only her surprise at the price but also her surprise at the belief that C_1 includes the proposition expressed. Consider the utterance in (55C) in the context of the following interaction:

(57) A: I would rather go to England in winter. I heard that tickets are so expensive in summer.
B: [= (55C)] Natsu no Igirisu iki no kōkū-ken wa sonna ni takai *mono ka*?!
'*Should* an airline ticket to England in summer be so expensive!?'

The utterance in (57B) [=(55C)] expresses the speaker's surprise at two distinct thoughts: (i) the high price, i.e., *An airline ticket to England is so expensive*; and (ii) the belief that C_1 includes *P*. By using *mono*, the speaker communicates that there is a conflict between the speaker's pre-existing assumption *An airline ticket to England in summer is not as expensive as the hearer suggested in the previous utterance* and the newly obtained assumption *An airline ticket to England in summer is so expensive*.

In addition, the speaker of (57B) expresses not only surprise but also doubt about two distinct thoughts: (i) the high price; and (ii) the belief that C_1 includes the proposition expressed. In other words, by using *mono*, the speaker expresses her surprise or doubt regarding the thought that C_1 includes the expressed proposition. I argue that the utterance in (57B) is interpreted as an interrogative rather than an exclamative only if the speaker's doubt is manifestly expressed.

On the contrary, the speaker of a clear case of exclamative such as (56) does not express her doubt but express just her surprise. Consider (56) in the following interaction:

(58) A (a customer): How much is a ticket to England?
B (an agent of a ticket office): It is just 90,000 yen now. The fare to Europe will be almost doubled in summer.
C (a customer): [= (56)] Natsu no Igirisu iki no kōkū-ken wa nante takai *mono ka*!
'How expensive an airline ticket to England in summer is! C_1 includes that thought (i.e., *P*), doesn't it?'

The utterance in (58C) is a clear case of an exclamative. It includes the explicit exclamative expression *nante* 'how/what a…!', and the speaker already has in mind the thought that C_1 includes the idea that a flight-ticket to England is so expensive. In (58), the speaker has accepted the travel agent's information as reliable and expresses her pure surprise at this information. By using *mono*, the speaker expresses her understanding that C_1 *includes* the information (*P*).

8.3 Degrees of Dissociation and Speaker Emotion

Some may wonder what is different about the speaker's emotional attitude when uttering a rhetorical question with surprise as opposed to a confirmatory surprise question. The speaker of an information-seeking question may express surprise as well as a desire for confirmation; the speaker of a rhetorical question may also express surprise. However, the surprise in a rhetorical question should be distinguished from that in a confirmatory surprise question. Recall (57):

(57) A: I would rather go to England in winter. I heard that tickets are so expensive in summer.
B: [= (55C)] Natsu no Igirisu iki no kōkū-ken wa sonna ni takai *mono ka*?!
'*Should* an airline ticket to England in summer be so expensive!?'

In (57B), the speaker's surprise may be at the gap between old information (i.e., the speaker's existing assumption that a summer ticket to England is not expensive) and newly received information (i.e., that the ticket is rather expensive). In addition to being surprised, the speaker of (57B) *wonders* whether the propositional content is true. The recognition of the wonder enables the hearer to recognize that speaker seeks information. The utterance in (57B) is therefore an information-seeking (confirmatory) question in which the speaker expresses not only wonder but also surprise.

Even if the utterance in (57B) were a rhetorical question, the speaker may still express surprise. However, in that case the speaker's surprise would not be from the gap between old and new information: The speaker of a rhetorical question should have strong enough confidence in the belief *The ticket is not expensive* to doubt the proposition expressed by the utterance, i.e., *The ticket is expensive*. Thus, if the utterance in (57B) were a rhetorical question, the speaker would be expressing surprise at the *hearer's* belief that the ticket is expensive — in other words, incredulousness at the huge gap between the speaker's and the hearer's beliefs.

How, then, is rhetoricity associated with speaker emotional attitudes such as *surprise*, *wonder*, *doubt*, and *disbelief*? As discussed in Chapter 5, discrepancy as rhetoricity can be explained in terms of a dissociative attitude on the part of the speaker towards the echoed source, i.e., what is implicated by the preceding utterances.

In an information-seeking use of (57B), the speaker's lower confidence in the thought *The ticket is expensive* means less dissociation. By contrast, in a rhetorical use of (57B), the speaker's strong confidence that the hearer's information is not true is expressed as a strong dissociative attitude. The recognition of this dissociative attitude functions as a strong clue to the rhetoricity of the utterance. This rhetoricity then involves a further dissociation: the speaker's dissociative attitude towards the interrogative mood of the utterance. Note that speaker emotions in *mono ka* interrogative utterances are recognized not as propositional attitudes but as attitudes towards the thought that *P mono da*. These two dissociations can be formulated as follows:

(59) Speaker's two dissociations in P *mono ka* utterances
   a. The speaker is dissociated from P *mono (da)*.
   b. The speaker is dissociated from the thought that the speaker is asking whether P *mono (da)*.

8.4 Conclusion

In both interrogatives and exclamatives, *mono ka* is not a fixed expression. Authors like Horn (1989) and McGloin (1976) have argued that *mono ka* can be considered an NPI licensing context, but what actually licenses NPIs seems to be the interrogative particle *ka*, consistent with the idea that *mono ka* is not a unit with a complex meaning but a combination of *mono* and *ka*. Therefore, *mono* and *ka* can be analyzed as communicating distinct meanings as individual markers.

Relevance theory can provide the necessary concepts for explaining *mono* (in *mono ka* constructions) and *ka*. In terms of explicit communication, both *mono* and *ka* are non-truth-conditional markers. However, *mono* encodes a conceptual meaning that *contributes to* the higher-level representation C_1 *includes* P, whereas *ka* encodes a procedural meaning which *constrains* the higher-level representation of the utterance. In her relevance-theoretic account, Itani (1993, 1995) observes that any combination of Japanese sentence particles is susceptible to this analysis. Itani (1993) focuses on the combination of attributive marker *tte* and interrogative/exclamative marker *ka* (e.g., *ka tte, ka tte ka*), but *mono ka* can be also combined with another marker, including the attributive marker *tte*:

(60) a. Children obey their parent's orders *mono tte ka*?
   'Children *should* obey their parent's orders, *you say?*'

b. An airline ticket to England in summer is so expensive *mono ka tte*?
'An airline ticket to England in summer is so expensive, *you say?*'

Either *tte* or *ka* can be used sentence-finally as shown in (60), but *mono* is not flexible: it encodes a conceptual representation and must be placed right after the propositional content. Therefore, neither of the following cases in which *mono* used sentence-finally are acceptable:

(61) a. Children obey their parent's orders *tte ka *mono*?
b. A flight ticket to England in summer is so expensive *ka tte *mono*?

Notes
1 Yoshimura (1999) claims that *demo*-appended expressions in Japanese, such as *itteki demo* 'one drop' + *demo*, are *bipolar elements* as defined by van der Wouden (1997): They appear only in weaker negative contexts, and not in either strong negative contexts (e.g., sentential negation with -*nai*) or positive contexts (e.g., monotone increasing contexts). Gotō (2007) further observes that this bipolar function of *itteki demo* allows the hearer to access a non-biased information-seeking reading of the interrogative utterance *Itteki demo nomimashita ka?* whereas its English equivalent *Did you drink a drop?* only allows a rhetorical reading.

Afterword

Rhetorical questions have attracted the research attention of many scholars due to the challenge of understanding speaker intention. This book is my contribution to this growing field.

The main research questions for this book were twofold: How can rhetoricity in interrogative utterances be defined? How is it recognized by the hearer? My answer to the first question is the *continuum of rhetoricity*, departing from the polarity-reversal-based analyses that many previous studies have focused on. My main research framework is Sperber and Wilson's relevance-theoretic approach to interrogative and ironical utterances, especially the concepts of *interpretive use* and dissociative speakers' attitudes. These concepts, and relevance theory more generally, allow rhetoricity to be explained as a continuum.

A rhetorical interrogative utterance is typically accompanied by an emotional attitude on the part of the speaker towards the proposition expressed by the utterance (e.g., sarcastic, mocking, irritated, self-deprecating, humorous, surprised, and so on). The cognition of rhetoricity, the topic of this book's second research question, involves the varying degrees of speaker emotion. Subtle nuances of emotion may be conveyed through non-verbal means such as tone of voice and facial expressions. Successful reading of these leads the hearer to the reading that accords with speaker's intentions.

Utterances in the ambiguous area between strongly information-seeking and strongly rhetorical interrogatives can lead the hearers to misunderstanding. The relevance-theoretic view answers the question of why speakers should choose such risky utterances: it may be a route to intimacy-oriented communication in which speaker and hearer cooperate to share the meaning the speaker intends to convey.

The relevance-theoretic analysis of utterances generally argues against Gricean and speech act theoretic dichotomic analyses based on the binary opposition of literal and non-literal meaning. According to Sperber and Wilson, any type of utterance can be interpreted by the same cognitive strategy of searching for an assumption that is optimally relevant in terms of balance between cognitive effect and processing effort. In understanding interrogative utterances, the hearer examines not only what thought is relevant enough to bring about some cognitive effect but also to whom that thought is relevant. Borderline utterances whose location on the continuum of rhetoricity is unclear may require more processing effort, but once the hearer's interpretation successfully agrees with the speaker's intention, cognitive effects can be achieved to offset the effort.

Based on the relevance-theoretic analysis of interrogative utterances, I argue that rhetoricity is rooted in the speaker's dissociative attitude towards the higher-level schema *The speaker is asking P*. In other words, rhetorical questions are ironical in a sense that the speaker adopts a dissociative attitude towards this higher-level schema, making them necessarily echoic to an extent. A typical rhetorical questions echoes an actual or predictable interrogative utterance seeking information. My research endorses Sperber and Wilson's echoic hypothesis of verbal irony in which dissociation is calculated by degrees, and so I argue that rhetoricity, too, can be determined by examining the degree of dissociation.

In summary, the answers to this book's two research questions are as follows. First, the concepts of rhetorical rating and information-seeking rating are dyadic: They mark the bipolar extremes of a continuum. Typically rhetorical questions have the lowest information-seeking rating, equivalent to the highest rhetoricity rating, which is itself recognized as the greatest dissociation from the higher-level schema *The speaker is asking P*. Second, rhetoricity can be recognized only when the interpreter or hearer recognizes the degree of the speaker's dissociative attitude. If an utterance's place on the continuum of rhetoricity is unclear, the hearer may search for more clues to achieve the relevant information.

We can also say with confidence that the speaker of a question whose rhetoricity is unclear intends to convey a preference for that risky strategy and to make it manifest between speaker and hearer that the hearer is chiefly responsible for determining the correct reading. Risky strategies like this may be preferred in some cases because the reward in terms of intimacy-oriented communication is greater: I predict that this will be found to be common in many languages, although this book only deals with English and Japanese. Cross-linguistic studies of preferences for risky utterances, including rhetorical questions, will require further research in broader discourse contexts.

References

Aristotle. (1924). *Rhetoric* (R. W. Rhys, Trans.) Retrieved from http://ebooks.adelaide.edu.au/a/aristotle/a8rh/ (Original work published ca 350 BCE)

Aristotle. (1960). Topics (E. S. Forster, Ed. and Trans.). In E. S. Forster & H. Tredennick (Eds. and Trans.), *Aristotle* (Vol. 2, pp. 272–739). Cambridge, MA: Harvard University Press. (Original work published ca 350 BCE)

Anno, K. (2003). "Hango" no mono ka bun no hyōgen kinō: Dōshiku o chūshin ni [The Expressive Function of Assertive MONOKA-Sentences]. *Bulletin of the International Student Center, Shizuoka University*, 2, 13–24.

Austin, J. L. (1962). *How to do things with words*. Oxford, England: Clarendon Press.

Bach, K., & Harnish, R. (1979). *Linguistic communication and speech acts*. Cambridge, MA: MIT Press.

Blakemore, D. (1987). *Semantic constraints on relevance*. Oxford, England: Blackwell.

Blakemore, D. (1992). *Understanding utterances: An introduction to pragmatics*. Oxford, England: Blackwell.

Blakemore, D. (1996). Are apposition markers discourse markers? *Journal of pragmatics*, 32, 325–347.

Blakemore, D. (1998). On the context for so-called discourse markers. In J. Williams & K. Malmkjaer (Eds.), *Context in language understanding and language learning* (pp. 44–60). Cambridge, England: Cambridge University Press.

Blakemore, D. (2002). *Relevance and linguistic meaning*. Cambridge, England: Cambridge University Press.

Blass, R. (1990). *Relevance relations in discourse: A study with special reference to Sissala*. Cambridge, England: Cambridge University Press.

Borkin, A. (1971). Polarity items in questions. *Chicago Linguistic Society*, 7, 53–62.

Bybee, J., Perkins, R., & Pagliuca, W. (1994). *The evolution of grammar: Tense, aspect, and modality in the languages of the world*. Chicago, IL: Chicago University Press.

Carroll, L. (with Gardner, M.) (2000). Through the looking-glass. In *Alice's adventures in Wonderland & Through the looking-glass*. New York, NY: Signet Classic. (Original work published 1871)

Carston, R. (1988). Implicature, explicature, and truth-theoretic semantics. In R. Kempson (Ed.), *Mental representations* (pp. 155–179). Cambridge: Cambridge University Press.

Carston, R. (1999). The semantics/pragmatics distinction: A view from relevance theory. In K. Turner (Ed.), *The semantics/pragmatics interface from different points of view* (pp. 85–125). Amsterdam, Netherlands: Elsevier.

Carston, R. (2002). *Thoughts and utterances: The pragmatics of explicit communication*. Oxford, England: Blackwell.

Cicero, M. T. (1949) De inventione [On invention] In H. M. Hubbell (Ed. and Trans.), *Cicero* (Vol. 2, pp. 1–346). Cambridge, MA: Harvard University Press. (Original work published 84 BCE)

Clark, B. (1991). *Relevance theory and the semantics of non-declaratives*. (Doctoral thesis, University College of London, England).

Clark, H. H. (1996). *Using language*. Cambridge: Cambridge University Press.

Clark, H. H., & Gerrig, R. J. (1984). On the pretence theory of irony. *Journal of experimental psychology: General*, 113, 121–126.

Clark, H. H., & Marshall, C. (1981). Definite reference and mutual knowledge. In A. Joshi,

B. Webber, & I. Sag (Eds.), *Elements of discourse understanding* (pp. 10–63). Cambridge, England: Cambridge University Press.

Driver, J. L. (1988). Vain questions. In M. Meyer (Ed.), *Questions and questioning* (pp. 243–251). New York, NY: De Gruyter.

Ekuni, K. (2005). *Akai nagagutsu* [Red boots]. Tokyo, Japan: Bungei Shunjū.

Etō, R. (Writer), Ninomiya, T. (Original creator), & Takeuchi, H. (Director). (2008, January 4–5). *Nodame kantabire: Shinshun supesharu in Yōroppa* [Nodame cantabile: New Year's special in Europe] [Television series]. Tokyo, Japan: Fuji Television Network.

Fogelin, R. (1988). *Figuratively speaking*. New Haven, CT: Yale University Press.

Fujii, S. (1998). What can "things" ("mono") do for propositional attitudes in Japanese discourse? In J. Verschueren (Ed.), *Pragmatics in 1998: Selected papers from the 6th International Pragmatics Conference* (Vol. 2, pp. 159–171). Antwerp: International Pragmatics Association.

Fujii, S. (2000). Incipient decategorization of MONO and grammaticalization of speaker attitude in Japanese discourse. In A. Gisle & F. Thorstein (Eds.), *Pragmatic markers and propositional attitude* (pp. 85–118). Amsterdam, Netherlands: John Benjamins.

Gotō, R. (1997). The analysis of focus particle *demo / mo* with minimal quantity expression *itteki*. *Kansai Linguistic Society*, 28, 316–326.

Grice, H. P. (1975). Logic and conversation. In P. Cole & J. Morgan (Eds.), *Syntax and semantics 3: Speech acts* (pp. 41–58). New York, NY: Academic Press.

Grice, H. P. (1981). Presupposition and conversational implicature. In P. Cole (Ed.), *Radical pragmatics* (pp. 183–198). New York, NY: Academic Press.

Grimm, J., & Grimm, W. (1949). Kaeru no ōsama [The frog prince]. In M. Kusuyama (Trans.), *Mori no kobito: Gurimu dōwa meisakushū* [Little folk of the forest: Collection of children's tales by the Grimm Brothers] (pp. 3–15). Tokyo, Japan: Komine Shoten. (Original work published 1812)

Gunlogson, C. (2001). *True to form: Rising and falling declaratives as questions in English*. (Doctoral dissertation, Unviersity of California, Santa Cruz).

Gutiérrez-Rexach, J. (1998). Rhetorical questions, relevance and scales. *Revista alicantina de estudios ingleses*, 11, 139–155.

Hall, A. (2004). The meaning of *but*: A procedural reanalysis. *UCL working papers in linguistics*, 16, 199–236.

Hamamoto, H. (1997). Irony from a cognitive perspective. In R. Carston & S. Uchida (Eds.), *Relevance theory: Applications and implications* (pp. 257–270). Amsterdam, Netherlands: John Benjamins.

Han, C.-H. (2002). Interpretation interrogatives as rhetorical questions. *Lingua*, 112, 201–229.

Hashimoto, K. (1982). Shūji gimonbun [Rhetorical questions]. *Gengogaku ronsō* [Working papers in linguistics, University of Tsukuba], 1, 33–47.

Horn, L. R. (1989). *The natural history of negation*. Chicago, IL: Chicago University Press.

Huddleston, R., & Pullum, G. K. (2002). *The Cambridge grammar of the English language*. Cambridge, England: Cambridge University Press.

Ichirō, Kitajima no kaikyo ni "Kimi wa sakana ka" [Ichiro shakes hands with Kitajima: "Are you a fish?"]. (2008, August 11). *Sanspo.com*. Retrieved from http://www.sanspo.com/beijing2008/news/080811/oado808111603018-n1.htm

Ifantidou, E. (2002). *Evidentials and relevance*. Amsterdam, Netherlands: John Benjamins.

Ifantidou-Trouki, E. (1993). Sentential adverbs and relevance. *Lingua*, 90, 69–90.

Ilie, C. (1994). *What else can I tell you? A pragmatic study of English rhetorical questions as discursive and argumentative acts*. Stockholm, Sweden: Almqvist & Wiksell.

Itani, R. (1993). The Japanese sentence-final particle *ka*: A relevance-theoretic approach. *Lingua*, 90, 129–147.

Itani, R. (1994). A relevance-based analysis of hearsay particles: Japanese utterance-final *tte*. *UCL working papers in linguistics*, 6, 379–400.

Itani, R. (1995). *Semantics and pragmatics of hedges in English and Japanese*. (Doctoral thesis, University College London, England).

Jeffreys, H. (1948). *Theory of probability* (2nd ed.). Oxford, England: Clarendon Press.

Josephs, L. (1976). Complementation. In M. Shibatani (Ed.), *Syntax and semantics 5: Japanese generative grammar* (pp. 307–369). New York, NY: Academic Press.

Kawakami, S. (1984). *Some fundamental studies on the semantic and pragmatic interpretations of English expressions*. Osaka, Japan: Osaka University Press.

Kiefer, F. (1994). Modality. In R. E. Asher (Ed.), *The encyclopedia of languages and linguistics* (pp. 2515–2520). Oxford, England: Pergamon Press.

Kreuz, R. J., & Glucksberg, S. (1989). How to be sarcastic: The echoic reminder theory of verbal irony. *Journal of experimental psychology: General*, 118, 374–386.

Kumon-Nakamura, S., Glucksberg, S., & Brown, M. (1995). How about another piece of pie: The allusive pretence theory of discourse irony. *Journal of experimental psychology: General*, 124, 3–21.

Lee-Goldman, R. (2006). *Rhetorical questions and scales: Just what do you think constructions are for?* Paper presented at the International Conference on Construction Grammar 4, Tokyo University, Japan.

Leggitt, J. S., & Gibbs, R. W., Jr. (2000). Emotional reactions to verbal irony. *Discourse processes*, 29, 1–24.

Lewis, D. (2002). Scorekeeping in a language game. In P. H. Portner & B. H. Partee (Eds.). *Formal semantics: The essential readings* (Vol. 7, pp. 162–177). Oxford, England: Wiley-Blackwell..

Manor, R. (1979). A language for questions and answers. *Theoretical linguistics* 6, 1–21.

Matsumura A. (Ed.). (1995). *Daijisen* [Great font of words]. Tokyo, Japan: Shōgakkan.

Maynard, S. K. (1993). *Discourse modality: Subjectivity, emotion and voice in the Japanese language*. Amsterdam, Netherlands: John Benjamins.

Maynard, S. K. (1995). Interrogatives that seek no answers: Exploring the expressiveness of rhetorical interrogatives in Japanese. *Linguistics*, 33, 501–530.

Maynard, S. K. (1997). *Danwa bunseki no kanōsei: Riron, hōhō, Nihongo no hyōgensei* [Possibilities for discourse analysis: Theory, method, and the expressiveness of the Japanese language]. Tokyo, Japan: Kuroshio Shuppan.

Maynard, S. K. (2005). *Danwa hyōgen handobukku* [Discourse expression handbook]. Tokyo, Japan: Kuroshio Shuppan.

McGloin, N. H. (1976). Negation. In M. Shibatani (Ed.), *Syntax and semantics 5: Japanese generative grammar* (pp. 371–419). New York, NY: Academic Press.

McGloin, N. H. (1986). *Negation in Japanese*. Edmonton, Canada: Boreal Scholarly Publishers and Distributors.

Murakami, H. (1991). *Dansu dansu dansu* [Dance, dance, dance] (Vol 2). Tokyo, Japan: Kōdansha Bunko. (Original work published 1988)

Murakami, H. (2001). The second bakery attack (J. Rubin, Trans.). In H. Murakami, *The elephant vanishes* (pp. 35–49). London, England: Vintage.

Nagano, M. (1986). *Bunshōron sōsetsu: Bunpōronteki kōsatsu* [Review of syntax: A grammatical inquiry]. Tokyo, Japan: Asakura Shoten.

Nakanishi, K. (2006). *Even*, *only*, and negative polarity in Japanese. In M. Gibson & J. Howell (Eds.), *Proceedings of the 16th Semantics and Linguistic Theory Conference* (pp.

138–155). Ithaca, NY: CLC Publications.

Nihon Kokugo Daijiten Dai Nihan Henshū Iinkai. (Ed.). (2000–2002). *Nihon kokugo daijiten* [Encyclopedic dictionary of the Japanese language] (2nd ed.). Tokyo, Japan: Shōgakkan.

Nishikawa, M. (2010). *A cognitive approach to English interjections*. Tokyo, Japan: Eihōsha.

Noh, E.-J. (2000). *Metarepresentation: A relevance-theory approach*. Amsterdam, Netherlands: John Benjamins.

Ōta, A. (1980). *Hitei no imi* [The meaning of negation]. Tokyo, Japan: Taishūkan.

Palmer, F. R. (2001). *Mood and modality* (2nd ed.). Cambridge, England: Cambridge University Press.

Pilkington, A. (2000). *Poetic effect*. Amsterdam, Netherlands: John Benjamins.

Progovac, L. (1993). Negative polarity: Entailment and binding. *Linguistics and Philosophy*, 16(2): 149–180.

Prus, R. (2010). Creating, sustaining and contesting definitions of reality: Marcus Tullius Cicero (106–43 BCE) as a pragmatist theorist and analytic ethnographer. *Qualitative sociology review*, 6(2), 3–50.

Quintilian, Marcus Fabius. (1856). *Institutio oratoria* [Institutes of oratory] (J. S. Watson, Trans.). Retrieved from http://rhetoric.eserver.org/quintilian/ (Original work published ca 95 BCE)

Quintilian, Marcus Fabius. (1920). *Institutio oratoria* [Institutes of oratory] (H. E. Butler, Ed. and Trans., Vols 1–4). Cambridge, London: Harvard University Press. (Original work published ca 95 BCE)

Quirk, R., Greenbaum, S., Leech, G., & Svartvik, J. (1985). *A comprehensive grammar of the English language*. London, England: Longman.

Rohde, H. (2006). Rhetorical questions as redundant interrogatives. *San Diego linguistic papers*, 2, 134–168.

Roy, A. M. (1978). *Irony in conversation*. (Doctoral dissertation, University of Michigan).

Sadock, J. (1971). Queclaratives, *Chicago Linguistic Society*, 7, 223–231.

Sasamoto, R. (2006). *The limits of classification: A relevance theoretic re-assessment of Japanese causal discourse connectives*. (Doctoral thesis, University of Salford, England).

Schaffer, D. (2005). Can rhetorical questions function as retorts? Is the Pope Catholic? *Journal of pragmatics*, 37, 433–460.

Schiffer, S. (1972). *Meaning*. Oxford, London: Clarendon Press.

Searle, J. J. (1969). *Speech acts*. Cambridge, England: Cambridge University Press.

Searle, J. J. (1975). Indirect speech acts. In P. Cole & J. L. Morgan (Eds.), *Syntax and semantics: Vol. 3. Speech acts* (pp. 59–82). New York, NY: Academic Press, 59–82.

Searle, J. J. (1979). *Expression and meaning: Studies in the theory of speech acts*. New York, NY: Cambridge University Press.

Seto, K. (1997). On non-echoic irony. In R. Carston & S. Uchida (Eds.), *Relevance theory: Applications and implications* (pp. 239–255). Amsterdam, Netherlands: John Benjamins.

Sperber, D., & Wilson, D. (1981). Irony and the use-mention distinction. In P. Cole (Ed.), *Radical pragmatics* (pp. 295–318). New York, NY: Academic Press.

Sperber, D., & Wilson, D. (1986). *Relevance: Communication and cognition*. Oxford, England: Blackwell.

Sperber, D., & Wilson, D. (1990). Rhetoric and relevance. In D. Wellbery & J. Bender (Eds.), *The ends of rhetoric: History, theory, practice* (pp. 140–155). Stanford, CA: Stanford University Press.

Sperber, D., & Wilson, D. (1995). *Relevance: Communication and cognition* (2nd ed.). Oxford, England: Blackwell.

Sperber, D., & Wilson, D. (1998). Irony and relevance: A reply to Seto, Hamamoto and Yamanashi. In R. Carston & S. Uchida (Eds.), *Relevance theory: Applications and implications* (pp. 283–293). Amsterdam, Netherlands: John Benjamins.

Stalnaker, R. C. (1999). Pragmatic presuppositions. In *Context and content: Essays on intentionality in speech and thought* (pp. 47–62). New York, NY: Oxford University Press. (Reprinted from *Semantics and philosophy*, pp. 197–213, by M. K. Kunitz & P. Unger, Eds., 1974, New York, NY: New York University Press)

Struyker Boudier, C. E. M. (1988). Toward a history of the question. In M. Meyer (Ed.), *Questions and questioning* (pp. 9–35). New York, NY: De Gruyter.

Tamaji, M. (2007). Rethinking typological universal, deontic > epistemic: The case of Japanese modal marker "monoda". *Takamatsu Daigaku kiyō* [Research bulletin of Takamatsu University], 47, 9–24.

Tanaka, L. (2006). Turn-taking in Japanese television interviews: A study on interviewers' strategies. *Journal of pragmatics*, 16, 361–398.

Tanaka, L. (2015). *Japanese questions: Discourse, context and language*. London, England: Bloomsbury.

Uchida, S. (1998). "No da": Kanrensei riron kara no shiten ["No da": A relevance-theoretic view]. In Konishi-sensei Sotsuju Kinen Ronbunshū Henshū Iinkai (Ed.), *Gendai Eigo no gohō to bunpō* [Grammar and usage of modern English] (pp. 243–251). Tokyo, Japan: Taishūkan.

Uchida, S. (2011). *Goyōron no shatei: Go kara danwa, tekusuto e* [The range of pragmatics: From words to conversation and text]. Tokyo, Japan: Kenkyūsha.

Uchida, S. (2013). *Kotoba o yomu, kokoro o yomu: Ninchi goyōron nyūmon* [Reading words, reading minds: An introduction to cognitive pragmatics]. Tokyo, Japan: Kaitakusha.

Utano, S. (1992). *Shiroi ie no satsujin* [The white house murders]. Tokyo, Japan: Kōdansha Bunko. (Original work published 1989)

Utsumi, A. (2000). Verbal irony as implicit display of ironic environment: Distinguishing ironic utterances from nonirony. *Journal of pragmatics*, 32, 1777–1806.

Uyeno, T. (1971). *A study of Japanese modality: A performative analysis of sentence particles*. (Doctoral dissertation, University of Michigan).

Van der Wouden, T. (1997). *Negative contexts: collocation, polarity and multiple negation*. London, England: Routledge.

Walton, D. N. (1988). Question-asking fallacies. In M. Meyer (Ed.), *Questions and questioning* (pp. 195–221). New York, NY: De Gruyter.

Wilson, D. (2000). Metarepresentation in linguistic communication. In D. Superber (Ed.), *Metarepresentation: A multidisciplinary perspective* (pp. 411–448). Oxford, England: Oxford University Press.

Wilson, D. (2006). The pragmatics of verbal irony: Echo or pretence? *Lingua*, 116, 1722–1743.

Wilson, D. (2009). Parallels and differences in the treatment of metaphor in relevance theory and cognitive linguistics. *Studies in pragmatics (Journal of the Pragmatics Society of Japan)*, 11, 42–60.

Wilson, D., & Carston, R. (2006). Metaphor, relevance and the "emergent property" issue. *Mind and language*, 21, 404–433.

Wilson, D., & Sperber, D. (1988). Representation and relevance. In R. M. Kempson (Ed.), *Mental representations: The interface between language and reality* (pp. 133–153). Cambridge, England: Cambridge University Press.

Wilson, D., & Sperber, D. (1992). On verbal irony. *Lingua*, 87, 53–76.

Wilson, D., & Sperber, D. (1993). Linguistic form and relevance. *Lingua*, 90, 1–25

Wilson, D., & Sperber, D. (2002). Truthfulness and relevance. *Mind*, 111, 583–632.

Wilson, D., & Sperber, D. (2012). Mood and the analysis of non-declarative sentences. In *Meaning and relevance*. Cambridge, England: Cambridge University Press. (Reprinted from *Human agency: Language, duty, and value*, pp. 77–101, by J. Dancy, J. M. E. Moravcsik, & C. C. W Taylor, Eds., 1988, Stanford, CA: Stanford University Press)

Yamazaki, M. (1996). In' yō/denbun no *tte* no yōhō [A descriptive study of the quotative particle *tte*]. *Kokuritsu Kokugo Kenkyūsho no Kenkyū Hōkokushū*, [NINJAL occasional paper], 17, 1–22.

Yamanashi, M. (1998). Some issues in the treatment of irony and related tropes. In R. Carston & S. Uchida (Eds.), *Relevance theory: Applications and implications* (pp. 271–281). Amsterdam, Netherlands: John Benjamins.

Yokoyama, O. T. (1990). Responding with a question in colloquial Russian. In M. H. Mills (Ed.), *Topics in colloquial Russian* (pp. 1–16). New York, NY: Peter Lang.

Yoshimura, A. (1999). *Hitei kyokusei genshō* [Negative polarity phenomena]. Tokyo, Japan: Eihōsha.

Yoshimura, K. (2007). *Focus and polarity:* Even *and* only *in Japanese*. (Doctoral dissertation, University of Chicago, IL).

Zarefsky, D. (2011). *Public speaking: Strategies for success* (6th ed.). New York, NY: Pearson.

Index

A
ad hoc concept   70-71
allusional pretense theory   103
answer   9, 19, 34, 41-43, 45, 50-51, 87
attributed thought   86
attributive   71

B
basic explicature   60, 76, 132

C
cognitive effect   56-57, 66-67, 69, 128
common ground   24, 27-28
complex question   34
confirmation question   11, 32-33, 62, 113
continuum   44-45, 88, 95, 116-117

D
desirable thought   65, 67, 87
discrepancy   90-93
dissociative attitude   72, 86, 89, 100

E
echoic hypothesis   85, 99-102
echoic utterance   72, 100
exam question   17, 36-37, 39, 42
explicature   58-59, 76
expository question   17-18, 50

F
felicitous condition   41-43, 49, 93-94

G
guess question   17, 36-37, 39

H
higher-level explicature   60-62, 76, 132-133

I
implicature   58, 63, 70
implicit display theory   103
information-seeking question   8, 11
interpretive resemblance   64

L
logical form   9, 17, 19, 46, 67, 87, 163, 169

M
metaphor   69-70, 73
metaphorical interrogative   16, 73
mutual manifestness   28, 109

N
negative polarity item   122, 153

O
optimal relevance   56, 89, 165

P
polarity reversal   2, 23
polarily reversed assumption   23, 95-97
principle of relevance   46, 56
propositional attitude   63, 89, 132

R
relevance theory   55
retort   34, 51-52
rhetorical question   1, 7-9, 19, 21-24, 32-33, 35-36, 48
rhetorical rating   32, 45, 87

rhetorically ambiguous question   40, 43

S

sentence-final expression (SFE)   119, 125-126, 129, 153, 157
speculative question   17-18, 37, 42-43, 156, 170
speech act theory   12, 86
surprise question   60-61, 145, 180, 182

T

tag questions   10
triply interpretive use   73
truth-conditional   76-81

U

universal desire   101-102

V

vain question   35-37
verbal irony   63, 71, 85-86, 90, 99, 101, 103

W

weaker implicature   70
wh-question   87

Y

yes-no question   87

後藤リサ（ごとう　りさ）

略歴

大阪府出身。
2012年奈良女子大学大学院
人間文化研究科博士課程修了。
博士（文学）。
関西外国語大学英語国際学部専任講師。

Goto Risa is an assistant professor in the College of Global Communication and Language, Kansai Gaidai University, Osaka, Japan. She received her Ph.D. from Nara Women's University in 2012.

主な著書

- "Relevance Theoretic Analysis of the Properties and Understanding Process of Rhetorical Questions," *Annual reports of Graduate School of Humanities and Science* (Nara Women's University) 26, (2011)
- 「アイロニーを伴う修辞疑問文発話の関連性理論による分析」『ことばを見つめて―内田聖二教授退職記念論文集―』（英宝社、2012）
- 「疑問文発話解釈における話者態度の高次のメタ表示」『関西外国語大学研究論集』第100号（2014）

Hituzi Language Studies No.3
Rhetorical Questions
A Relevance-Theoretic Approach to Interrogative Utterances in English and Japanese

発行	2018年2月16日　初版1刷
定価	10000円＋税
著者	©後藤リサ
発行者	松本功
ブックデザイン	白井敬尚形成事務所
印刷所	三美印刷株式会社
製本所	株式会社　星共社
発行所	株式会社　ひつじ書房

〒112-0011　東京都文京区
千石2-1-2　大和ビル2F
Tel: 03-5319-4916
Fax: 03-5319-4917
郵便振替 00120-8-142852
toiawase@hituzi.co.jp
http://www.hituzi.co.jp/
ISBN978-4-89476-883-3

造本には充分注意しておりますが、
落丁・乱丁などがございましたら、
小社かお買上げ書店にて
おとりかえいたします。
ご意見、ご感想など、小社まで
お寄せ下されば幸いです。